A MESSIANIC RABBI'S STUNNING
SUPERNATURAL JOURNEY TO ZION
AND THE LIFE-CHANGING TREASURES
HE UNCOVERED ALONG THE WAY

UNMASKING
THE CHALDEAN
SPIRIT

RABBI ZEV PORAT

Co-author of the bestseller *The Rabbi, The Secret Message, and the Identity of Messiah*

Foreword by Pastor Carl Gallups
Amazon Top 60 bestselling author

DEFENDER

CRANE, MO

UNMASKING THE CHALDEAN SPIRIT: *A Messianic Rabbi's Stunning Supernatural Journey to Zion and the Life-Changing Treasures He Uncovered along the Way*
by Rabbi Zev Porat

Defender Publishing
Crane, MO 65633
© 2022 Zev Porat

ISBN: 9781948014533

A CIP catalog record of this book is available from the Library of Congress.

Cover design by Jeffrey Mardis.

Dedicated to the glory of Yeshua,
the revealer of wonders and mysteries.

⊶

For my precious wife, Lian.
You are always there for me.
~Zev Porat

Acknowledgments

My special thanks to my dear brother and ministry partner Pastor Carl Gallups and his wife, Pam. You are like family to me. This book could not have been accomplished without you.

Also to Pastor Carl's wonderful congregation at Hickory Hammock Baptist Church in Milton, Florida, as well as the membership of Redeemed Ministries in Cleveland, Alabama, where Brandon serves as associate pastor and the director of the Redeemed Rehab Ministries.

My deepest gratitude to Tom and Nita Horn, SkyWatch TV, and team. And to Angie Peters—a terrific editor.

Thank you, Diane Roblin Lee, for a ton of tremendous help and wonderful support from the very beginning of this work.

My sincere appreciation to Pastor Caspar McCloud for standing with, and praying for, the global ministry endeavors of Messiah of Israel Ministries.

Thanks to all those who so faithfully and selflessly serve on the Messiah of Israel Ministries team.

And a very special thanks to my brother Haim and his wife, Sarah Levy.

CONTENTS

Part IV: From a Simple Exploration to a Startling Revelation

Part V: Out of the Darkness and Into the Light

Part VI: From Jacob's Ladder to Bethlehem

Part XII: From the Beginning to the End

FOREWORD

For many years, it has been my honor to minister alongside Messianic Rabbi Zev Porat throughout the United States and Israel. I know of no other Messianic rabbi who possesses the unique depth of Hebraic credentials that he does.

Zev was born and raised in Israel. He speaks Hebrew as his first language. He was raised in the most Orthodox rabbinical community in Israel, and perhaps in the entire world: B'nai Barak. His family line on his father's side includes renowned rabbis—some were even judges in the rabbinic courts of Israel. On his mother's side of the family are those who served in top positions in the Netanyahu Israeli government.

Zev also served in the Israeli military—even though he was legally exempt from serving—then graduated from an Orthodox yeshiva that credentialed him to minister as a Sanhedrin rabbi of Israel. Zev's grandparents actually had the former prime minister of Israel, Ariel Sharon, spend the night in their home on one occasion. These are the types of connections Zev has to all things Israel.

Zev, of course, has long-time and profound contacts inside the Israeli Orthodox Jewish community—from top to bottom—including very personal ties with the most renowned rabbi in Israel's history, the late Rabbi

Yitzhak Kaduri. You'll read more about that stunning association a little later on. But, in spite of his decidedly Orthodox Jewish pedigree, Zev still found his way to the light of Jesus Christ.

Zev's first passion is for his fellow Jews to also know Yeshua as Messiah. But, at the same time, he does not neglect his calling to assist in equipping today's church at large—both Jews and non-Jews—in order to bring them to a richer understanding of the biblical texts, especially as those Scriptures relate to their deeper Hebrew context and interconnections.

To this day, Zev inserts himself into harm's way—without fear or hesitancy—showing up in Orthodox communities and in synagogues, as well as on the streets and sidewalks of many Israeli cities, and at the Kotel (Western Wall), in order to take the gospel message directly to where his fellow Jews frequently congregate. In so doing, he has led numerous Orthodox Jews to Yeshua as Messiah. That number also includes several well-known Israeli rabbis and a Muslim imam.[1] Zev's Kingdom exploits are well documented in photos, print stories, media reports, books, newsletters, and videos.

Zev's zeal for the message of Yeshua doesn't stop there. He's paid a dear price for his devoted outreach. He is frequently attacked by Jewish anti-missionary organizations and other groups of people with similar mindsets. I've witnessed some of those attacks firsthand while he was ministering the Word. He's been vilified, called a liar, and even threatened with death. Several of his own dear family members have cut off ties with him because of his faith in Yeshua, and as a result, he has been disinherited. He has even had his property damaged by those attempting to silence his message. Zev has been spit upon and had rocks thrown at him because of his refusal to renounce Yeshua as Messiah. In spite of all this, he persists in the power of the Lord's strength and grace, exhibiting great faithfulness.

Zev and his ministry—Messiah of Israel Ministries—are now known all over the world. He has appeared on major US and European media programming, including television, radio, and well-known podcasts. In addition, he has authored this book and coauthored another one released through a prominent Christian publisher. He preaches and teaches in churches and Bible prophecy conferences in various nations, including Messianic Rabbi Jonathan Cahn's church in New Jersey, the church I pastor in Northwest Florida, Redeemed Ministries in North Alabama, and hundreds of congregations in underground churches throughout Asia.

Zev's primary message is about recovering God's contextual Word from the demonic influence and confusion of the globally pervasive *Chaldean spirit*—the brutal last-days spiritual deception that Rabbi Zev will define in the pages that follow. As he accomplishes this task, you're in for some stunning surprises and rich treats of biblical understanding.

Throughout this excursion, you'll begin to connect many points of Scripture—from the Old Testament through the New—like you've probably never done before. Major details regarding the birth, life, death, and resurrection of Yeshua/Jesus will come to light with a richer perspective. You'll also begin to more deeply appreciate the Pauline concept of the "one new man." And you'll find out how to faithfully and powerfully *make it to the end*, especially in these unquestionably prophetic days in which we are living. All of these things, and so much more, will bring you into a deeper understanding of the genuine message of God's glorious Word, from cover to cover.

I pray that the Lord Jesus Christ will bless this incredible journey you're about to take.

—Carl Gallups
Senior pastor and bestselling author

Jesus said to them,
"Therefore every teacher of the law who has become
a disciple in the kingdom of heaven is like
the owner of a house who brings out of his
storeroom new treasures as well as old."

~Matthew 13:52

PART I

FROM ORTHODOX JEW TO MESSIANIC RABBI

I would later realize that it had all been a part of God's divine test. I also learned that you can't outgive the owner of "the cattle on a thousand hills."

> I have no need of a bull from your stall
> Or of goats from your pens,
> For every animal of the forest is mine,
> And the cattle on a thousand hills.
> I know every bird in the mountains,
> And the insects in the fields are mine.
> If I were hungry I would not tell you,
> For the world is mine, and all that is in it.
>
> ~Psalm 50:9–12

1

THE TEMPTATION

I almost couldn't believe those words
actually blurted out of my mouth.

His straightforward manner stunned me.

He peered over the rim of his reading glasses and looked down at me while seated behind his huge desk and said, "Zev, your grandfather has left you a substantial portion of his estate. I have the paperwork right here before me."

I was sitting in the plush office of our family's attorney in the Orthodox town of Bnei-Brak, Israel, where my people had lived for generations. My grandfather's funeral had only been a week earlier. Of course, I knew I was the oldest of all the grandchildren, but I didn't know that I was at the top of the list to receive the lion's share of his inheritance, especially in light of the monumental shift my life had recently taken.

Before the attorney's calmly spoken words made their full impact upon me, the lawyer went on to outline that my renowned rabbi grandfather had become extremely wealthy over his lifetime. I was aware that he had been a man of considerable means, but I had no personal knowledge of the extent of his wealth. Now I was about to find out. Was it tens of thousands? A hundred thousand? Several hundred thousand? I didn't know. At this point in my life, even a measly couple of hundred dollars would have provided welcome relief.

I gulped as I attempted to swallow back the burst of shock and anticipation that welled up in my throat. My grandfather had been dear to me. However, because of a long estrangement—the details about which you'll read in the following pages—I hadn't heard from him in quite a while. Sadly, because of that separation, I wasn't even allowed to attend his funeral. Yet, here I sat with his attorney, who was telling me that my grandfather had left me what would probably amount to a hefty inheritance. Boy was I in for a shock.

"As the eldest son of your immediate family," the lawyer said, "your grandfather left you the part of the inheritance that would have gone to your father, had he not died before him. Therefore, your portion is 1.5 million dollars in cash, for a total of approximately 40 million dollars in various properties and other tangible assets."

He smiled slightly as he slid the paper across his desk—one finger guiding it to its resting place in front of me. As I looked at the legal document that would change my life forever, he tapped the signature line with his pen to indicate where I should sign.

The lawyer's words overwhelmed me. Could this really be true? Could all my financial woes be over for the rest of my life, with the simple signing of my name? This amount of money was surreal. I could never even in my wildest dreams have imagined having that much.

I picked up the pen to sign the document, my head spinning and sweaty hands shaking. I wanted to put my name on that line before anybody changed their minds.

ONE THING MORE

As I touched the tip of the pen to the paper, the lawyer spoke again. "Zev, there's only one condition to this inheritance agreement," he said. "And it's an important one. Without it, the whole thing is off."

I held my hand still and sucked in a deep breath. I had a dreaded feeling the other shoe was about to drop. Of course, *there's always a catch.*

"Here's the situation," he said. "You must renounce this crazy stuff about Yeshua.[2] You are embarrassing your family and your Jewish tradition. Simply live a good Jewish life, and your grandfather's wealth will be yours. If you don't agree to do that, you'll receive nothing."

My jaw clenched. I froze, remembering that fitful night of spiritual battle not too much earlier when I had finally surrendered my life to Yeshua. Sitting in that ornate office, pen in hand, I thought back to what had felt like a jolt of electricity running throughout my body the night I had been transformed—*born again.* In the immediate moments of those swirling memories I answered the lawyer.

"I won't do it. I'll *never* deny Yeshua. I simply cannot."

I almost couldn't believe those words actually blurted out of my mouth. *All that money. All that freedom. All that potential influence.* The temptation was certainly present. I heard that serpent-like "voice" in my head: *You fool!* But, even in the depths of my soul, I was convinced that I should, indeed, be standing upon my words of faith.

With a look of utter disbelief, our family's attorney glared above the rim of his glasses again, paused, took a deep breath, then snapped. "Zev— *just sign the paper.*"

He fidgeted, then continued. "Look, Zev, I'm only a lawyer. I'm not a rabbi. I don't care *what* you do with your life, and I certainly don't care about your religious beliefs. Just sign the paper so my job can be done here. Your financial problems will be over, and you'll be set for life. Later, when all this dies down, you can always go back to your Yeshua stuff. You can even do it now—secretly, if you want. Who will know?"

There it was again. In those words, there was a temptation I had heard many times before. It came from the evil one: *Who will know? Who will care, when it's all said and done?*

But, I knew fully well "who" would know.

I spoke up again. "I will know," I said. "The *Lord* will know. I will not put my name to a document that renounces Yeshua as Messiah. I'm sorry, but I won't do it." The lawyer sat stunned, his mouth hanging open for a second.

I rose from my chair and informed him, "You can keep the money."

As I stood waiting for a response, the lawyer shook his head and shrugged his shoulders. "Oh well," he said. "If you don't sign this paper, that money will be transferred to the rest of your family. None of it will be yours."

"If that's God's will, so be it," I replied. "But tell my family that it was really Yeshua who gave them the money. By me not renouncing His name, they are now rich."

I went to the door, and as I passed through it, I became peacefully aware that I was leaving behind a huge part of my past. For a while, the whole experience seemed like a dream. Had I really just turned down forty million dollars?

I would later realize the entire affair had all been a part of God's divine test. I also learned you can't outgive the owner of "the cattle on a thousand hills." But it would be much later before I fully understood these things. Right then, I knew I was beginning a new journey. Humanly speaking, it was one that *could* go very badly. And that's exactly how it began—obviously, as yet another part of the test.

Let me back up a bit and tell you how that journey unfolded.

2

HERITAGE

*It wasn't until many years later when it dawned on me,
and I recognized their answers as flawed understanding.*

I was born and raised in the small city of Bnei Brak, the most ultra-Orthodox city in Israel. Orthodoxy was in my genetic makeup, which is no easy hurdle to overcome. Bnei Brak is a place where even saying the name "Yeshua" or walking down the street with a Bible that includes the New Testament can be an offense worthy of stoning. It's a city of famous rabbis where many black-garbed, bearded men spend their entire lives studying in the *yeshivot*—a rabbinical preparation school.

Never doubt, the power and legacy of direct ancestral lines are as important as physical currency in the life of a religious Jewish person. My lineage was the finest. My father, grandfather, great-grandfather and several other ancestors were respected rabbis. Several were even *dayans*—judges of rabbis who presided in the rabbinical courts of Israel.

My grandfather who left me the inheritance, Rabbi Pinhas Porat, had escaped from the Holocaust in Poland. His entire family had been exterminated in the gas chambers when he was a teenager. As he fled, eventually landing in the Republic of Belarus, he met and helped two other women—sisters—escape the murderous horrors of the Nazi death camps. One of the women died in the midst of the long, arduous journey. The other eventually became my grandmother by marrying Pinhas Porat.

My mother's father, Zev Goldman, was a member of the Knesset in the Likud party,[3] now headed by Benjamin Netanyahu. So, my mother's side has family in the Israeli government, while the people affiliated with the government on my father's side are Sanhedrin rabbis who hold powerful sway over the inner workings of the Israeli halls of institutional power. Because of these family lines of significant influence, I have both secular and religious connections in the Israeli government.

My grandfather arrived in the land of Israel in 1946. In 1948, at the time of Israel's rebirth, he became a distinguished leader of the Orthodox rabbinate, the ruling elite. For this reason, my access to Holocaust survivors and connections important to my work with the Jews of Israel are enviable. I have the freedom to contact people, go places, and walk through open doors through arrangements that would otherwise be impossible. It's amazing how God is using my heritage and the resultant connections to people who want nothing to do with Yeshua for the purpose of furthering His Kingdom.

OFF TO THE UNITED STATES

I was not raised only in Israel. Our family moved to the United States when my father became the principal of a Hebrew day school and the chief rabbi of a synagogue in southern California. Consequently, I grew up speaking fluent Hebrew and English.

As the son of an influential rabbi, I wasn't allowed to do most of the things other kids were doing, so I didn't have many friends. It was a lonely time in my life, and during that period I also got my first taste of my father's abject hatred of the name of Jesus.

One day when I was thirteen years old, a group of Christians were passing out tracts containing the gospel message of salvation. They were gathered across the street from our school. My father became furious when he saw them. "Those people are dangerous," he told me. "God will be angry with you if you even *mention* the name of Jesus. It is blasphemy against Judaism and all we stand for." So, I was trained to be especially afraid of the name of Jesus.

QUESTIONING

Despite all the religious trappings of our family life, I never felt the personal presence of the God of Abraham, Isaac, and Jacob. My overriding feeling instead was of suffocating bondage to tradition. Because of this, I became increasingly miserable.

Whenever I asked my elders about not being able to feel the presence of God in my life, they chastised me for my inadequacy, specifically in relation to the Jewish Sabbath requirements. They said I simply needed to study the Sabbath laws more intently and apply myself with greater diligence. That was their only answer to my honest questions. It wasn't until many years later, as the truth dawned on me, that I recognized their answers reflected a deeply flawed understanding of the truth of God's Word. Their response was associated with what Jesus was talking about in Matthew 12:1–8, Mark 2:23–28, and Luke 6:1–5: "They glorify the Sabbath more than the Sabbath maker."

While my father was alive, he sent me to Orthodox schools whether I was in the United States or in Israel. I wore the big black hat, had long side curls, and looked like I was walking straight toward the future my family expected.

Even though I was raised to continue our honored rabbinical family line, I never really wanted to be religious. There were just too many rules, too much misdirected intensity. I felt no urging from God to pursue that path.

Looking back, I now see God's genuine calling upon my life. He put all the connections in place that I would need—associations and open doors—to fulfill the ministry He had for me. I understand how He prepared me to take the message of Yeshua to the Jews of Israel. However, it took many years of the Holy Spirit working in my life before I was ready to step into His plan and purposes.

In spite of all this, I could have never guessed what was just down the road.

3

THE WITNESS

At the same time I was running away from God,
I was seeking peace with Him, but not finding it.

I was sixteen years old when my father died of a sudden heart attack while we were in America. We returned to Israel and buried him in Ponevezh Cemetery in Bnei Brak, the most venerated rabbinic cemetery in Israel. It was reserved for prominent rabbis and renowned religious members of the Israeli military.

At my father's passing, my grandfather—the one who eventually intended to leave much of his wealth to me—stepped into my father's role, making sure I studied the Torah and the Talmud. He wanted me to become an authorized Sanhedrin rabbi like the other males in my family. Although I loved him dearly, I felt trapped.

MAKING CHANGES

Ultra-Orthodox Judaism didn't fit me, so I began to quietly rebel. I took off my big black hat, cut my side curls, shaved my beard, and joined the Israeli army. My grandfather arranged to have me drafted into the army with special privileges, including time off several times a week to complete my studies in the yeshiva.

I reluctantly submitted to my beloved grandfather's wishes and became an authorized Sanhedrin rabbi, just like my family expected. You can imagine their delight as well as my deepening anxiety in my intensely conflicted heart.

BAD DECISIONS

Because of the spiritual and emotional pain this struggle was causing me, I started going to taverns, looking for relief in alcohol. That extremely unwise decision eventually led to drunkenness, fighting, and exploring the darkest offerings of the Internet.

My anger and frustration with life grew almost boundless, to the extent that I assaulted a police officer who arrived on the scene to break up one of my many bar fights. Then, in the midst of the ensuing court proceeding, I threatened the presiding judge. Obviously, I wasn't thinking very clearly in those days. But God's hand was still upon me, whether I knew it or not.

Thanks to my grandfather's ability to clean up the growing mess, he stepped into the fray and kept me out of jail. He even arranged to keep the reports of my criminal exploits and court proceedings out of the newspapers as well. I can assure you, that feat was almost supernatural in and of itself. I can still envision how those headlines would have read under any other circumstances: "Prominent Rabbi's Grandson Assaults Police Officer, Threatens Judge." Of course, that would have been a disaster for our family, as well for as my own life and future. The Lord was patiently and graciously preserving me and preparing me for what was to come.

━◆━

Because of the management skills I developed in the army and my fluency in English and Hebrew, once I completed my military stint, I landed a great job with Granulox, a German medical company where I managed thirty-seven employees and earned five times the national average salary in Israel. I bought a new car and kept all my bills paid. But all that wasn't enough for me. I wanted more—more money, more jewelry, a more expensive car, and nicer clothing. Without realizing it, I was trying to fill a hole that had formed in the cavernous recesses of my continually blackening soul. So I supplemented my income with a second job as the evening reception clerk in a high-end hotel, where I met a woman named Lian.

LIFE-CHANGING ENCOUNTERS

Lian was a top chef from Shanghai who was, with a tour group from China, participating in a food expo at the hotel's convention center. Once we met, we bonded almost immediately and married ten months later in spite of the fact that, spiritually speaking, we were at different ends of the universe. In fact, our home decor included an eclectic mix of images and statues of Buddha from her background and numerous pictures of long-bearded rabbis from mine.

As the décor of our home reflected, nothing was spiritually clear to me in those days. At the same time I was running away from God, I was also seeking peace with Him, but in all the wrong places—and I was not finding it. My dissatisfaction with life ate at me every moment of every day. So, I began to search the Internet for answers. In an online chat room that I stumbled into, I met an American Christian named Todd who patiently explained the gospel of Jesus Christ to me after discovering the fact that I had studied to be a rabbi. As a Jewish person, I was very clear about not wanting to hear about the New Testament or, for that matter, anything at all about God. I became angry with Todd, rejecting everything he tried to explain about Jesus. My Jewish upbringing caused me to bristle at the truths Todd revealed.

"Don't speak to me about such things," I insisted. "I'm a Jew. I am running away from God. I have no need for Him in my life." Yes, I actually told Todd I was *running away from God.*

However, over a period of four years, Todd taught me about Messiah by using the Old Testament, which he knew very well. With his guidance, I started to understand key messianic passages such as Isaiah 53, Isaiah 9, Micah 5, Psalm 2, Psalm 110, Psalm 22, and Isaiah 7:14.[4] Each of these passages is still important in my own ministry to this day.

Had Todd been one of those Christians who majored on the supernatural and mere "experiential" aspects of Christianity, I wouldn't have been ready for it. I needed the nuts and bolts of the Old Testament to secure my mind to the truth of the New Testament and the gospel message. God knew Todd was just the person I needed…at just the right time.

⊷⊷

After the first couple of years of my exposure to the teachings about the Messiah, I started having trouble sleeping. My spiritually induced insomnia grew increasingly worse, and I realized I was going to have to do my own investigation into the whole business. *Just who is the genuine Jewish Messiah?* I combed through libraries, studied the history of Christianity and Judaism, and became thoroughly confused as I searched for the answer to my question. I fell under strong conviction to find the truth, and I couldn't get away from it. It became impossible to hide from God's presence in my quest.

I started waking up in the middle of the night as the Holy Spirit began to give me visualizations of what I had been studying. It was as though the Bible verses I had read came to life. I began to understand that these experiences were what the Bible calls "visions."

But then I would hear a voice that would say, "Yeshua is the Messiah of the *Gentiles*. He is *not* the Jewish Messiah. Stay away from Him. Go the other way. Pay no attention to this teaching. *You are Jewish*. That's all you need."

I now know that voice came from the demonic realm, but at the time, I thought I was going crazy. I needed help. And I knew just where to turn.

4

THE VOICE

I fell to my knees beside my bed, weeping.

Like any good Jewish person, I decided to go straight to the rabbis for help. *Certainly they would have the truth.* All my life, this is what I had been taught—and it was a convenient road for me to take. After all, my entire family was filled with rabbis. And if the ones in my own family weren't enough, each of them had personal relationships with scores more. So, I was off to see the prominent rabbis of Israel.

SEEKING ANSWERS

First I went to my grandfather. Without mentioning anything about Yeshua, I showed him some of the Scriptures Todd had shared with me. I asked for his thoughts on the New Covenant in relation to Isaiah 53, Isaiah 7:14, Micah 5:2, and Jeremiah 31:31.

Then I asked, "Who is this baby in Micah 5:2?"

At this, my usually calm grandfather became very nervous. His apprehension told me something was wrong. I knew I was onto something. I had to find out what was going on. I wanted a straight answer. Who was this child in existence before the foundation of the world, who would one day be the ruler of Israel? *Who was this baby?*

When even my highly respected rabbi grandfather couldn't answer the question, I interviewed a series of thirty-two other rabbis over a two-year period of researching and digging. In those interviews, I received twenty-six *different* answers to my question.

In Judaism, a rabbi's voice is almost like that of God; when he speaks, it is with authority that few question. When I received all of those different answers concerning one simple passage of Scripture, I knew I had hit a huge snag, as far as Judaism was concerned.

Eventually, I met with the chief rabbi of Israel who, at that time, was Israel Lau. Years earlier, he had flown from Israel to California to conduct my bar mitzvah.

"I've interviewed thirty-two rabbis and have received twenty-six different answers to this same question," I told Rabbi Lau. "Why would this be?" I asked. "Isn't there just one Word of God?"

"Zev," he said, "it's okay, because there are seventy faces to the Torah—seventy different answers to the Scriptures."

This answer made it clear that the "all-knowing" rabbis were just as confused on the subject as I was. Could it really be that all the "difficult" biblical questions had *seventy* answers? This seemed a convenient way to avoid answering a hard question. I knew God had to be revealing something through this unclear response from Rabbi Lau.

COUNTING THE COST

Nevertheless, the truth was being confirmed. I knew—after four years of research on the Internet, discussions with Todd, numerous conversations with the rabbis, and two years of subjective research and further evaluation—that Yeshua was indeed the Messiah of Israel.

But I was a Jew. Believing in this truth would cause me to lose my family, my friends, my job, and maybe even my life. So I dared not do it. Believing in Yeshua simply was not a realistic option; I loved my family too much to cross that line.

⊷✧⊶

I am about to share with you the defining moment of my life and faith, my very own "burning-bush" experience. To this day, I am convinced of its Heaven-sent reality. It was an eternally life-changing experience that still strengthens me.

The night after I met with Rabbi Lau, a very cold night after I had gone to sleep, I was awakened at about 3 a.m. shaking and sweating heavily. It felt like tingling electricity was flashing through my body. Over my head, I could see a bright light shrouded in a shiny cloud. The only thing I could think of in that frightening but marvelous moment was the glorious cloud through which God revealed Himself to the children of Israel as they were departing from Egypt. Was this bright cloud just above my head in the wee hours of the morning the *shekinah* glory of God's presence?

All I knew for certain was that something supernatural was happening. In that critical moment of a very real crisis of belief, I heard the *voice*. It became audible, and it shouted to the depths of my soul.

The voice (in Hebrew) said, "Zev, *Zev*." I couldn't believe what I was hearing. It continued, "Isaiah 53 which you have been studying so diligently—this is the *Messiah of Israel*. Isaiah 53 is Yeshua. It is true."

I was stunned. My shaking became violent, almost uncontrollable. It took me a while to regain my composure. I fell to my knees beside my bed, weeping. I called out for Yeshua to save me and receive me as His own. At that moment, I was transformed—born again. Because of that experience, I have never turned back to my old life.

As soon as this happened, I shook Lian awake, screaming, "Lian. *It is true!* The Messiah of Israel is Yeshua!" She had seen and heard nothing;

still a Buddhist, she said, "Go back to bed, Zev. The guy from the Internet is brainwashing you."

She tried to roll over and go back to sleep, but I wouldn't have it. "No, Lian. Listen to what I'm telling you! Yeshua is the Messiah. I know it now!" When she realized that the whole bed was wet from my sweating—on this very cold night—she knew something significant had truly happened.

Within a week of exploring the Scriptures with me, she renounced her Buddhist beliefs and was also born again in Yeshua. Our previously "dark" house was now becoming a house of light for both of us. We got rid of our idols of deception and became the "one new man" spoken of in Ephesians 2:14–18—a Jew and a Gentile, together as one.

We were now not only husband and wife, but brother and sister in the Lord.

5

THE REJECTION

*I had been a believer for less than two years and,
except in my relationship with my wife, I felt quite alone in my faith.*

After that night, I was on fire for Yeshua. I had heard the voice of God.

The Lord had told me—one on one—that Yeshua was indeed the long-awaited Messiah of Israel. I had no more wondering. No more ambivalence. No more holding back simply because I was Jewish, because I was afraid to suggest this possibility to others, or because my rabbinic connections were insisting otherwise. Yeshua was my Messiah. This was my road-to-Damascus revelation.

I was so full of excitement that I often had a hard time containing myself. I was overflowing with the Spirit of God and felt that I *had* to tell people what Yeshua had done in my life. But whenever I tried to share that I had finally discovered who the Messiah really is, I was met with severe persecution. The entire Orthodox community rejected me. I was cursed, spat upon, stoned, and reviled almost everywhere I dared to even speak the name of Yeshua. I was like Joseph, who had experienced a personal encounter with God; I was trying to tell my "brothers" about it. Instead of being interested or happy about my experience, they attacked me and attempted to destroy me. I now know that, like Joseph, I was being humbled by the Lord Himself.

In my family, I started by sharing my newfound faith in Yeshua with my mother. I hoped she would show a certain understanding and a shared joy. However, I was once again met with anguish and fury.

"Your father is twisting and turning in his grave because of what you have done," she said. "You are blaspheming the name of your family. You are supposed to be a rabbi. You are supposed to continue our tradition. How can you do this to us?"

I pleaded with her, "But Mom, it's in the Jewish Bible. Let me sit with you and I'll show you. Bring your Bible, and I'll show you that Yeshua is the Messiah—born in Bethlehem, raised in Nazareth. This is the Messiah of Israel."

"Go be a missionary," she said. "But don't share your 'teaching' with me."

She paused, leaned in, and lowered her voice almost to a whisper. I sensed what I thought to be a slight softening of her heart. In that moment, she said, "However, I *will* eventually talk with you about these things, but only in the presence of a rabbi."

SCORNED

I soon discovered that my mother's "softening" heart was simply a clever motherly ruse. She had only concocted another idea about how to get me to renounce Yeshua. She took me to Rabbi Yoseph Stiglitz in Netanya who was a deprogrammer—one who helps parents explain to their children who have begun to believe in Yeshua that it is against the teachings of the Old Testament and Judaism.

Rabbi Stiglitz began by explaining that Yeshua Himself did not fully trust God. The proof was that He cried out on the cross, "My God, my God, why hast Thou forsaken me?"

I shook my head, explaining that Yeshua prayed that because He was God's once-and-for-all-time sacrificial Lamb. "Besides," I said, "Yeshua was quoting King David's words in Psalm 22."

My God, my God, why have you forsaken me?...

But I am a worm and not a man, scorned by everyone, despised by the people. **All who see me mock me; they hurl insults, shaking their heads. "He trusts in the Lord," they say, "let the Lord rescue him. Let him deliver him, since he delights in him."**

Dogs surround me, a pack of villains encircles me; **they pierce my hands and my feet.** All my bones are on display; people stare and gloat over me. **They divide my clothes among them and cast lots for my garment.** (Psalm 22:1, 6–8, 16–18; emphasis added)

The rabbi was astonished; he may not have even known those specific words were in that passage. He turned to my mother. "He's brainwashed," he said. "He's finished. I can't help him."

As a result of that meeting, my mother didn't speak to me for two long years. After that, she relented and agreed to see me as long as I wouldn't talk to her about the Bible.

My grandfather was next. This was a man I loved more than words can express. He had stepped into the void left when my father died, and he had made sure I lacked nothing. I had more respect and love for him than I did for anyone else. When I began to share with him my precious knowledge that Yeshua was the Messiah of Israel, my grandfather—by this time a frail, old man—shot out of his chair, opened the glass cabinet behind him, and shouted, "*Goy* ["Gentile"]! Traitor! Get out of here!"

He pulled plates from the cabinet and started hurling them at me. My shirt was torn and my head was streaming with blood when I ran out of his home to head straight to the hospital for stitches. To this day, a scar on my forehead left by a plate that hit its mark reminds me of the overwhelming pain I endured—not from the gash, but from my grandfather's rejection of me and my faith in Yeshua. That was the last time I ever saw him. I tried, once, to call him, but he said, "Deny Yeshua, or don't ever call me again."

Then there was my sister and her husband, a rabbi. They responded to my effort to share my faith with them by filing an injunction against me in the rabbinical court. I was ordered to stay one hundred meters away from their seven children—my beloved nieces and nephews. If anyone asks my sister about me today, she says nothing about my faith in Yeshua, only that I died. Every six months, she and her husband renew the order against me.

My aunt's response took a different twist. In an effort to encourage me, she tried to give me money for a psychiatrist, saying, "Your family shouldn't reject you, just because you're sick." When I declined her offer, she left.

ANOTHER STUNNING BLOW

After almost two years of being a Messianic believer, I received a call from Rafi Ben Hamo, the CEO of Granulox, where I had been employed for more than fourteen years. After work on many days, once I was born again, I shared the news of Yeshua with anyone who was willing to talk with me.

Rafi wore a knitted skullcap signifying that he's a traditional Jew. One day, he called me into his office for a "talk."

"Zev, sit down," he said. "I've been hearing things about you."

"What kinds of things?" I asked.

"You've been talking about *Yeshu*." ("Yeshu" is the extremely derogatory pronunciation of *Yeshua* that a nonbelieving Jewish person uses. It's almost like a curse word.[5])

"You'd better stop this," Rafi insisted. "You're going to turn this place into a cult."

"First of all," I said, "if I've been doing anything to jeopardize my job, please tell me. I don't speak about Yeshua at work; I do it *after* work."

"I don't want you to do it *at all*," he contended.

"Well, other people who work here, like Moshe or David, talk about football or basketball after work," I said. "What's the difference?"

"You're brainwashing people," he answered. "I won't allow it. Come back in the morning to talk to me. I'll give you your options then."

I went back to Rafi's office the next morning as he asked. He looked at me—solemnity written all over his face—and said, "What's it going to be?"

I looked straight at him. "Are you still asking me to deny the Lord Yeshua?"

"Yes I am." His words were exacting, his voice firm.

"I simply can't do it," I said, holding my ground.

"Then you're *out of here*, Zev." He glared at me with a resoluteness in his eyes I had never seen before. And then, just like that, he terminated my fourteen-and-a-half-year career…in two minutes.

"Go to your office, clear your desk, and return your car keys," he instructed. "You're leaving: no compensation, no salary, and no pension. That's it."

When I told my colleagues at work what happened, they were shocked and saddened. I had enjoyed great relationships with them for all those years.

"He can't do this," they protested. "This isn't legal. He can't fire you without compensation. It's wrong."

Of course I knew they were right. I also knew I had grounds for a lawsuit.

I had been a believer for less than two years and, except for my relationship with my wife, I felt quite alone in my faith. I left the office in tears and was still crying when I got home to Lian. Not knowing what to do, I prayed for two days. Then the Lord led me to the Scripture, "Vengeance is mine" (Deuteronomy 32:35).

I knew, right then, that God was telling me not to challenge my legal rights, but to pray for the salvation of my boss. I started looking for a new job in management, but with no success. No one would recommend me.

The friends I had before I became a believer drifted away when I no longer went to bars with them. Others left me simply because of my faith in Yeshua. I really could have expected no less of them. After all, even my own dear family had left me, some of them even telling their friends that I was no longer living.

But this was still only the beginning; more rejection would follow.

6

BEACH BUMS

The officer told me I was crazy, released my handcuffs, and left.

Eleven months went by after I lost my dream job at Granulox. I couldn't find meaningful employment anywhere. At least we still had our apartment and a little bit of savings. *Surely, things will turn around soon,* I thought. But they didn't.

One day, as I was reading 2 Thessalonians 3:10, which says: "If a man doesn't work, he shall not eat," I understood that God was telling me something very important: "If you can't find the job you want, if you can't find a job in management, you must take any job, because any job is a blessing."

HARD TIMES

So, I found employment in a place where no one cared what I believed: I became a dishwasher. The manager of the little restaurant where I was hired was an Arab. He hated Jews, and now he finally had a Jew under his thumb. He shouted at me every day: "Faster, *faster*, wash. *Wash.*" I endured his harshness and tried to do the best job I knew how to do, hopefully to open doors of future communication and witness opportunities.

Eventually, our apartment lease expired. Without enough left in the bank to pay the rent, we bought an old, cheap car in which we could store our meager belongings, and we bought a tent. Then we headed for the beach on the Mediterranean Sea. We were now homeless.

Each of us took turns doing a three-hour, night-watch shift while the other slept—guarding our tent and its enclosed belongings from prostitutes, thieves, drug addicts, and drunks prowling the beach. We took cold showers in the public facilities in the early morning hours. We continued living this way for three and a half months. I didn't know this relatively short period of life could seem so incredibly long while we were in the midst of it, but I had committed the unpardonable Jewish sin. I had become a follower of Yeshua, the most detested name in Israel and among the Jews. I was considered an utter disgrace by almost everyone I knew. To them, I deserved what I was getting. At times, I felt like a modern-day Job, except he at least had three friends. Lian and I had none, but we had each other…and we had the Lord. For us, that was enough.

While the first night or two of camping in a tent on the shore of the Mediterranean might sound romantic, I can assure you the glamour quickly dwindled as the reality of our homelessness and our absence of real friends sank in. First, days went by, then weeks, then months. Time crawled along like a turtle plodding through a trough of quicksand. At times, the ordeal was humiliating. But we kept our eyes on Yeshua and continued forward. We believed that He would, in His own timing, intervene on our behalf.

WISE WORDS

One day, in the midst of all that was going on, Lian turned to me and said, "We believe in Yeshua. *Right?* Doesn't the Bible say that God will take care of us? Doesn't the Bible say we are blessed?"

I thought about it for a minute. "You know, God *does* have a blessing for us," I said. "He has a plan for us. God is not the one who put us here on the beach. He is not the author of evil, but He *has* allowed it. There's a reason for this. We'll be blessed. We'll see it soon."

So, I continued washing dishes knowing that God was, somehow, in control of the entire mess, because our hearts and lives were totally His.

INTERVENTION

A few months later, I felt the Lord saying, "I didn't challenge you to preach the gospel only when you are living in a hotel or a penthouse, or when you are rolling in money and have plenty of the things of this world. I told you to preach the Gospel *in season and out of season*." So, after my dishwashing hours, I started going out on the beach and sharing the good news with people. *Any* people. *Anyone* who would listen. I received many different reactions to my message about Yeshua and salvation in Him, but I seldom had a positive encounter.

Once, during our early days on the beach, when I was sharing with an elderly religious Jewish man, he suddenly punched me in the eye. Confusion ensued, and several people near the altercation believed I was the one who had hit the older man. Of course, that wasn't true. But I couldn't convince them otherwise, and they called the police, who handcuffed me when they arrived.

I managed to make the officer understand that I'd been sharing the Bible with the fellow when he hit me. The man finally admitted to the assault, saying, "He's a *goy*. Get him out of here—he's a traitor."

When the officer suggested that I could sue the attacker and would probably easily win a settlement, I refused to press charges. "God bless this man," I said. "He doesn't know what he's doing." The officer told me I was crazy, released my handcuffs, and left.

So there I was, a Messianic Jew sporting a nasty black eye, living homeless on the beach with my wife, hated by my family, fired from my high-paying job, disenfranchised of all my benefits, disowned by all my former friends, working as a dishwasher for an Arab who hated me, and desperately looking for a better job.

But Lian and I had found the Pearl of Great Price, Yeshua the Messiah, and we would never turn back. Nothing this world had to offer could compare in value. We were still full of His joy, and that joy never left us...even in the midst of our time of testing and tribulation.

The next day, I would find out why.

7

SEVEN DAYS OF BLESSING

They pulled out a check for an amount equivalent
to $27,000 in US currency.

The morning after the altercation, I received a phone call from a man who told me that I should go to our family lawyer's office. I figured all my relatives would be there, and I knew they would be shocked at my appearance. I prepared for the worst.

However, as it turned out, I showed up at the attorney's office, but was the only one present. It was at this meeting that I learned—as related in the opening chapter—that my refusal to renounce Yeshua had effectively cut me off from my grandfather's hefty inheritance, as well as severed all ties with my family.

The day after I saw the lawyer—on a Thursday morning—I took a bus to Jerusalem and went to the Garden Tomb. We had now been living on the beach for almost four months. As I sat at the site praying and crying, a man from Australia walked up to me. "Are you a Messianic Jew?" he asked.

How could he know that? When I said "yes," he said, "The Holy Spirit just told me to come over here to talk and pray with you."

I appreciated this man's sensitivity. At his request, I told him about my situation and explained how I'd gotten the black eye. We wept together. Then he said, "The Lord Yeshua is going to bless you. You'll see."

After that, we exchanged contact information, shook hands, and parted. I couldn't have known at the time that this conversation and prayer of blessing would be *day one* of a week that would encompass a supernatural outpouring of five straight days of divine blessing.

A MOTHER'S REACTION

Despite my mother's disapproval of my choices, she continued to accept calls from me. I was her firstborn, and she still liked it when I would phone her at the beginning of the Sabbath evening to wish her a good Sabbath rest: "Shabbat Shalom." After not reaching out to her for a few weeks, I finally called one Friday evening. She asked why I hadn't done so sooner.

"We're living on the beach," I said. "We don't have a home anymore."

I fully expected a loving, mothering, sympathetic response. Instead, she said, "This is what you deserve."

But she wasn't finished with her chastisement. "I told you not to believe in that *Yeshu* guy," she said. "This is punishment from God. I warned you about this, and now you have lost everything—your friends, your job, your home, your family—*you lost everything*."

"God is going to bless me," I said. "He has a blessing for me. You'll see it one day, I promise."

"Meshuga. *Crazy*," she said. "*This* is a blessing?" She hung up.

The very next night—the Sunday after the Sabbath—close to midnight, seven ultra-Orthodox Jews from the well-known, highly influential anti-Messianic organization Yad L'Achim[6] and two other rabbinical political officials showed up at our tent. I was sure they had come to break my legs. That would not have been an unusual visit in extreme cases like mine.

However, they spoke in conciliatory tones and finally assured me, "Zev, we are not here to fight with you; we are here to talk with you. You made a mistake. You are supposed to be a rabbi. We forgive you. *Come with us.* We'll put you back in a yeshiva; we'll get you a place to live." Then one of the men pulled out a check for an amount equivalent to $27,000 US dollars. "Take this and come with us."

"Thank you," I said, "and I pray that God will bless you, but I will never deny my Lord Yeshua."

Their faces went red. Wads of spit aimed at me began spewing from their mouths. They cursed Yeshua, turned their backs to me, and stomped through the sand, muttering and fuming as they stormed from the beach.

A Series of Supernatural Events

Nevertheless, the blessings of the Lord upon our life had actually begun two days after that meeting with the man from Australia. After those two days, we received five straight days of what I believe to be direct interventions from Heaven. At the end of those divine instances, it had been a total of seven days since the Australian man I had met at the Garden Tomb had spoken a word of blessing over me.

Here's how those five days unfolded:

Day 1: I received a phone call from an insurance company. The representative said he and his colleagues had been looking for me for some time because they had, for about ten years, had a check for 48,000 shekels (about $13,000 US) that belonged to me. I knew right then that the phone call and the check were from Heaven. That same day, Lian and I got the money, and that evening—believe it or not—we found an apartment for rent.

Day 2: We got a call from the family Lian had been working for, managing large VIP banquets. The father of the family had left for the United States and had left Lian a bonus of $14,000 US.

Day 3: Lian and I had the same dream from the Lord. Through that dream, we understood that we needed to give a tithe (10 percent of our recently acquired funds) to the Lord and His work. So we went to the Garden Tomb ministry in Jerusalem to do just that.

Day 4: We received yet another phone call, this time from someone who said, "Mr. Porat, you were here looking for a job eleven months ago. Are you still looking?" The caller was from the Ministry of Defense, and the offer was for a good management position in the Israeli army. I said I was still interested, and they employed me.

Day 5: Still another phone call came. Another Messianic believer had met the man from Australia, who had told him about us and had given him our number. He invited us to worship the Lord with him.

So...at the end of one week, God had protected us from a physical assault on the beach, given us finances, led us to a place to live, provided a great job, and connected us to a new brother in the Lord. Blessings after blessings were starting to pour out upon us.

The anti-Messianic Yad L'Achim organization had tried to buy us with money and position, but when we declined, Yeshua blessed us for standing firm. Even their "persuasive" emissaries, cursing, and stone-throwing had failed to turn us from our faithfulness to the Lord of Hosts.

The following Sabbath, I called my Mom and greeted her. "Shabbat Shalom."

She responded to my greeting with a warning. "We tried to help you," she said, "but you won't help yourself." That's when I realized it was she who had sent the late-night visitors to my tent.

Seven months later, the Lord called me to leave the job with the Ministry of Defense and begin a full-time ministry to the Jewish people of Israel. I took a step of faith and began to serve the Lord. Thus began Messiah of Israel Ministries. To this day, our calling is to share the news of Yeshua everywhere: on the streets, in synagogues, in mosques, in private homes, through Internet videocasting, and on websites, as well as in discipleship programs, through television and radio interviews, via print media articles, in conference preaching, on tours, and in joint ministry efforts with other like-minded believers—wherever the Lord leads.[7]

We also visit Holocaust survivors and those doing Aliyah[8] in Israel, blessing them with basic necessities of life and bringing them the truth of the gospel of Yeshua the Messiah. We now—in person—preach the gospel all over the world—primarily in Israel, but also in Europe, in many places in Asia, and in the United States.

This is a ministry calling for which we are unspeakably grateful. Yeshua has entrusted us with a global outreach and an eternally significant task. And the adventure of that heavenly assignment continues to take unbelievable turns.

8

A RABBI—TO BE OR NOT TO BE

If I say I'm a rabbi, they'll listen;
if I say I'm a pastor, they won't listen. This is the Jewish way.

Before we go farther down the road of our exploration, let me address an important consideration. Every now and then, someone will ask why I use the title "rabbi." Many refer to Matthew 23 as their point of biblical concern. Their argument is that "Jesus said His followers shouldn't call themselves 'rabbi'." At first glance, this apprehension seems justified. Let's have a look at that admonition by Yeshua Himself.

> [Jesus said to them,] "But you are **not to be called 'Rabbi,'** for you have one **Teacher,** and you are all brothers. And **do not call anyone on earth 'father,'** for you have one Father, and he is in heaven. **Nor are you to be called instructors,** for you have one Instructor, the Messiah." (Matthew 23:8–10; emphasis added)

As with all Scripture, we must examine this verse in its proper context. What was the purpose of Yeshua's pronouncement? Who was He talking *to,* and why? What do the rest of the Scriptures have to say about this?

How do biblical scholars and language experts understand the passage? When we study these matters in their proper context, we find our answer.

In Matthew 23, Yeshua had been admonishing the Pharisees regarding their pride and their impious desire to be addressed as though they were worthy of the highest prestige among the "lowly" people around them. However, the word "rabbi" in Hebrew simply means "teacher of the Scriptures."[9] Of course, we know teaching is a biblically specific ministry gift.

> **So Christ himself gave** the apostles, the prophets, the evangelists, the pastors **and teachers** [rabbis]. (Ephesians 4:11; emphasis added)

If that passage was written in Hebrew, it would say:

> So Christ Himself gave the apostles, the prophets, the evangelists, the pastors and **rabbis.**

Jesus' point in Matthew 23 was an effort to redirect His disciples towards *humility* in God's service. The idea of people seeking titles in order to elevate themselves above others is ungodly. However, there is a difference between seeking a title and *receiving* one for the practical purposes of opening legitimate ministry opportunities with specific groups. And that is the consensus among scholars who understand Hebrew customs, as well as the original language nuances.[10]

While I've never actively sought the title of "rabbi," that designation is still upon me within the Jewish culture, because I am a Jewish teacher of the Word of God. If I say I'm a rabbi, the Jews will listen to my teaching. If I say I'm a pastor or a preacher, they won't; they will completely shut me down. This is the Jewish way.

I do not use the title "rabbi" for prideful purposes. The moniker is simply a tool to help me spread the message of salvation, especially in Israel, and even within the Jewish community outside of Israel. The title, when used to speak of me or introduce me, accommodates the culture without violating anything Jesus commanded in order to keep the doors open to the preaching of the gospel.

This was the same heart the Apostle Paul had:

> To the Jews I became like a Jew, to win the Jews. ...To the weak I became weak, to win the weak. **I have become all things to all people so that by all possible means I might save some.** (1 Corinthians 9:20–22; emphasis added)

I'm very careful how I teach and preach. I don't purposely implant rabbinical/legalistic Jewish cultural teachings into my faith, life, or biblical message. Nor do I mix into my teaching the interpretations or practices of the unbelieving Orthodox Jewish rabbis or the writings of their ancient forefathers, unless I use those sources to give context to Hebrew thought and cultural practices, or to the intricacies of ancient Jewish history.

My only desire is to teach and preach the entire Word of God in its proper context. That perspective is centered on everything that has been and will be fulfilled in the life, ministry, death, resurrection, and return of Yeshua.

Sometimes I find that I upset those who are deeply entrenched in the Hebrew Roots movement. At other times, I offend those in the highly westernized, "Gentile-roots" Christian church. But, I cannot be concerned about those things. When one stands on the Word of God, centered in and interpreted through Jesus Christ, that person is going to offend somebody, somewhere—*always*. Such is my life.

Rabbi Paul of Tarsus is the one who told us: "Where the Spirit of the Lord is, there is liberty" (2 Corinthians 3:17). I try to walk in that same God-given liberty and deliver others from the bondage of unbelief—or even misbelief. Paul was talking about liberty from man-made laws, rituals, rules, and regulations, as well as freedom from a life that is in bondage to empty religiosity and the vainglorious interpretations of Scripture crafted only to meet ambitions or long-held traditions. These characteristics basically defined the Yeshua-denying Judaism of Paul's day, and they define ours as well.

Even before Paul, Jesus had also sternly rebuked the Pharisees for their culture-driven religious customs and rules, especially those that nullified the genuine Word of the Lord and took it out of context.

And Jesus continued, **"You have a fine way of setting aside the commands of God in order to observe your own traditions. …** Thus you nullify the word of God by your tradition that you have handed down. And you do **many** things like that." (Mark 7:9–13; emphasis added)

Why would I want to copy the "many things" that they did, and that some are even still doing in our day? We have to make a decision: Are we following Yeshua and His fulfillment of the Word or are we following man's customs, rules, and self-serving regulations? I've made my decision, regardless of the persecution that I might suffer for doing so. I pray you have as well.

ANOTHER SUPERNATURAL LINK

In the early days of persecution my wife and I endured, and in the heart-breaking losses of personal relationships, we had no idea that our lives would soon be intricately entwined with the message of the world's most revered Orthodox rabbi, Yitzhak Kaduri.

Many have rightly described Kaduri as the most revered rabbi in all of Israel's long history…all the way back to the beginning of the rabbinical system. But, surprising to many people outside Israel, he was also a man with whom we shared deep family and ministerial relationships.

That same rabbi, in early 2007, would deliver a seemingly peculiar message—written in a note—by his own hand. That note would turn out to be a message that would eventually send shock waves reverberating around the world. The fallout would forever shake the underpinnings of Jewish orthodoxy.

And, in time, I would be caught in the very heart of the frenzy.[11]

PART II

FROM REVELATION TO AN IMPROBABLE MINISTRY CONNECTION

How precious to me are your thoughts, oh God.
How vast is the sum of them.
Were I to count them,
they would outnumber the grains of sand—
when I awake, I am still with you.

~Psalm 139:17–18

9

THE RABBI WHO STUNNED THE WORLD

His followers would soon receive the shock of their lives.

In 1898, in the midst of the unfolding tumultuous history of the Jewish people, a baby boy was born into the home of a respected Iraqi rabbi and his wife. The couple named their child Yitzhak.

They could not have known at the time that a monumental event in this child's life—over a hundred years into the future—would overturn the moorings of Judaism. And who in the world could have imagined that my newfound destiny in Jesus Christ, as well as my eventual global ministry, would be so tethered to his? Only the Lord God, the creator of Heaven and earth, could have known and orchestrated such a thing.

KADURI'S EARLY YEARS

Having eventually settled in Palestine in the early 1920s, Yitzhak Kaduri became an Orthodox rabbi who navigated the early years of the formation of the Jewish state of Israel and became a recognized religious leader, particularly among ultra-Orthodox and North African Jews. Thousands visited him to ask for advice.[12]

He gradually emerged as a significant force in Israeli politics in the 1990s. His endorsement of Benjamin Netanyahu was considered crucial to the Likud leader's 1996 election as prime minister. In 2000, Kaduri claimed he had seen a vision in which Heaven was shown to have favored the then little-known Moshe Katzav for president over former Prime Minister Shimon Peres, and so once Katzav won that bid, Kaduri came to be regarded as a prophet who could predict future events.

Once he acquired a taste for politics, it seemed he was everywhere, using his voice to influence the establishment of housing developments, to promote "Jewish values," and to endorse marketing ploys that were used to sway Israeli elections. He was always "there," making suggestions in reference to peace bids with Israel's enemies, Syria and Iran, as well as influencing certain territorial changes. Many, like the Israeli sausage factory team that flew him in by helicopter to bless their business, cashed in on Kaduri's name and reputation.[13]

Known for his seemingly photographic memorization of the Old Testament, the Talmud, and other Jewish writings—right up to the day of his death—Rabbi Kaduri quickly became a revered yeshiva teacher. He was an icon among Jewish sages, as well as among other celebrities and rabbis who had kept the Jewish faith alive even before the State of Israel was born.

In 2002, he surprised his followers when he claimed that the *true* Messiah had appeared to him in a vision. He claimed he knew the name of the Messiah who was soon to come. He eventually wrote that name in a note[14] that he indicated was not to be shared with the world until one year after his death. He publicly proclaimed this revelation, along with his strict instructions about its release, during the 2005 Yom Kippur services in his own synagogue. News of his pronouncement was carried in mainstream Israeli news sources.

Rabbi Yitzhak Kaduri was 108 when he died from pneumonia on January 28, 2006. By that time, "small, bent and wizened, invariably draped in the white robes of an oriental Jewish kabbalist," he had become a widely known, familiar figure. Everyone in Israel and many around the world recognized his face from images that graced coffee mugs and "dangled from rearview mirrors of taxis scuttling between Tel Aviv and Jerusalem."[15]

Rabbi Kaduri successfully kept the world holding its collective breath for an entire year after his death. His followers, millions of them, and everyone else who had heard about the mysterious note were waiting for the unveiling of the secret he had supposedly handwritten and sealed in an envelope about five months before he died.

What would the note say? What was the name of the Messiah? His followers would soon find out.

10

THE NOTE

The Messiah note revelation created a huge collection
of problems for the Orthodox Jews.

The following words were written in Rabbi Kaduri's Messiah note. The words are translated into English, but they were, of course, originally penned in Hebrew—the only language the rabbi spoke.[16]

> Concerning the letter abbreviation of the Messiah's name, **He will lift the people and prove that his word and law are valid.** This I have signed in the month of mercy.

It's uncertain who initially deciphered the code or precisely when that process occurred. However, only after the note had been displayed for several weeks on Kaduri's website was the original, promised message finally revealed.

The key to its unlocking had been there all along. Rabbi Kaduri had inserted the clue, hidden in plain sight, in the first portion of the first sentence: "Concerning the letter abbreviation of the *Messiah's name*."

To the non-Jewish eye, the key might not have been that obvious. However, this veiled clue pointed to an ancient Hebrew custom of using an acrostic-style method of emphasizing words or letters of the Hebrew alphabet. The first letter of a word in a paragraph or passage served as the marker for that selection.

Acrostics of this nature are found, for example, in the book of Psalms—in chapters 25, 34, 37, 111, 112, 119, and 145. The well-known passage of Proverbs 31:10–31 is also an acrostic, as is Lamentations chapters 1–4.

These examples, as they appear in the Scriptures, are not necessarily meant to reveal a hidden code. Rather, they employ a distinctive Hebrew literary practice of declaring that the words of the writing are particularly important and should be carefully examined for their deep truths. However, in Rabbi Kaduri's case, it is apparent that he meant for the acrostic procedure to apply only to a certain portion of his note, to decrypt a hidden revelation within the note: *the name of the true Messiah.*

The "secret key" portion of the note was immediately followed by a selection of six Hebrew words: *Yarim ha'am veyokhiakh shedvaro vetorato omdim.* Those words translate in English to: "He will lift the people and prove that his word and law are valid." This was the conspicuously separated portion of the note that was to be used to decipher the Messiah's name.

When the first letter of each of those Hebrew words is strung together—from right to left, as the Hebrew language is properly read, and with the appropriate vowel sounds included—they spell the word *Yehoshua.* This is the older, long-form rendering of the Hebrew word *Yeshua*—or, as most English-speaking people pronounce the name, Jesus.

There it was, displayed before the eyes of the world. Once it was properly decrypted, Rabbi Kaduri's message finally revealed what he had promised his followers: the name of the true Messiah.

But there was still one monumental problem. To any Orthodox Jewish person, that name was an abomination. For the last two thousand years, this had been the very name the Jews had passionately tried to discredit. Now, their most famous Orthodox rabbi was telling them that this name was, in fact, the one that should be revered above all others. How were they going to deal with this theological nuclear explosion?

SALVATION

The Messiah note revelation created a huge collection of problems for the Orthodox Jews. The Hebrew words *Yehoshua* and *Yeshua* are effectively the same name, derived from the same Hebrew root of the word "salvation," as documented in Zechariah 6:11 and Ezra 3:2.

Yehoshua is the word for "Savior," and *Yeshua* is the word for "salvation." They convey the same meaning and are equivalent to the Greek *Iesous* (Jesus). Over eighty times the word *Yeshua*, meaning "salvation," appears in the Old Testament. This means the presence of Jesus is found throughout the Bible, from beginning to end, every time that word/name is used.[17]

This is one of the biggest reasons the rabbis warn their congregants not to read the Scriptures for themselves and claim the Jewish people need to rely on the rabbinical interpretations. The rabbis are afraid the Jewish population will begin to connect the biblical dots and eventually discover that Yeshua is indeed Messiah.

Rabbi Kaduri's son, David Kaduri, actually admitted that his father's final year was focused on the visions of the Messiah and that he had said Messiah was coming soon. But when the note was opened in January 2007, he and the Yeshua-hating Jews were horrified. How could this be?

David claimed the note must have been a forgery. The ultra-Orthodox Jews from his seminary in Jerusalem argued that their master did not leave the exact solution for decoding the Messiah's name. They did everything they could to discredit the revelation that, if believed, would change everything for the Jewish people.

I later learned Rabbi Kaduri had shared his knowledge of Jesus as the Messiah with a small circle of his most trusted disciples, and they were the ones who had authenticated the note. My knowledge of this fact came to me directly from one of Kaduri's students. Interestingly, Kaduri was still living, and while the Jewish world was commending the elderly rabbi as the greatest of all the rabbis in Israel, he was also teaching several members of his "inner circle" about Yeshua as Messiah—the greatest "sin" a Jewish person can commit.

Rabbi Kaduri was resolute in his belief that the world was in its prophesied last days, and he was passionate about making sure the Jews knew the genuine Messiah had already come. He was adamant that Messiah's true name is *Yeshua.*

It seemed Rabbi Kaduri and I had both committed that same, unforgivable Jewish sin.

11

QUESTIONS

Two important intertwined questions invariably
arise when I am sharing this remarkable account.

On a cold day in January 2016, President Moshe Katzav of Israel
spoke the eulogy at Rabbi Kaduri's funeral. The service drew a
massive crowd of well over two hundred thousand mourners from around
the world.

The aftermath of Kaduri's "Messiah revelation" sparked a global awakening. The "Kaduri Revival," as I like to call it, is still gaining momentum
today. It is a prophetic movement of God. Jews all around the world are
coming to Jesus Christ as Messiah in response to Rabbi Kaduri's note.

The global Church of born-again believers is also hearing the truth
of this supernatural account, and revival is breaking out in various underground movements, especially in Asia. As a firsthand witness to this phenomenon, I am still in awe that the Lord of Heaven would include me
and my ministry in this amazing occurrence.

Two important intertwined questions invariably arise when I share
this remarkable account: Why didn't Rabbi Kaduri immediately present

his revelation to the world? And why did he tell his ministry officials to wait a full year after his death to release the note?

In answer to the first question, Kaduri knew that if he had shared his knowledge with the world immediately, he would have been summarily discredited; no one would believe him. The authorities and the largely Orthodox news media in Israel would have squashed the story, and the matter would have been over, forever. (Yes, we have "fake news" in Israel, too.)

Remember, for a Jewish person to say Jesus is the true Messiah is an outrage and practically unforgivable within the Orthodox community. Also, preaching Yeshua as Messiah is an offense that draws the penalty of stoning. He could have been killed. If that happened, the vision most certainly would have died with him.

Don't forget this important detail as well: Kaduri was not entirely keeping the matter a secret. Before his death, he had revealed this earth-shattering vision with almost a dozen of his select students. To this day, they are believers in Yeshua as Messiah.[18]

The second question—about why Kaduri did not want the note released until a year after his death—is answered like this: In major sects of Judaism, in the year following a death, the legacy, reputation, and credibility of the deceased are formally established. People write articles, tributes, books, and even songs about the life and deeds of the person being mourned.

Kaduri was wise. He knew his message would be harder to discredit once his overall impeccable legacy had been "carved in stone." After his death, the message would not just be his word; it would be his word *framed by his solid-gold reputation for speaking truth and wisdom.* Telling his ministry team to wait a year before opening and posting the note was a brilliant move.

Also, consider this important tidbit: Before Rabbi Kaduri became a believer, he taught Kabbalah. That ancient system of spiritual practice and twisted biblical interpretations is riddled with demonic mysticism and even out-and-out forms of witchcraft and occultic practices. Kabbalah often elevates its own "sacred" texts and commentaries above the Torah. Witchcraft—the sin of rebellion—operates wherever it can. Kabbalah is still influential among a large sector of Orthodox Judaism in Israel and around the world.[19] While it is true that Kaduri was a Kabbalist rabbi, God chose him as the conduit for the greatest message ever to be given to those who had, for centuries, awaited the coming of the Jewish Messiah. This choice was not an endorsement of mysticism. Rather, it was God in the act of crushing Satan under His foot. In much the same way that God chose the Christian-killing, church-persecuting Saul of Tarsus to write almost half the New Testament and have a direct hand in starting almost all of the churches in the Roman Empire during the first decades of its existence, Yahweh used yet another unlikely rabbi in these last days—Rabbi Kaduri.

HEAVEN-SENT PLAN

God ensured that the top teacher of Kabbalism embraced Yeshua as Messiah and then planned the most effective way to establish the name of Yeshua as the long-awaited Messiah of the Jews, a way that was certain to get that message to the world. The chapter you are now reading, once again, fulfills that supernatural, Heaven-sent plan.

It's also important to note that in the last eight months of his life, Kaduri no longer taught Kabbalah. I know this for a fact. I was living in the midst of the turmoil of this startling revelation. I witnessed the transformation in Rabbi Kaduri's life and within his overall ministry approach. I have documented that observable phenomenon many times on television, via radio, and in print. Remember, our family knew him well. The divine connection between our family and Kaduri's ministry caused my life to turn a sharp corner, a turning point from which there would be no departure.

12

WHO COULD HAVE KNOWN?

Rabbi Kaduri's life and mine would be inextricably intertwined.

Rabbi Kaduri's discovery of Yeshua as Messiah set the stage for my personal ministry to the Jews. When I was growing up, he was a frequent visitor in our home, a beloved friend of our rabbinic family, and part of the overall fabric of my life. For the non-Jewish readers, this would be similar to someone like Billy Graham or Franklin Graham being a frequent guest in your own home or in the home of one of your close family members. My father and my grandfather were good friends with Rabbi Kaduri; they esteemed him as supremely righteous. They moved in the same rabbinical circles of important people in Israel, as well as in the United States.

As a child, I thought nothing of this relationship with Rabbi Kaduri; I took it for granted. I had no idea what it would mean to me in later years. It was within the context of that elite culture and associations that God began to order my steps and ministry. Growing up with the name of Yeshua understood as being one to openly revile, I could never have imagined that both Rabbi Kaduri and I would, one day, believe in Yeshua as Messiah. In addition, at the time, I could never have been convinced *by anyone* that both Rabbi Kaduri and I would serve as emissaries of the same message to the Jewish people around the world: *Yeshua is indeed the Messiah.*

One more thing: How could I have dreamed my direct connection to the Kaduri saga would burst open the many doors of opportunity that would otherwise never have been unlocked? This book is just one example of those divinely opened doors.[20]

Who could have known that Kaduri, at the end of a lifetime of teaching occultism and refuting the claims of Yeshua, would eventually proclaim the truth of the gospel message? Who would have guessed that God's plan for Israel would be revealed through the Kaduri years? It was unthinkable. *Only Yahweh could have known.* And only Yahweh could have made it happen.

> How precious to me are your thoughts, O God. How vast is the sum of them. Were I to count them, they would outnumber the grains of sand—when I awake, I am still with you. (Psalm 139:17–18)

The very idea of Rabbi Kaduri having a supernatural revelation of Yeshua as Messiah, then teaching that revelation to his yeshiva students, would have seemed crazy. But then, for him to leave the disclosure of his divine revelation in a handwritten note on his personal website was the stuff of fiction novels. Yet every bit of what I have related, *and more*, happened. The truth of that story is now thoroughly documented.[21]

THE GOAL

It's one thing to accept the revelation of Yeshua as Messiah, and it's something else to walk in the revelation of it and move forward in the authority He gives us. So, what does God want us to do now?

How do we navigate the perilous times ahead? How can we find the genuine footsteps of Yeshua/Jesus so we can follow Him, both spiritually and physically? How do we wade through the demonic deception that constantly surrounds us? How are we to effectively avoid the false teachings of the "doctrines of demons" (1 Timothy 4:1) that pull at us, attempting to lead us astray and drive us into deeper and deeper darkness?

Jesus has not hidden the truth from us. Yet, He never promised us that the work of Kingdom ministry would be easy. In fact, He was quite clear about it. Sometimes, the battle would be brutal. Often the walk is grueling. But the ultimate goal is clear:

> Then Jesus told his disciples, "If anyone would come after me, let him deny himself and take up his cross and follow me." (Matthew 16:24)

And so it was that Rabbi Kaduri's life and mine would be inextricably intertwined in the Kingdom work of advancing the gospel message that Jesus Christ is Lord and Messiah. Only Heaven's throne itself could have arranged such a thing.

13

JOURNEY TO ZION

My entire life's journey, since coming to Jesus/Yeshua as Messiah and Lord, has been to trace the genuine treasures of biblical truth.

The subtitle of this book speaks of my own "journey to Zion." The word "Zion" is biblically rich; it's the designation the Bible first gives to Jerusalem, also known as the City of David.

Nevertheless, David captured the fortress of Zion, the City of David. (2 Samuel 5:7)

The word is often used as a pejorative, as in, "Oh, you're one of those crazy Zionists, aren't you?" What they mean to convey is they are not a supporter of Israel's right of return to the land or the national sovereignty of the State of Israel itself. So, for those who do support these biblical truths, the term is not negative at all. It's coined by God.[22]

However, "Zion" isn't only the word God Himself uses to describe Jerusalem; He also uses it to designate *those who love Him* and seek an abiding and personal relationship with Him.

This is **what the Lord, the God of Israel, says:** "I have heard your prayer concerning Sennacherib king of Assyria. This is the word that the Lord has spoken against him:' 'The Virgin **Daughter of Zion** despises you and mocks you. The **Daughter of Jerusalem** tosses her head as you flee.'" (2 Kings 19:20–21; emphasis added)

God also speaks of Zion as the place He chose to install the ultimate rule and reign of Jesus Christ, His Messiah, and our salvation. That place encompasses Jerusalem, all of Israel, and even the unseen realm of Heaven's throne—Paradise.[23]

For these reasons, born-again believers speak of being with God in Paradise as our "journey to Zion." That understanding is beautifully expressed in the hymn, "We're Marching to Zion," by Isaac Watts:

First stanza:

Come, we that love the Lord,
And let our joys be known;
Join in a song with sweet accord,
And thus surround the throne.

Refrain:

We're marching to Zion,
Beautiful, beautiful Zion;
We're marching upward to Zion,
The beautiful city of God.[24]

In Psalm 2, Yahweh rebukes the rebellious nations and their kings. He chastises them for thinking they can band together, under Satan's influence, and defeat the purposes of Heaven's throne, which He calls Zion.

Why do the nations conspire and the peoples plot in vain? The kings of the earth take their stand and the rulers gather together against the Lord and against his Anointed One. "Let us break their chains," they say, "and throw off their fetters."

The One enthroned in heaven laughs; the Lord scoffs at them. Then he rebukes them in his anger and terrifies them in his wrath, saying, "**I have installed my King on Zion, my holy hill.**" (Psalm 2:1–6; emphasis added)

The *Encyclopaedia Britannica* describes Zion like this:

Zion appears in the Old Testament 152 times as a title of Jerusalem. It appears seven times in the New Testament and five times in quotations from the Old Testament....

Mount Zion is **the place where Yahweh, the God of Israel, dwells** (Isaiah 8:18; Psalm 74:2), the place where he is king (Isaiah 24:23) and where he has installed his king, David (Psalm 2:6).

It is thus **the seat of the action of Yahweh** in history.[25] (Emphasis added)

The last sentence of that encyclopedia entry is the one that carries the fullest meaning of this book's subtitle. My life's journey, since coming to Jesus/Yeshua as Messiah and Lord, has been to trace the treasures of biblical truth regarding Yahweh's work among His creation throughout history. This is especially so regarding His birth, life, ministry, crucifixion, and resurrection—the crux of the entire gospel message.

As I set out on that personal journey to Zion, I ran into incredible discoveries—the uncovering of deep biblical mysteries that I believe were directed by the Holy Spirit of God. On top of that, the Lord began to bring several of those biblical revelations to life by taking me right to the places of their fulfillment. What I've found along the way of this journey has defined my entire life and ministry. And now I want to share what I've found with you.

Part III

From the Chaldean Spirit to the Unmasking

Look among the nations, and see; wonder and be astounded. For I am doing a work in your days that you would not believe if told. For behold, I am raising up the Chaldeans, that bitter and hasty nation, who march through the breadth of the earth, to seize dwellings not their own.

~Habakkuk 1:5, 6

14

ONE NEW MAN

He came for the Jew first, and Yeshua gave His life for them...first.

Belief in the "eventual" coming of the Messiah is one of the fundamental tenets of the Jewish faith. But, the Jewish people desperately need to understand that Messiah has *already* come, and has provided genuine salvation for them through Yeshua. As a born-again and, therefore, a "completed" Jew, I am deeply stirred by the critical need of the Jewish people to recognize Jesus as their Messiah and to know of His great and abiding love for them.

However, a number of God's people don't understand that there are really *four kinds* of Jewish people:

1. **Secularized Jews.** These, as would be the same among almost any ethnic group of people, simply don't believe in *anything*. Or, sometimes they claim to believe in *everything*. This group includes everyone from atheists and agnostics to those who believe in some variety of universalism.
2. **Cultural Jews.** These have DNA that proves their ethnicity, but they aren't particularly religious, except during some of the major

traditional Jewish holidays. This is much like a certain number of Christians around the world showing up at church only for Christmas, Resurrection Day, a wedding, or a funeral.

3. **Committed Religious Jews.** These hold to their Jewish faith through consistent practice of its traditions, rituals, and rabbinically developed rules. They regularly attend synagogue, practice the teachings of the rabbis, and faithfully celebrate all the major feast days. However, even this group is divided into different "denominations" of Judaism—similar to the subgroups of the Christian faith system. Jewish denominations range from the ultra-liberal to the ultra-Orthodox and include almost every view in between.

4. **Completed Jews.** Also known as Messianic Jews, these hold a belief that is solidly founded in Yeshua as Messiah. That born-again belief framework brings them into the *true family* of God (Romans 11).

A CLOSER LOOK AT MESSIANIC JEWS

Born-again Jewish brothers and sisters don't give up their "Jewishness" by serving Yeshua as Lord and Messiah; rather, they, of all people, most fully understand that Yeshua truly did fulfill all the prophecies of Messiah as outlined in the Old Testament (the *Tanakh*) and the biblical feasts of the Lord (Leviticus 23). Through these truths, they understand by the Holy Spirit that Yeshua is the Messiah the Jewish people have long awaited. The part of the present-day Church that is not Jewish should never forget that when God sent His Messiah, He came for the Jewish people first, and Yeshua gave His life for them *first*. As I like to say, "Not to the Jew *better*, but to the Jew *first*."

Therefore, while Jewish people certainly would "give up" parts of their past "Jewishness" that held them in slavery to the "teachings of the rabbis"—they *do not give up* their Jewish foundations. In fact, they often find those foundations to be greatly enhanced. Messianic Jews know the truths underlying the message of the Old Testament prophecies, feasts, and teachings. In so believing and understanding, they then become a part of what the Word of God identifies as the "one new man," Jew and Gentile together in Jesus Christ, under the New Covenant of His shed blood.

> **For he himself** is our peace, who **has made us both one** and has broken down in his flesh the dividing wall of hostility by abolishing the law of commandments expressed in ordinances, that **he might create** in himself **one new man in place of the two,** so making peace, and might **reconcile us both to God in one body through the cross,** thereby killing the hostility. (Ephesians 2:14–16; emphasis added)

WHAT SECULARIZED, CULTURAL, AND COMMITTED JEWS NEED

Secularized Jews, as well as cultural Jews and even deeply committed religious Jews, need the amazing message of the love of God through Jesus Christ—the true Messiah of Israel. They must understand that Yeshua is for them, *first.* But, that message will now largely come from the Church—*the one new man*—under the true Lamb of God, *Yeshua Ha Mashiach.*[26] Now is the time—especially in these unprecedented prophetic days.

The Apostle Paul, foreseeing our own prescient times, said it like this:

> For if you [Gentiles] were cut from what is by nature a wild olive tree, and grafted, contrary to nature, into a cultivated olive tree, how much more will these, the natural branches, be grafted back into their own olive tree.
>
> I do not want you to be ignorant of this mystery, brothers and sisters, so that you may not be conceited: Israel has experienced a hardening in part until the full number of the Gentiles has come in and **in this way** all Israel will be saved. As it is written: "The **deliverer will come from Zion**; he will turn godlessness away from Jacob." (Romans 11:23–26; emphasis added)

The *Pulpit Commentary's* take on that passage elaborates on the wonderful truth of what Paul wrote.

> In what follows next the eventual **coming of the Jewish nation into the Church** is not only anticipated as possible or probable, but **foretold prophetically.** Paul announces it **as a "mystery,"** which his readers may be ignorant of, but which he wishes them to know. By the word [mystery], as used by Paul, is meant **something hidden from man in the Divine counsels till made known by revelation** (see 1 Corinthians 2:7, 10; 1 Corinthians 15:51; and, in this Epistle, Romans 16:25, 26–a passage which expresses clearly the apostle's meaning in his use of the word).[27] (Emphasis added, parentheses in original)

Maybe you're asking, at this point, something like: "But does this truth from Romans 11 then mean that the Church has *replaced* the Jews as God's chosen people?" No, it certainly does not. In fact, it proclaims just the opposite, in every contextual way.

That leads us to one of the most despicable lies from the evil one. That lie is still slithering through some of the halls of institutional Christianity, even today…especially today.

15

THE LIE

God chose a specific people through whom He would carry
His Word to the earth. For that task, He chose Israel.

The Scriptures are clear. Not only have the ethnic Jews been given a
double portion of God's covenant blessings (Isaiah 40:2), but also,
when believing Jews and Gentiles come together, they create a holy
dwelling place—a holy temple—for His Spirit (Ephesians 2:11–22).
That dwelling place is called "Israel." It is the spiritual Israel, *which is the
Church*. The two are *one and the same* under the blood of Jesus. They are
called the "one new man."

> Therefore, remember that formerly **you who are Gentiles**
> by birth and called "uncircumcised" by those who call them-
> selves "the circumcision" (which is done in the body by human
> hands)—remember that at that time you were separate from
> Christ, **excluded from citizenship in Israel** and **foreigners to the
> covenants of the promise**, without hope and without God in the
> world. But now in Christ Jesus you who once were far away have

been brought near by the blood of Christ. (Ephesians 2:11–13; emphasis added)

Having abolished in his flesh the enmity, even the law of commandments contained in ordinances; for to make in himself of twain **one new man,** so making peace; And that he **might reconcile both unto God in one body** by the cross, having slain the enmity. (Ephesians 2:15–16, NKJV; emphasis added)

In him **the whole building** [Jew and Gentile together] is joined together and rises **to become a holy temple in the Lord.** (Ephesians 2:11–13, 21; emphasis added)

DANGEROUS DECEPTION

The idea that somehow the *Church has replaced Israel*[28] is a prime example of the prophesied last-days demonic deception. And it's centered on blatant anti-Semitism. The Scripture speaks to this special kind of demonic and "ignorant conceit." Have a look at one powerful sample of the biblical clarity on this matter. It's from Paul's letter to the Romans:

I ask then: **Did God reject his people? By no means.** I am an Israelite myself, a descendant of Abraham, from the tribe of Benjamin. **God did not reject his people,** whom he foreknew....

Again I ask: Did they stumble so as to fall beyond recovery? **Not at all.** Rather, **because of their transgression, salvation has come to the Gentiles** to make Israel envious....

I do not want you to be ignorant of this mystery, brothers and sisters, **so that you may not be conceited...**

As far as the gospel is concerned, they are enemies for your sake; but **as far as election is concerned, they are loved on account of the patriarchs,** for **God's gifts and his call are irrevocable.** (Romans 11:1–2, 11, 28–29; emphasis added)

God's Word equates spiritual Israel with the Church. The two entities are the same. Further, Paul declares that salvation itself first issued forth out of Israel:

> I do not want you to be ignorant of this mystery, brothers and sisters, so that you may not be conceited: Israel has experienced **a hardening** in part until the full number of the Gentiles **has come in** [come in to the body of believers in Yeshua, the Church], and in this way **all Israel** [spiritual Israel; also known as the Church] **will be saved.** (Romans 11:25–26; emphasis added)

Barnes' Notes on the Bible:

> Shall be saved—Shall be recovered from their rejection; be **restored to the divine favor**; become followers of the Messiah, and **thus be saved as all other Christians** are.[29] (Emphasis added)

Meyer's New Testament Commentary:

> **Will be saved**, unto **Messianic salvation**, by their **conversion to Christ** [which then equates saved Jews and saved Gentiles—the Church—as "all Israel"].
>   …consequently not the [Second Coming itself], because the conversion of **all Israel** must be antecedent to this, **but rather** that especially efficacious self-revelation of Christ in **the preaching of His gospel** (comp. Ephesians 2:17).[30] (Emphasis added)

CHOSEN PEOPLE FOR A CHOSEN MISSION

God chose a specific people through whom He would carry His Word to the earth. For that task, *He chose Israel.* He chose the Jewish people. Therefore, we must never forget that it was through the Jewish people that the original Word of God came.[31] Along with that Word came the last-days prophecies, many of which we're living through now. And every single writer of Scripture was Jewish.

Not only that, but when God *did* send His Son, He was clothed in Jewish flesh. And don't forget that the early church was made up almost entirely of Jewish believers. It was the Jewish believers who first preached the gospel of Jesus Christ to the world.

> Then what advantage has the Jew? Or what is the value of cir-cumcision? Much in every way. **To begin with, the Jews were entrusted with the oracles of God.** (Romans 3:1–3; emphasis added).

Humanity—especially today's church—owes a great debt of gratitude to the Jewish people for protecting the Scriptures throughout the wars and upheavals of the centuries. But, the deceptive and lying demonic spir-its of Satan's dark kingdom are tasked with turning the world away from the Jewish people, as well as the prophetically returned nation of Israel. That prophesied end-time lie is alive and well today; it's yet another stark proof of the prophetic times in which we're living.

16

THE CONUNDRUM

*These issues are no small matters to the
Jewish people who are not yet believers in Jesus as Messiah.*

We face a double-pronged problem in trying to reach the Jewish people in today's Israel and around the world. First, the purely ethnic Jews have been deceived by their cultural blindness concerning the gospel of Yeshua. They've been raised in a world that teaches them from childhood to loathe the name of Yeshua as well as the New Testament documents that lay out the account of His life, ministry, death, and resurrection.

Second, the Jews of a more spiritual/biblical nature—those who regularly practice their faith—have also been led astray. Their blindness has come through the workings of a particularly devious spiritual deception and false rabbinical teachings. That evil spirit is one that tries to rob the Jewish people of their true biblical inheritance and presents to them a different gospel—a system of "good works." They believe they are *saved* by rigidly obeying the "law" and the Orthodox Jewish customs, especially in the way it is taught by their own rabbis and largely the same way it was taught in the New Testament days of the early church.

71

HOLY PLACES?

Believe it or not, a huge part of the demonic lie affecting the Jewish people as a whole has been reinforced by the presence of the so-called *holy places* throughout the nation of Israel, especially those that are tourist traps, having been designated as *bona fide* holy sites. This is primarily orchestrated by the Roman Catholic Church and, occasionally, by folks in other denominational faith systems.[32] The Jewish population of Israel, by and large, wants nothing to do with these impositions. They consider the Roman Catholic religious system, in particular, to be steeped in idol worship and false holy sites that are superimposed upon the distinctive and rich history of Israel and Judaism.

I understand that what I'm saying here might not be too popular, but please believe that I am stating the absolute truth. I hear this sentiment almost every day on the streets of Israel. I was born and raised among Israel's Jewish people, and I live among them to this day. They are my people. I am one of them in the deepest of ways, both through DNA as well as through my Orthodox training from birth. Trust me when I say this is *precisely* what they talk about and how they feel in regard to this important spiritual matter.

The Jewish people also identify the Roman Catholic Church as having deeply ingrained historical roots involving direct persecution against the Jews. Additionally, they quite often classify *all* Christians as a part of that overall Roman Catholic system.[33] These issues are not small matters to the Jewish people who are not yet believers in Jesus as Messiah. The hurdles they must scale in order to believe are enormous—*humanly insurmountable*—and they run demonically deep, which, as promised, brings us to the next important biblical revelation.

17

UNDERSTANDING THE CHALDEAN SPIRIT

*Since time immemorial, the term "Chaldean spirit"
came to be associated with a certain
kind of hideous demonic rampage.*

The Lord is using supernatural tools like the Kaduri Revival and various ministries such as Messiah of Israel and several other organizations in Israel and around the world that truly have the best interest of the Jewish people at heart. Those of us involved in these efforts are faithfully proclaiming Yeshua as Messiah in the proper context of Old Testament foundations and its messianic revelations. These endeavors might be labeled as the positive side of God's work in this area.

Conversely, on what some might label as the more negative side of His work, He's also using another specific vehicle to achieve His goal. It's an instrument of testing and discipline. It is a separating process that God has used since the most ancient of Old Testament times.

HABAKKUK

For example, in Habakkuk's day, the Lord chose the *Chaldeans* for the task of separating the faithful from the unfaithful, or "the wheat from the chaff" (Matthew 13). And, as we'll discover in subsequent chapters of this book, there is a reason He chose the Chaldeans in particular. It is in this sense that I and numerous renowned biblical scholars often refer to their Heaven-prompted but demonically manipulated exploits as being accomplished through the "spirit of the Chaldeans."[34]

Here is what God instructed Habakkuk to tell the Jewish people of his time:

> Look among the nations, and see; wonder and be astounded. For I am doing a work in your days that you would not believe if told. For behold, **I am raising up the Chaldeans**, that **bitter and hasty** nation, who march **through the breadth of the earth, to seize dwellings not their own.** (Habakkuk 1:5, 6; emphasis added)

But, there's something else to this truth. This "raising up" of the Chaldeans in the days of Habakkuk also had a dark spiritual aspect. The Chaldeans were steeped in practices of the occult and all the vile evil attached to it. This lifestyle was foundational to their civilization, and the Jewish people around the world are particularly familiar with this fact.

From the *Jewish Encyclopedia*:

> It was **from Chaldea that the name "shedim" (evil demons) came to the Israelites**, and so the sacred writers intentionally applied the word in a *dyslogistic* [noncomplimentary] sense to the Canaanite deities.[35] (Emphasis added; parentheses in original)

Being a native-born Hebrew speaker, I can attest that in the Modern Hebrew language, the word "Chaldean" (Hebrew: *kasdim*) is frequently used to mean ghosts, demons, or spirits—because of the grammatical, biblical, and historical connections to the word. The historic connections come from the fact that the Chaldeans were known for practicing astrology, the magic arts, and divination.[36]

DARK PRINCE, DARK SPIRITS

Satan is the grand prince of those Chaldean spirits, and through his authority over that corrupted demonic host, he continues to storm throughout the earth stealing what does not belong to him, arrogantly believing he can somehow thwart the work of God. I believe the Chaldean spirit makes up the bulk of Satan's army—especially in the last days, and especially against the Jewish people, as well as against the Church.

Nevertheless, God *will* turn everything around for His own purposes. He always does. Yet, He still *allows* that same demonic spirit to act as a sort of divine "weed eater." In this way, the tares are continually pulled from among the wheat, right until the time of the last-days harvest. Jesus has never hidden this great truth from us.

> He answered, "The one who sowed the good seed is the Son of Man. The field is the world, and the good seed stands for the people of the kingdom. **The weeds are the people of the evil one, and the enemy who sows them is the devil.** The harvest is the end of the age, and the harvesters are angels. **As the weeds are pulled up** and burned in the fire, so it will be at the end of the age. The Son of Man will send out his angels, **and they will weed out of his kingdom everything that causes sin and all who do evil."** (Matthew 13:37–41; emphasis added)

> For it is time for judgment **to begin with God's household;** [the Church] and if it begins with us, what will the outcome be for those who do not obey **the gospel of God?** (1 Peter 4:17; emphasis added)

The Chaldean spirits are ominously dark in origin, fiercely loyal, and faithful in continuing to serve Satan throughout the ages. This is true whether they are posing as humans—as in the "appearance" of a dead relative in a séance—or as some other ghostly apparition that is "summoned" forth at the command of someone immersed in the occult. These spirits can also work through teachers of false doctrine, as well as by simply exerting their spiritual influence in the ongoing war that is waged in the arenas of the human mind and soul (Romans 12:1–3; 2 Corinthians 10:5; 1 Timothy 4:1).

We know the centermost battle of the universe, according to God's own Word, is spiritual warfare against Israel. It started in Israel where the Garden of Eden was first laid out, and it's going to end in Israel where the Garden of Eden is ultimately reclaimed and divinely revealed (Revelation 21–22).[37]

Satan knows these truths, and, as I've already stated, he *knows* his days are numbered.

> But woe to the earth and the sea, because the devil has gone down to you. He is filled with fury, because he knows that his time is short. (Revelation 12:12)

Never doubt: The battle is always over the *firstborn*, which is spiritual Israel, the "one new man" (Ephesians 2; Romans 11; and Revelation 12). So we know Satan will attack anyone who has anything meaningful to do with Israel, especially if it involves the salvation of the Jewish people. The evil one will try to steal what does not belong to him.

> The thief comes to steal, kill, and destroy. (John 10:10)

That *stealing-killing-destroying* agenda is brought about through the Chaldean spirit. Satan and his demonic horde will never give up until they are ultimately defeated at the Second Coming of our Lord Jesus Christ.

18

THE SPREAD OF DARKNESS

The spirit of the Chaldeans grows
in influence throughout the world.

In several places in the Scriptures, we are given insight concerning the demonic hierarchy of Satan's kingdom.[38]

Ephesians 6:10–12 is a well-known passage about the demonic realms against which we battle. Sadly, many believers are unaware that these interdimensional realms exist. For this reason, these believers are ill prepared to deal with the very real warfare that frequently comes their way.[39]

Because we cannot literally see into the halls of those spiritual dimensions in the same way we see the physical world around us, we tend to think we're battling only the people and circumstances we can observe with our earth-bound eyes. We're often oblivious to the dark forces that are actually controlling those people, circumstances, and situations.

Finally, be strong in the Lord and in his mighty power. Put on the full armor of God so that you can take your stand against the devil's schemes. For our struggle is not against flesh and blood but against the rulers, against the authorities, against the powers of this dark world and against the spiritual forces of evil in the heavenly realms. (Ephesians 6:10–12)

Jesus said, "For judgment I have come into this world, so that the blind will see and those who see will become blind." Some Pharisees who were with him heard him say this and asked, "What? Are we blind too?" Jesus said, "If you were blind, you would not be guilty of sin; but now that you claim you can see, your guilt remains." (John 9:39–41)

For though we live in the world, we do not wage war as the world does. The weapons we fight with are not the weapons of the world. On the contrary, they have divine power to demolish strongholds. (2 Corinthians 10:3–4)

Unseen Realms

While some of our struggles are indeed deeply seated within our own fallen carnal desires and the sin-filled earthly institutions of our societies, our underlying battles begin within the realms of unseen principalities. These demonic entities try to maneuver the things of this world through us by influencing, manipulating, and/or controlling certain areas of our lives.

Think of it like this: There may be times when you've traveled through an area and felt a repressive darkness. Yet, in other areas where you've been, there's no perception of anything especially dark that affects your spirit in the same way. For instance, there are certain cities around the world where greed, lust, and even murder seem to prevail. In fact, often the bulk of their economies is built upon those fleshly allurements, resulting in their manifested outpouring over that locale. Those who are spiritually discerning can actually feel the presence of those entities while in those places. A number of biblical scholars believe that when people come into *agreement* with the ruling spirits in an area—for example, by wantonly indulging in the gambling and prostitution of that city—and then they travel to another location, they might very well carry that spirit with them.[40]

Barnes' Notes on the Bible:

> Infidelity and wickedness, like **an evil spirit** in a possessed man, were **appropriately at "home" in them**. If driven out, they would find no other place so comfortable and undisturbed as their bosoms. **Everywhere they would be, comparatively, like an evil spirit going through deserts and lonely places, and finding no place of rest. They would return, therefore, and dwell with them.**[41] (Emphasis added)

Pulpit Commentary:

> With **the connotation of distance traversed** (John 4:15; Acts 9:38), but probably **"goes about,"** i.e. **to different spots** (cf. Luke 9:6; Acts 8:4, 40; Acts 20:25, **like a rumor being spread abroad,** Luke 5:15), in **restless wandering.**[42] (Emphasis added)

The *Pulpit Commentary* correctly characterizes this demonic manifestation as "a rumor being spread abroad, from person to person, in restless wandering." This is at least one manner through which the spirit of the Chaldeans grows in influence throughout the world. Its *modus operandi* is to take what does not belong to it, then continually expand its grip upon various territorial holdings.

Or—also like a rumor—this spirit endeavors to take a kernel of truth and twist it until the reality is finally obscured in falsehood. In all of this, the demonic spirit seeks to establish itself as the ultimate authority over humanity, especially attaching to the multiple institutions of God's legitimate work upon the earth—like government, technology industries, marriage, education systems, and so forth. Does any of this sound familiar? Is our current state of global affairs beginning to make more sense now?

The prophet Habakkuk declares that it is the Chaldean spirit that

God actually *allows* to do its work of sifting, deceiving, and manipulating among those who do not desire to follow His Word and His ways. In the same way, the Scripture speaks of people finally being "given over" to certain demonic forces. Consider, for example, the "spirit of fear" mentioned in 2 Timothy 1:7 and the "spirit of depravity" found in Romans 1:28.

And so it is that, right in the midst of our times, one can see this same type of demonic spirit operating throughout the world, even in the core of the institutional church (some would say *especially* in the midst of the institutional church). We are currently witnessing this prophesied phenomenon reaching an apex across the planet.[43]

> The **Spirit clearly says** that **in later times** some will abandon the faith and **follow deceiving spirits** and **things taught by demons**. (1 Timothy 4:1; emphasis added)

Here's one sample of what Jesus had to say about the matter:

> [Jesus said to them] "Listen then to what the parable of the sower means: When anyone hears the message about the kingdom and does not understand it, **the evil one comes and snatches away** what was sown in their heart." (Matthew 13:18–19; emphasis added)

There's yet another surprising biblical connection related to the matters we've just explored, and it's linked from the earliest pages of the Bible to the very last pages, right up to the "end of all things."

19

FROM THE BEGINNING

No place on earth is safe from being
hijacked by the spirit of the Chaldeans.

The Chaldeans are also known in the Bible as the Babylonians. In fact, the geographical designation "Chaldea" is simply another name found throughout the Bible for Babylon (and also for Shinar).[44]

But here is how this becomes especially relevant for our own prophetic days: Accounts of the depraved spirit of Babylon are recorded throughout the Old Testament, and they continue to be reported all the way into the very last chapters of the book of Revelation. Also, ancient Babylon was located in the area of what was known in the antediluvian days as the greater region of early Eden.[45]

Spiritually speaking, this demonic Chaldean spirit was first evident in the garden that God had established in the land of Eden, the place where Heaven's throne met the earthly creation. It was there from the beginning, when the enemy first plotted to steal God's family along with His entire newborn creation.[46]

CHALDEA AND BABYLON

Chaldea was also the geographical setting for the ancient disaster of the
Tower of Babel, after the days of Noah's Flood. The Bible calls that area
the "plain of Shinar." It turns out, then, that Babel was the earthly command center for the great battle in Heaven when Satan and his demons
once again—after the Garden of Eden and the Flood of Noah—thought
they would somehow dethrone God, the Creator of the Universe.[47]

So, when we speak of the Chaldean spirit, it's actually another name
for the Babylonian spirit. The two phrases can be used interchangeably.
This is the demonic spirit that permeated Ur of the Chaldeans, the land
we know today as Iraq.[48]

Pulpit Commentary:

Like Jeremiah and Ezekiel, Isaiah knows the **people as Chaldeans**
(Kasdim), **the capital as Babylon.**[49] (Emphasis added)

Barnes' Notes on the Bible:

Behold **the land of the Chaldeans**—This is a very important
verse, as it expresses the source from where these calamities were
coming upon Tyre; and as **it states some historical facts of great
interest respecting the rise of Babylon.**[50] (Emphasis added)

While Ur was a specific geographical area, the demonic powers at the
controls of the earthly thrones of that region were doing all they could
to rob God of His own people and of His authority over them. Because
there is no place of rest for demonic spirits, they continue throughout the
generations, controlling geographical areas as well as the people who open
the doors of their lives to areas of demonic control. The Chaldean spirit
is as active as ever, as increasingly despicable depravity continues to pour
out upon the earth. Even the biblical prophecies concerning the very last
of the final days bear out this fact.

The rest of mankind who were not killed by these plagues **still did not repent** of the work of their hands; **they did not stop worshiping demons**, and idols of gold, silver, bronze, stone and wood—idols that cannot see or hear or walk. **Nor did they repent** of their **murders, their magic arts, their sexual immorality or their thefts.** (Revelation 9:20–21; emphasis added)

Even in the Modern Hebrew, the word "Chaldean" is also used for "astrologer, witch, sorcerer, or magician"—the depravity we just read about in that passage from the book of Revelation. This symbolic use of the word "Chaldean" was also true of the ancient Hebrew language. Obviously, that term speaks to the overall character of the people and the demons associated with them—a people thoroughly steeped in wickedness of a very deep and dark occultic nature.[51] Understanding the direct demonic connection to the word "Chaldean" clarifies our use of the terms "the spirit of Babylon" and "the Chaldean spirit" as we move forward.

Next, we'll uncover another striking biblical discovery concerning this spirit. It's one with distinct ties to the book of Revelation and end-time prophecy, much of which, I believe, correlates to our own prophetic days.

20

THE HAUNT OF DEMONS

The book of Revelation warns that this same evil spirit remains at work in the world, right up to the end, and its purposes have not changed.

Even as we come to the final chapters of the Word of God, we run right into the Babylonian/Chaldean spirit of demonic evil in the book of Revelation. It is an evil that eventually sweeps the entire planet. And it is this spirit that is unarguably the laser focus of God's coming wrath. That spirit is connected directly to the days of the Antichrist kingdom, Satan's ultimate deception and masquerade.

It should therefore come as no surprise to the attentive student of God's Word that this Chaldean spirit is called the "Mother of Prostitutes" in Revelation 17. It is figuratively tied to Sodom, Egypt, and even Jerusalem—which, by taking into account the larger narrative of Revelation, we come to understand that the demonic spirit spoken of is actually the spirit of Babylon/Chaldea. And, that spirit is specifically tied to Rome.

> And their dead bodies shall lie in the street **of the great city** [Babylon/Chaldea], which spiritually is called Sodom and Egypt, where also our Lord was crucified. (Revelation 11:8; emphasis added)

Meyer's New Testament Commentary:

Many…have concluded from a comparison with Revelation 16:19, Revelation 18:15, etc. that also in this passage **the great city is nothing but Babel, i.e., Papal Rome.**[52] (Emphasis added)

Barnes' Notes on the Bible:

So far as the language is concerned, it might apply either to Jerusalem **or to Rome**…though, as the reference is rather to Christians than to the ancient people of God, **it must be admitted** that it would be **most natural to refer it to Rome.**[53] (Emphasis added)

Jamieson-Fausset-Brown Bible Commentary:

The great city—eight times in the Revelation elsewhere used of BABYLON…. **Babylon** marks its idolatry, **Egypt** its tyranny, **Sodom** its desperate corruption, **Jerusalem** its pretensions to sanctity on the ground of spiritual privileges, while all the while **it is the murderer of Christ** in the person of His members. **All which is true of Rome.**[54] (Emphasis added)

KINGDOM OF ANTICHRIST

The book of Revelation warns that this same evil spirit remains at work in the world, right up to the end, and its purposes have not changed. Its ultimate attempt to duplicate Yahweh's kingdom will be manifested during the last-days reign of the Antichrist kingdom, as outlined in Revelation 13 and following. And interestingly enough, this evil empire will be the main focus of the outpouring of God's wrath in the very last days. Revelation calls that Antichrist kingdom "Babylon (Chaldea) the Great" and specifically links it to *impure spirits.*[55]

WOMAN OF EVIL

Then the angel carried me away in the Spirit into a wilderness. There I saw a woman sitting on a scarlet beast that was **covered with blasphemous names** and had seven heads and ten horns. The woman was dressed in purple and scarlet, and was glittering with gold, precious stones and pearls. She held a golden cup in her hand, **filled with abominable things and the filth of her adulteries.**

The name written on her forehead was a mystery: BABYLON THE GREAT, THE MOTHER OF PROSTITUTES, AND OF THE ABOMINATIONS OF THE EARTH. I saw that the woman was drunk with the blood of God's holy people, the blood of **those who bore testimony to Jesus.** (Revelation 17:3–6; emphasis added.)

THE HAUNT OF DEMONS

"Fallen. Fallen is **Babylon** the Great." She has become a **dwelling for demons** and a haunt for **every impure spirit,** a haunt for every unclean bird, a haunt for every unclean and detestable animal. For all the nations have drunk the maddening wine of her adulteries. The kings of the earth committed adultery with her, and the merchants of the earth grew rich from her excessive luxuries."

By your **magic spell** all the nations were led astray.

In her was found **the blood of prophets and of God's holy people,** of all **who have been slaughtered** on the earth. (Revelation 18:2–3, 23–24; emphasis added)

In an in-depth article on this topic, theologian, pastor, and major-media biblical pundit Mark Driscoll[56] reveals the following:

God creates a Kingdom that is called His bride. Satan counter-feits with a kingdom that **is called Babylon**, the "mother of pros-titutes" (Revelation 17:5). **The spirit of Babylon is at work in every nation and generation.**

For this reason, **the last book of the Bible, Revelation** is closely connected to Daniel as they both have prophecy about the end of human history and beginning of eternity with the Second Com-ing of Jesus Christ. **Long after the nation of Babylon had ceased to exist, Revelation reveals that the demonic spirit of Babylon remains at work in the world.**[57] (Emphasis added)

Robert Morris,[58] pastor of the largest congregation in the Dallas-Fort Worth metroplex, one of the largest churches in the United States, attests:

> **The name Chaldean means "wanderer." The root of the word means "to lay waste or to destroy."** The historical Chaldeans conquered lands, robbed people of their money and goods, and stole the next generation—the young future leaders—brainwash-ing their minds and morals. **The metaphoric Chaldeans of Paul's day—and today—were demons with the same destructive aims** and strategies. **They want to take control of territories that aren't theirs.**[59] (Emphasis added)

The only boundaries known to the spirit of the Chaldeans are those established by God. He will allow the influence of that demonic spirit to go only as far as He permits, and only for His ultimate and divine purposes.

For example, that same depraved Chaldean spirit destroyed the people of Sodom and Gomorrah. But it didn't stop there. Its trail of destruc-tion cut a wide swath through Nazi Germany when Hitler and many of his closest cohorts immersed themselves in the occult, sexual perversion, and drug abuse, inextricably tying their destinies to the Chaldean spirits that sought to take what did not belong to them. They carried out their dark exploits by tempting fallen humanity through impure activities and attachments until they finally controlled them.

These demonic principalities run rampant through drug cartels, the sex-trafficking trade, the porn industry, the anti-God school curriculum, the entertainment industry, the halls of government where insatiable power and lust and greed are present, and so on. The Chaldean spirit is globally pervasive.

These are the Chaldean spirits of wickedness of which I speak. No place on earth is safe from being hijacked by the spirit of the Chaldeans. No message is safe from being infected by its counterfeit. Observe yet again the Apostle Paul's reminder of this deeply spiritual phenomenon:

> The Spirit clearly says that in later times some will abandon the faith and follow **deceiving spirits** and **things taught by demons**. (1 Timothy 4:1; emphasis added)

As we draw ever closer to the end of the age, I am convinced the Lord is allowing the Chaldean spirit increasing freedom, with more diversity to its activities. Once again, He's using that dark kingdom as a tool, a sifting agent, to separate the chaff from the wheat. However, the Lord has effectively put His hooks into the jaws[60] of these impure spirits, sealing their fate in the soon-coming final judgment.

In our continued biblical quest for deeper truth, I'll now show you several more examples of how this demonic deception works, not only throughout the affairs of the world's power brokers, but particularly in the hearts and minds of the modern Jewish people as well as within the deceived portions of today's church.

PART IV

FROM A SIMPLE EXPLORATION TO A STARTLING REVELATION

The great dragon was hurled down—that ancient serpent called the devil, or Satan, who leads the whole world astray. He was hurled to the earth, and his angels with him.

~Revelation 12:9

21

THE DARK HARBINGER

We both saw it. I'll never forget it for the rest of my life.

After I was saved, I didn't just pick up a Bible and start preaching; I went through a lengthy and challenging process of sanctification.[61]

When a person of my background comes to faith in Yeshua, it's a very different experience than that of one who has grown up in the United States or in any other part of the world where the gospel of Jesus Christ is rather well-known and tolerated among the general populace. However, because of my strict Orthodox background, I had no prior knowledge of who Yeshua really was. In fact, as I've stated earlier, when I was growing up, my entire Jewish culture was heavily anti-Jesus. To this day, the Orthodox Jewish culture in Israel is still that way.

Once I was born again, I immersed myself in discovering the basics of who Jesus truly was *and is*. However, I was clueless about what was really in the pages of the New Testament and how they related to the Old Testament Scriptures.

> For [Paul] vigorously refuted his Jewish opponents in public debate, proving from the Scriptures that Jesus was the Messiah. (Acts 18:28)

I went through twenty-six months of severe persecution after accepting Yeshua, but I had the fire of the Holy Spirit in me keeping my faith alive, whether I knew it or not. However, I *did* know that I desperately needed something else. So, I decided that I should go on a journey—but not just any journey. I wanted to see and experience where Yeshua had walked.

All the Talmudic knowledge I had gained as a Sanhedrin-trained Orthodox rabbi and all my years of rabbinic study ultimately served to my advantage. In fact, this has aided even my most current efforts of evangelism among the Jewish people. But, at that time in my young Christian life, I still had to clean out the "leaven of the Pharisees" from my own life (Matthew 16:5–12). This was a huge endeavor, one that is still a part of the continual process of sanctification. It is a day-by-day journey of Spirit-led separation: leaving behind the "old man" and putting on the "new man" in Jesus Christ.

> Therefore, if anyone is in Christ, the new creation has come: The old has gone, the new is here. (2 Corinthians 5:17)

During those days, I had no clue what a Baptist, a Protestant, or a Roman Catholic[62] was; all I knew was Orthodox Judaism. I needed to learn about Christianity and the life of Yeshua. So Lian and I followed the signal flag of an Arab tour guide as we traipsed through the streets of Jerusalem. We had set out on a trek to go where all the tourists in Israel go. *Surely, we could find biblical truth on a journey of this type.*

Boy, were we in for a big surprise.

THE WAY OF SUFFERING

Our first stop was the Via Dolorosa in Jerusalem, where the guide offered to show us the so-called 14 Stations of the Cross.[63] As we went from station to station and eventually came to where the disciples supposedly laid the body of Christ, I knew in my spirit that something was wrong, even though I didn't know what it was.[64]

So, I started flipping the pages of the Bible I had in my hand, looking for the exact locations of these Stations of the Cross within its pages. They weren't there. But the enemy tried to fool me by making me think I couldn't find the stations because I didn't know my Bible well enough. I thought it was *my* problem.

Then, when we arrived at the location where the guide proclaimed Mary's original handprint was still on the wall, my spirit again became deeply unsettled. Looking back, I understand that the Holy Spirit was using that strange feeling to teach me, to protect me.

At the Church of the Holy Sepulcher, there was a long line of people waiting to get in. A priest with incense was walking among the people, who were kissing a piece of cement where Yeshua's body supposedly had been laid. At that time, I didn't have a clue what they were doing.

Finally, we reached the site that was said to be Jesus' grave. It was like a tomb, except it was full of candles; a man wearing black clothes was inside. I didn't want to go in because I sensed evil. I can't explain the reason, but everything in my soul cried out, *"Something isn't right."* I decided to go home and study my Bible some more.

A WARNING

On our way home, Lian and I sat down for a few minutes near the exit of the Holy Sepulcher and—I know this may be hard to believe—in that moment, we were horrified at the sight of a woman dressed in black, with a dark hood covering her hair. She appeared to be a physical, living entity—with one great exception. She looked like she wore the robes of a priest, but she had no discernable body inside the clothing. And, she was sitting/floating on the air.

I know what you're thinking: *This guy is nuts!*

I don't blame you. If my wife hadn't also seen this and been equally startled, I wouldn't be telling you about it now. I would have thought I was dreaming or going mad. An experience like that isn't something you can just run out and tell the world, but what we saw in that moment shook us to the core. We talk about it with each other to this very day.

The apparition of that woman slowly turned toward us and shot us a revolting smirk, as if she knew who we were and was boasting about her right to be there. Her eyes were pure evil, and deeply black. When I looked at her, I felt like I was looking at the harlot of Babylon herself (Revelation 17:3–6).

I told Lian I wasn't going back to that place ever again—to this day, I've never returned. Even when I'm asked to speak on tours of that site, I politely refuse.

I believe God allowed us to experience this apparitional revelation as a part of bringing me to the point where I am today. Sadly, millions of tourists have been going to the Via Dolorosa for years without knowing its demonic power.

I know with almost certainty one thing: Jesus didn't carry His cross in that place. As you will discover through several other chapters of this book, He carried the cross somewhere else entirely; it wasn't even in the same direction of the Via Dolorosa.

THE MASQUERADE

Tourists and pilgrims from all over the world visit Israel to see all the well-known landmarks. Many come to receive a blessing, but they sometimes end up in areas of genuine demonic activity, whether they "see" or "feel" it or not. In fact, most of the time, Satan doesn't want us to be aware of his very real presence, even as we come into direct contact with it.

You can bank on this: Satan *always* has a counterfeit. And he's always at work in the Holy Land. He believes this territory, in particular, is *his*. He's a thief. He's a liar. He's a murderer. He claimed the territory in Eden. He claimed it on the top of the Mount of Olives and in Bethlehem. In several following chapters, you'll discover the archeological, historical, and contextual biblical truths of these very important assertions.

Satan knows he can't deceive believers simply by telling them Jesus is not the Messiah; that won't work in most cases. However, he can deceive them by pointing them to the *wrong messiah*...and leading them along wrong paths. In so doing, he dilutes the Word of God, waters down the gospel, and robs God's children of the victories and the power of Yahweh's truth.

22

THE CHALDEAN IMPRINT

Do you now see how pervasive and
insidious this dark spiritual force really is?

The Babylonian/Chaldean spirit continually promotes Satan's counterfeit gospel, luring misinformed sheep away from the Shepherd
and into treacherous territory. In the process of thinking they're on a spiritual pilgrimage, Jews like me—*who believe in Messiah*—still fall into the
trap and go to those places because they simply don't know anything different. We have a responsibility to shine the light of biblical truth upon
these travesties.

> We know that we are children of God, and that **the whole world is
> under the control of the evil one.** (1 John 5:19; emphasis added)

> The great dragon was hurled down--that ancient serpent called
> the devil, or **Satan, who leads the whole world astray.** He was
> hurled to the earth, and his angels with him. (Revelation 12:9;
> emphasis added)

The light of a lamp **will never shine in [Babylon]** again…. By your magic spell **all the nations were led astray.** (Revelation 18:23; emphasis added)

⊢◆⊣

The tourist industry in Israel is, for the most part, run by the Roman Catholic Church. In the next chapter, I'll explain why that is. In spite of this, many congregants—and even a good number of spiritually astute leaders of today's Roman Catholic Church—are well aware of the powerful doctrinal disagreements that have arisen within the halls of Catholic ecclesiastical government.[65] And it hasn't gotten any better through the centuries.

Even its most modern doctrinally adulterated influences continue to span the globe with increasingly false teaching. Don't believe it? Look at just a few of the headlines issued from the Vatican in our own days. Do you see the Chaldean spirit at work in these stories?

(December 2020) *NPR*: Vatican OKs Receiving COVID-19 Vaccines, Even If Research Involved Fetal Tissue

The Vatican says that it's "morally acceptable" to receive a vaccination for COVID-19, **even if the vaccine's research or production involved using cell lines derived from aborted fetuses,** given the "grave danger" of the pandemic.[66] (Emphasis added)

In that proclamation, the pope aligned the Catholic Church, in a watered-down spiritual agreement, with the demon of abortion—infant murder. But that's not all.

(October 2020) *The Catholic Sun*: In New Film, Pope Francis Affirms Gay People "Are Children of God," Expresses Support for Legalizing Civil Unions

"**Homosexual people** have **a right to be in a family. They are children of God** and have **a right** to a family. **Nobody should be thrown out** or be made miserable over it," the pope, speaking in Spanish, says in the film, Catholic News Service reported. "**What we have to create is a civil union law. That way they are legally covered.**"[67] (Emphasis added)

In that pronouncement, the pope allied the Roman Catholic Church with the spirit of Sodom and Gomorrah. This is also the demonic spirit that the New Testament connects with the very last days.[68]

Now when they have finished their testimony, the beast that comes up from the Abyss will attack them, and overpower and kill them. Their bodies will lie in the public square of **the great city**—which is **figuratively called Sodom and Egypt**—**where also their Lord was crucified.** (Revelation 11:7–8; emphasis added)

Most judicious interpreters understand Rome to be the "great city" of that passage—or the biblical "Babylon." Notice that the figurative characteristics of this mysterious city are tied to Sodom and its desperate corruption, as well as to Egypt and its hideous reputation for oppressive slavery of God's people. It also correlates to Jerusalem as the literal place where Jesus was crucified, but, solely in the sense that the crucifixion could have only taken place with the distinct legal permission of Rome's authority. The imagery is pretty hard to miss if the searcher understands the biblical context and its relationship to history.[69]

But there's still more to this picture as it relates to current connections.

(March 2019) *Reuters*: "**Conversion Is Not Your Mission,**" Pope Tells Catholics in Morocco:

Pope Francis told the tiny Catholic community in predominantly Muslim Morocco on Sunday that **their mission was not**

to convert their neighbors **but to live in brotherhood with other faiths.**[70] (Emphasis added)

Here the pope attaches the Roman Catholic Church to the spirit of *universalism.*[71] This false teaching of developing "brotherhood" with people of faiths that deny the lordship of Jesus Christ is also directly contrary to the clear teachings of God's Word.

Do not be yoked together with unbelievers. For what do righteousness and wickedness have in common? Or what fellowship can light have with darkness? What harmony is there between Christ and Belial [Satan, or the demonic]? Or what does a believer have in common with an unbeliever? What agreement is there between the temple of God and idols? For we are the temple of the living God. (2 Corinthians 6:14–16)

This heresy is nothing less than the demonic spirit of the "different gospel" the Apostle Paul spoke about in Galatians. But that different gospel had already taken a very serious turn way back in October 2015, when Pope Francis stepped over yet another biblical line of scriptural truth.

(October 2015) *Independent U.K*: Pope Francis Assures Atheists: You Don't Have to Believe in God to Go to Heaven:

In comments **likely to enhance his progressive reputation,** Pope Francis has written a long, open letter to the founder of La Repubblica newspaper, Eugenio Scalfari [a staunch atheist], stating that **non-believers would be forgiven by God if they followed their consciences.**

Responding to a list of questions published in the paper by Mr. Scalfari, who is not a Roman Catholic, Pope Francis wrote:

"You ask me **if the God of the Christians forgives those who don't believe** and **who don't seek** the faith. I start by saying— and this is the fundamental thing—that God's mercy has no limits if you go to him with a sincere and contrite heart. **The issue for those who do not believe in God [atheists] is to obey their conscience. Sin, even for those who have no faith, exists when people disobey their conscience.**"[72] (Emphasis added)

In that article, it appeared as though the pope erroneously declared that even atheists, as long as they obey their conscience, can enter the Kingdom of God. A large number of Catholics and Evangelicals alike saw the apparent underlying message of the pope's declarations. Of course, Scripture clearly refutes this false, *Chaldean-infused* claim.

Not everyone who says to me, "Lord, Lord," will enter the kingdom of heaven, but only the one who does the will of my Father who is in heaven. (Matthew 7:21; emphasis added)

Such teachings come through hypocritical liars, whose consciences have been seared as with a hot iron. (1 Timothy 4:2; emphasis added)

The heart [conscience] **is deceitful** above all things, and **desperately sick** [if not redeemed through Jesus]; who can understand it? (Jeremiah 17:9; emphasis added)

PERPETUAL BATTLE

Do you have a little better understanding now of how pervasive and insidious this dark spiritual force really is, even among some of the most famous "Christian" tourist sites in Israel? Do you perhaps understand more clearly when I speak of how hard it is for Jewish people to become born-again believers in Yeshua, especially while they are living in the midst of the original ground zero of spiritual warfare?[73]

That battle still rages today in the land of Israel. I live and minister right in the middle of it every single day. I assure you it's real, and exceedingly wicked. Sadly, according to God's Word, the spiritual warfare of *deception* will continue to exhibit its fury right up until Yeshua's return.

Now, I'll keep my earlier promise about further discussing the "holy places." I'll reveal the dark secret as to why Israeli leadership, by and large, seems to have an affinity for those *holy sites* even though they claim to have a great disdain for the faith system that operates almost every one of them.

23

ROMAN ISRAEL

*My fervent passion for finding genuine biblical truth
was originally wrapped in righteous frustration.*

Years of deception, misunderstanding, and false teaching have blown over the pearls of God's Word and Yeshua's genuine footsteps, obscuring truth from the spiritual eyes of our understanding. The Chaldean spirit, seeking to rob the family of God of the richness of His glory, has hidden God's treasures from view, carefully constructing a trail of plastic gems and counterfeit treasures to throw believers off track.

This is the reason tourists from around the world traipse through groomed gardens and groves, cathedrals and caverns, following guides who convince them that "Jesus did this here, and He did that there, and something else happened over there, and Mary put her handprint in the concrete over here...and, oh yes, please put your money in the jar on your way out." To a born-again Jewish person whose eyes have been opened to this charade, it is a sad thing to behold.

However, the truth is that Israel doesn't really care about those sites. Most of the rabbis in Israel don't know the difference between a Catholic and a Lutheran, a Pentecostal, a Baptist, or anyone else. To them, everybody who is a "Christian" believes in the pope. That's what they've been taught since childhood throughout more than fifteen hundred years of generations.

Remember, I grew up among those rabbis. I was raised in the most Orthodox of rabbinical communities in a family steeped in Jewish orthodoxy. And, as already related, I even attended and graduated from a Sanhedrin training school—a yeshiva. I can assure you, the majority of the Israeli rabbis don't know the differences between the various understandings of institutionalized "Christianity."

Therefore, anything to do with Jesus is all about tourism, as far as the average Israeli is concerned. And, in the long run, that tourism is especially lucrative for the Israeli government and the rabbinical institutions attached to it. So, they tolerate—even welcome—it. That's why they appear to wholeheartedly promote it.

It's also important to understand that Israel sells the rights to sites and tourist facilities to the highest bidder. Not always, but most often, the extravagantly wealthy Roman Catholic Church wins those bids. To put it simply, *money* controls and builds tourism in Israel. Eighty percent of the places people go in Israel, even if they *were* places Yeshua walked, have been spiritually muddied by the demonic grip of financial opportunism.

Are you now beginning to see how, and why, the kingdom of darkness gets involved in all of this? Power, wealth, possession of property, and dominance of the "narrative" within the borders of Israel—all of these are weapons in Satan's arsenal. Even sites that haven't been sullied by the Roman Catholic Church are vulnerable simply because we're living in the end times.

INFLUENCE BEHIND THE INSTITUTIONS

The *Chaldean principalities* are increasingly moving in to occupy areas that are not their own (Habakkuk 1:6). The more they can occupy an area and blur the genuine sites and the biblical truths associated with them, the more they can draw increasing numbers of people away from the deeper truths of the person and mission of Yeshua. This is why we must do our due diligence in exposing the falsehoods and uncovering the truth. It's hard work and often unpopular, as it will sometimes unseat long-held traditions and false notions.

In my newfound faith in Yeshua, the question burned within me: How could I undo thousands of years of Chaldean deception and introduce people to the real Yeshua Jesus in this idol-draped, Roman-influenced Israel? I knew I had to dig deeper into Scripture and trust God to lead me to the genuine locations of the birth, life, crucifixion, and resurrection of Yeshua/Jesus. I knew I must do this not merely to eliminate barriers to belief for my Jewish brothers and sisters, but also for the throngs of non-Jews also searching for the truth.

MY PURSUIT

So, I began my quest to find and follow *the real footsteps* of Yeshua. Scripture has been my ancient map, but uncovering its layers continued to send me on an extraordinary treasure hunt. The more I searched, the more evident it became that Satan, through the Chaldean spirit, has stomped his footprints over the genuine ones...almost *everywhere*.

Could it be that the *spirit of the Chaldeans* has used the Roman Catholic Church[74] as a vehicle for disinformation, propaganda, and counterfeit evidence of the life of Christ throughout the land? A number of believers as well as scores of renowned biblical scholars who have taken a similar spiritual journey believe the answer is *yes*.

I did not set out on my search with a negative spirit of rejection, looking to discredit people of various faith systems. All I wanted was the biblical truth—in its proper context and backed up by legitimate archeological and historical findings. I knew that if my efforts to find this kind of truth were to be authentic, I needed revelation from the Spirit of God, especially from the Scriptures, to confirm or reject my conclusions. I prayed, "God, show me the truth...show me the *real* footprints of Yeshua."

In this matter, my heart was pure. I had marching orders from Yahweh and an insatiable thirst for His verification of the facts.

It was in this way that I set out on my mission. What I discovered along the way transformed the very depths of my faith in Yeshua. That quest also threw even more fuel on the flames of my ever-deepening love for searching out the nuggets of gold buried within the pages of God's Holy Word and all over the countryside of Israel.

PART V

OUT OF THE DARKNESS
AND INTO THE LIGHT

The Word gave life to everything that was created, and his life brought light to everyone. The light shines in the darkness, and the darkness can never extinguish it.

~John 1:4–5

24

Spiritual Archaeology

The artifacts I unearthed changed my life forever.

Archaeology can be a demanding profession. A successful archaeologist must begin with a fiery passion for discovery. Often the process takes years of meticulously brushing bits of sand from hidden clumps, hoping against hope to find exciting pieces of evidence of whatever is being sought out.

But before the tip of the archeologist's trowel ever kisses the ground, the passion and curiosity that drive the seeker must be refined through years of study and preparation to prevent wasting time on unnecessary excursions. Through those years of study, skills are developed, tools are gathered, and information is examined, analyzed, and weighed.

A Passion-Driven Pursuit

Spiritual archaeology is similar to the traditional variety of the science. Digging deep and getting to the truth of Scripture demands passion—soaked with much study and preparation. It also entails collecting the proper tools and reliable sources of knowledge, a healthy dose of perseverance, and a heart saturated in the anointing of the Holy Spirit.

During the years God was preparing me for the quest that has consumed my life, I was unaware of His ultimate purpose. It humbles me now to feel His passion for His people burning in my own heart. I know that my own pressing desire to find and reveal the truths of God's Word, as well as the biblically accurate steps of Yeshua, and my need to expose the deception of the Chaldean spirit flow from the very heart of God. These are *His revelations*—His spiritual archaeology. The Lord God is disclosing these discoveries to us, the true believers, and the "one new man." I'm convinced He's doing these things even more so in these unprecedented and prophetic times.[75]

> Those who are wise will shine like the brightness of the heavens, and those who lead many to righteousness, like the stars for ever and ever. But you, Daniel, roll up and **seal the words** of the scroll **until the time of the end**. Many will go here and there to increase knowledge. (Daniel 12:3–4; emphasis added)

Since the days in which Daniel wrote those words, we are humanity's first generation to see the words of that prophecy happening—and at breakneck speed. Deep mysteries of God's Word are being brought to bursting light. The sands of time are blowing away, finally revealing what has been there all along…waiting to be discovered, and only in our times.

DIGGING DEEP

After all the experiences I've shared in the preceding chapters, I knew it was time to pick up my spiritual shovel and start digging for the truth on my own. I wasn't supposed to just play around in the sand, building pretty sandcastles to earn approval, seeking the acclaim of men. I was supposed to dig deep, maybe even unearth a few old bones of false teaching and expose them to the world.

I knew this task wasn't going to be popular. But, the Lord had certainly prepared me for it. After all, practically everyone who had previously been a part of my life, even most of my loved ones, already hated me. What did I have to lose? I was now doing the work of the Kingdom of Yeshua and being unspeakably blessed in the midst of it. I pray that the retelling of my ever-continuing journey to Zion blesses your life as well.

25

LEAVING THE LAND
OF THE CHALDEES

*It is a trek that takes us right through the middle
of Satan's current territory.*

When people ask how to pray for Israel, I usually respond with
an important question: "Do you know who Israel is?" I ask this
because if a person doesn't know who Israel actually is, they're not going
to know how to pray for Israel. Let me explain.

Abraham, the human father of the people termed "Israel," left Ur of
the Chaldees ("Ur" means "the light" and "of the Chaldees" means "of
the Chaldean area") and went to Canaan. God told him to leave that
area. Only Jesus—the Living Word of God—is the true Light. *Ur was a
counterfeit light.* Satan is the great impostor, the masquerader disguised as
a messenger of light, even though he is the prince of darkness and death.

And no wonder, for Satan himself masquerades as an angel of
light. (2 Corinthians 11:14)

God had to take Abraham out of the land where the realm of darkness had been abiding for a long time. God couldn't make an eternal covenant with Abraham until he was willing to leave the stronghold of the demonic realm that dominated the land of the Chaldeans. It is that same spirit of the Chaldeans, under the direction of Satan, the great masquerader, that still sets out to deceive the people of God and frustrate His Kingdom work.

FORMIDABLE ROADBLOCK

God called Abraham out of the fake light of Satan into the true light of the coming gospel of Jesus Christ. But, Satan effectively said, "I'm going to thwart this heavenly maneuver. I'll simply bring my Chaldean-spirit army directly into the heart of Israel. We'll deceive God's people *there*."

Thus, the Chaldean/Babylonian spirits are working overtime. They're still in Israel to corrupt the promise given to Abraham, and they will do everything they can to impede the power of that promise. As a result, the vast majority of the Jewish people in Jerusalem that I try to speak with about Yeshua point to the "Christian" tourist sites and say, "We don't want anything to do with that."

It's a hard roadblock to get around. So, this is how I tell people to pray for Israel: Pray that they may finally see the light of Yahweh—the light that is the gospel of Jesus Christ, the only One who brings true life.

When Lian and I saw that demonic spirit of witchcraft right before our physical eyes at the Church of the Holy Sepulcher, I believe the Lord allowed us to experience the reality of the spiritual warfare in Israel. *Now we know what it really is.* It's deeply authentic, it's powerful, it's tangible, and it's vile. And the Lord was leading us away from our very own land of Ur of the Chaldees into the light of God's truth.

POWER FOR THE JOURNEY

Our Lord Jesus Christ has not left us without the divine power we need for this earthly journey and mission. It is a trek that takes us right through the middle of Satan's current territory, one that eventually will no longer be his. It is a place that will soon belong to us.

> **But when he, the Spirit of truth, comes, he will guide you into all the truth.** He will not speak on his own; he will speak only what he hears, and he will tell you what is yet to come. He will glorify me because it is from me that he will receive what he will make known to you. **All that belongs to the Father is mine.** That is why I said the Spirit will receive from me what he will make known to you. (John 16:13–15; emphasis added)

> Now **if we are children, then we are heirs—heirs of God** and **co-heirs with Christ,** if indeed we share in his sufferings in order that we may also share in his glory. (Romans 8:17; emphasis added)

> Blessed are the meek [the born again], for **they will inherit the earth.** (Matthew 5:5; emphasis added)

> **Blessed and holy are those** who share in the first resurrection [the born again]. The second death has no power over them, but **they will be priests of God and of Christ and will reign with him for a thousand years.** (Revelation 20:6; emphasis added)

> And [Jesus] has **made us to be a kingdom and priests** to serve his God and Father—to him be glory and power for ever and ever. Amen. (Revelation 1:6; emphasis added)

> But you are a chosen people, a royal priesthood, a holy nation, God's special possession, that you may declare the praises of him who **called you out of darkness into his wonderful light.** (1 Peter 2:9; emphasis added)

The promises are right there in God's Word. He has not hidden them from us. Satan knows what those promises are. He wants to keep us from them. He'll pull out all of his deceptions to keep us from it. *This is war.*

We'll begin our spiritual archeological journey by examining the character who is the supreme commander of the realm of darkness—Satan himself. We must know exactly what, *and who,* we're up against. You might be shocked by what you're getting ready to see.

Let's start digging.

26

RIPPING OFF THE MASK

Satan was one of the trusted members of God's
heavenly court, the Divine Council.

Who is this Satan figure we talk about so much? Do we understand the chasmic depth of his evil and his power?

The multilayered lament concerning the king of Tyre found in Ezekiel 28 turns out to be an unveiling of the character of the ancient serpent himself (Revelation 12:9). From that passage, we gain a lot of knowledge about Satan, the enemy of God's people. And, of course, he's not a red imp with scaly skin and horns holding a pitchfork, as he's often depicted in literature and cartoons.

A STELLAR CREATURE

What we learn in the narrative of Ezekiel 28 is that Satan was the highest-ranking, most-trusted member of God's heavenly court, the Divine Council.[76] In his arrogance, Satan shamefully chose to exalt himself above the Creator. Because of that rebellion, God basically said to him, "Look at all you were created to be. Look how beautiful you were; how perfect, and divinely exalted you were—and you've thrown it all away, because of your pride and iniquity." Ezekiel 28 actually turns out to be God's lament over the fallen nature of His most magnificent creation.

Let me state the matter simply, but in a much more dramatic way than you've probably ever considered. Satan was to Yahweh in Paradise what Judas was to Jesus on earth. Get the picture now? God's heart was crushed when Satan betrayed Him in the Garden of Eden. Yeshua's heart was broken when Judas betrayed Him in the Garden of Gethsemane.

Have a look at that passage in Ezekiel, beginning with the first two verses:

The word of the Lord came to me: Son of man, **say to the ruler of Tyre,** "This is what the Sovereign Lord says: In the pride of your heart you say, I am a god." (Ezekiel 28:1–2a; emphasis added)

COMPOUND PROPHECY

As we get to verse 13, the object of the prophecy changes. From this point forward, none of the rest of Ezekiel 28 can contextually be used as a description of the earthly king of Tyre. Instead, the attention turns to Satan, the real power behind the throne of the king of Tyre.

You were in Eden, the garden of God; every precious stone was your covering…. The workmanship of your timbrels and pipes was prepared for you on the day you were created.

You were the anointed cherub[77] who covers; I established you; you were on the holy mountain of God; you walked back and forth in the midst of fiery stones. You were perfect in your ways from the day you were created, till iniquity was found in you.

By the abundance of your trading you became filled with violence within, and you sinned; therefore I cast you as a profane thing out of the mountain of God; and I destroyed you, O covering cherub, from the midst of the fiery stones.

Your heart was lifted up because of your beauty; you corrupted your wisdom for the sake of your splendor. (Ezekiel 28:13–17, KJV; emphasis added)

A number of scholars agree that Ezekiel 28, although it begins with a divine disapproval leveled against the king of Tyre, eventually changes into a picture of Satan himself—the real power at work behind the earthly throne of the king of Tyre. This kind of shift in a prophetic passage is known as a compound prophecy and is found throughout the Scriptures.[78]

Here are a few scholarly observations about Ezekiel 28 (as well as Isaiah 14, which we'll examine in the following chapter) and its direct connection to Satan.

Coffman's Commentaries on the Bible notes the compound characteristic of this passage:

> **There is not a line of this that can be applied to any other being who ever lived, except Satan.** It was that garden where Adam and Eve had been placed by the Lord, and into which Satan appeared as an intruder to seduce Eve and precipitate the fall of the human race. **After this clause, the rest of the description must be applied to Satan.** The application is clear enough. **Just as Satan lost his place in the mountain of God, the king of Tyre, and all other proud kings, shall lose their place** in the destruction God prepares for them.[79] (Emphasis added)

Jamieson, Fausset, and Brown Commentary:

> The language, **though primarily here applied to the king of Tyre,** as similar language is to the king of Babylon (Isaiah 14:13, Isaiah 14:14), **yet has an ulterior and fuller accomplishment in Satan** and his embodiment **in Antichrist** (Daniel 7:25, Daniel 11:36, Daniel 11:37, 2 Thessalonians 2:4, Revelation 13:6).[80] (Emphasis added)

Bible Exposition Commentary:

The use of the word "cherub" (Ezekiel 28:4–6) suggests that **we're dealing here with an angelic creature,** also the fact that he had been "upon the holy mountain of God" (v. 14). This **sounds a great deal like the description in Isaiah 14:12 ff.** Satan began as an obedient angel but rebelled against God and led a revolt to secure God's throne.[81] (Emphasis added)

F. F. Bruce's New Layman's Bible Commentary:

This passage in Ezekiel has contributed details to **the picture of the fall of Satan.**[82] (Emphasis added)

Now for one of the biggest surprises about Satan's formerly exalted position.

27

THE ANGEL OF MUSIC[83]

The array of instruments that adorned Satan's unfallen condition does not escape the attention of the majority of biblical scholars.

In Andrew Lloyd Webber's internationally famous musical, *The Phantom of the Opera*,[84] a young chorus girl named Christine Daae gets voice lessons from a shadowy "music teacher" she calls the "Angel of Music." Christine is convinced that this teacher is the angel her dying father promised to send to help complete her musical training.

As the musical progresses, we discover that what Christine believed to be an angel sent by her father is nothing more than a deranged madman—living in the hidden underworld of the theater—who wants to possess her for his own selfish desires. The Angel of Music is nothing but *evil* masquerading as *good*, using music to lure his unknowing victim into his clutches.

In the production, a number of people see the Angel of Music as a metaphor of the alluring work of Satan upon all who succumb to his Garden of Eden whisperings. Shocking to some students of the Word is the fact that the Bible addresses this tempting characteristic of the evil one. And, like the Phantom of the Opera, it's not a pretty picture at all.

TAMBOURINES AND FLUTES

Let's have another look at verse 13 of Ezekiel 28, noting the highlighted words:

> **You were in Eden, the garden of God**; every precious stone was your covering.… The workmanship of **your timbrels and pipes** was prepared for you on the day you were created. (NKJV; emphasis added)

This verse reveals an important piece of information. Satan, the fallen cherub, was created "with" *timbrels and pipes*. The passage speaks of the instruments of praise that were an integral part of his being, in much the same way that our own vocal chords are often used as the ultimate "instruments" of praise when we worship the Lord in song. Apparently, these instruments were designed for that guardian cherub alone, and were an actual part of his person to be used in his role as the worship leader of Heaven.[85]

The Hebrew word for "timbrel" refers to a percussion instrument such as a tambourine. The Hebrew term translated as "pipes" denotes a wind instrument, like a flute—something one blows through to make a sound. It can also be used to reference the hole, or boring, that would be employed in making wind instruments, or even in making fine jewelry—particularly the hole/setting in which a gem might be placed.

Even Isaiah 14—a passage we'll more closely examine in the next chapter—mentions the sound of Satan's stringed instruments, specifically the harps:[86]

> All your pomp has been brought down to the grave, along with **the noise of your harps.** (Isaiah 14:11; emphasis added)

The instruments that adorned Satan's unfallen condition do not escape the attention of the majority of biblical scholars. Following are samples of similar observations:

Guzik Bible Commentary—Enduring Word:

The workmanship of your **timbrels and pipes** was prepared for you: **Before his fall, Satan had a significant role in the music of heaven,** surrounding God's throne.[87] (Emphasis added)

Christian Apologetics and Research Ministry:

It is quite possible that…Satan, was originally an angel whose purpose was to be involved in the worship of God. The case can be made from Ezekiel 28. In the Hebrew, the word for "settings" is **toph** which means timbrel, which is *a musical instrument*. Likewise, the Hebrew word for "sockets" is **neqeb** and means "pipes, grove, and hole."[88] (Emphasis added)

Jamieson, Fausset, and Brown:

Tabrets—tambourines. Pipes—literally, "holes" in musical pipes or flutes. Created—that is, in the day of thine accession to the throne. Tambourines and all the marks of joy were ready prepared for thee ("in thee," that is, "with and for thee").[89] (Emphasis added)

Now have a look at Psalm 150, noting the highlighted portions indicating words and phrases found in other passages that are related directly or indirectly to Satan's pre-fallen state:

Praise the Lord [Hebrew: "hallelujah"]. Praise God in his sanctuary; **praise him in his mighty heavens.** Praise him for his acts of power; praise him for his surpassing greatness. **Praise him with the sounding** of the trumpet, praise him with the harp and lyre, **praise him with timbrel** and dancing, **praise him with the strings and pipe,** praise him with the clash of cymbals, praise him with

resounding cymbals. Let everything that has breath praise the
Lord. Praise the Lord. (Psalm 150; emphasis added)

So, when God created that guardian cherub, He also created percussion instruments, wind instruments, and stringed instruments within the
cherub's body itself, or at least very unique instruments that were made
available only for his use in leading the worship of Yahweh in Heaven. To
this day, all instruments fall into one of these three categories: percussion,
wind, and stringed.[90]

INSTRUMENTS OF PERSUASION

Never doubt that Satan was, formally, the chief worship leader of the
divine realm. He knows about religion. He also knows about false worship. And he definitely knows about the power of music over the human
mind and soul. To dramatically emphasize this assertion, have a look at
NPR's 2011 article, "'The Power of Music' to Affect the Brain":

> Science all but confirms that **humans are hard-wired to respond
> to music.** In *The Power of Music*, Elena Mannes says scientists
> have found that **music stimulates more parts of the brain than
> any other human function.** That's why she sees so much potential
> in **music's power to change the brain** and affect the way it works.
>
> Archaeologists have discovered **ancient flutes**—one of which
> is presumed to be **the oldest musical instrument in the world.**
>
> "And remarkably," Mannes says, "this flute, when played, pro-
> duces these **amazingly pure tones.**"[91] (Emphasis added)

Satan is the inventor of false gods and false religions, and he knows
how to spread all of those falsehoods among fallen humanity. He understands how to speak to our souls through demonically empowered music
and instruments and how to lure us into sin and wickedness—through
demonically inspired musical methods.

He also knows how to hypnotize those who are not sealed with the Holy Spirit. Like the Pied Piper, he plays his flute of deception. And almost all of humanity, like lost sheep, follow after him—headed to the slaughter.

This is our enemy. This is the leader of the Chaldean troops of our day.

28

THE ANGEL OF ARROGANCE[92]

Satan's unbounded pride desires God's throne and
all the power and glory that belongs to it.

Satan's rebellion was what got him kicked out of Heaven. He wanted
to be worshiped and exalted over and above the throne of Yahweh. He
wanted to be the sole possessor and ruler of all Yahweh had created.

Isaiah 14 gives us yet another striking picture of the drama of Satan's
expulsion from the presence of God's throne. And it gives us added insight
into the heart of our most dreaded enemy.

How art thou fallen from heaven, O Lucifer[93] son of the morning.
How art thou cut down to the ground, which didst weaken the
nations. (Isaiah 14:12, KJV)

Like Ezekiel 28, Isaiah 14 is a compound prophecy. And, as its sister
passage in Ezekiel, the scholars see it as a clear picture of Satan. Even the
ancient Jews understood the passage in that light.

Lange's Commentary on the Holy Scriptures:

Even as early as the LXX [Septuagint—Hebrew Scriptures translated into Greek by Jewish scholars] **this passage seems to have been understood of Satan.** It points that way that **they change the second person into the third** [another compound prophecy]…

　　And this is the aim of Satan and of his earthly sphere of power, the world-power, **which culminates in Antichrist** (Daniel 11:36; 2 Thessalonians 2:3).[94] (Emphasis added)

A number of respected biblical scholars see Isaiah 14's connection with Satan's fall from Heaven. They know it is a prophecy with a multiple message.

Arno Gaebelein is just one example:

Behind this…king…looms up Satan, who energized that wicked and false king. The description of him who was "Lucifer," the light-bearer, and his fall.[95] (Emphasis added)

Mr. Gaebelein is exactly right in his commentary entry. Even though Isaiah 14 begins by talking about the king of Babylon, it transforms into a meticulous disclosure of what really happened with Satan.

Now that we know about the Chaldean/Babylon demonic spirits—with Satan as their king—we see this connection even more clearly. So, Isaiah 14 also serves the double purpose of showing that the truth Paul presented in Ephesians 6 is very real. There are demonic powers behind kings and kingdoms. Our battle indeed rages within our flesh-and-blood world, but, like Paul states, we must think beyond what we can physically see to understand that behind the curtain of our dimension are powers of darkness that orchestrate much of what goes on in the religious and political realms of our earthly existence.

Here are a few more examples from the scholars who understand Isaiah 14 in this same way.

E. W. Bullinger:

[This is a] **divine revelation of** Him Who knows what **Satan "said in his heart."**[96] (Emphasis added)

H. A. Ironside:

The fall of Lucifer portrays the fall of Satan. The passage **links very closely with Ezekiel 28**, which should be carefully considered in the effort to understand this fully. These words cannot apply to any mere mortal man. Lucifer (the light-bearer) is a created angel of the very highest order, identical with the covering cherub of Ezekiel 28. He was, apparently, the greatest of all the angel host and was perfect before GOD until he fell through pride. It is of him our Lord speaks in John 8:44.[97] (Emphasis added)

Warren Wiersbe:

In the fall of the king of Babylon, **he saw the defeat of Satan,** the "prince of this world," who **seeks to energize and motivate the leaders of nations** (John 12:31; Ephesians 2:1–3). Dan 10:20 indicates that **Satan has assigned "princes"** (fallen angels) to the **various nations so that he can influence leaders** to act contrary to the will of God. **This highest of God's angels tried to usurp the throne of God** and capture for himself the worship that belongs only to God (Matt 4:8–10).[98] (Emphasis added)

FIVE ARROGANT DECLARATIONS

In Isaiah 14, Satan declares what are known as his five "I wills" (Isaiah 14:13–14). In these words, observe Satan's abject conceit and his agenda. You and I are mere pawns in his greater plans. To Satan, humanity is nothing more than something to be possessed and enslaved. That's why the Bible says that, without Jesus, we are slaves to sin and darkness. But in Jesus Christ, we are free and no longer under the yoke of that slavery and the eternal death it brings.

Following is that biblical snapshot of Satan's heart and soul:

I will ascend into Heaven. I will exalt my throne above the stars of God.[99] I will sit on the mount of the congregation on the furthest sides of the north. I will ascend above the heights of the clouds. I will be like the Most High. (Extracted from Isaiah 14:13–14; emphasis added)

God's response to Satan's haughtiness was swift, straight to the point, and catastrophic.

[But God said] You shall be brought down to Sheol, to the lowest depths of the pit. (Isaiah 14:15)

Your pomp will be brought down to Sheol and to the sound of stringed instruments. (Isaiah 14:11)

It had to be a sad day for God. Imagine His disappointment. Satan, the original guardian cherub, was no small player in Yahweh's overall creation plan. Only three archangels, chief angels of the highest order, are mentioned in the Bible. Satan was one of them.[100]

VICIOUSLY RELIGIOUS

This is who we are "wrestling against" (see Ephesians 6:10ff). Satan is the former divine worship leader of the throne of God, perfect in beauty and wisdom, the original chief guardian and divine governor of the Garden of Eden. At one time, he was chief among all the angels of Heaven.

Now, in his fallen state and with a Heaven-decreed death sentence hanging over his head, he is *viciously religious*. He knows how to manipulate our souls and minds with music and the serpent-like hissings of his words and promises, as well as with the beguiling nature of his beauty and wisdom. He truly is our adversary. He hates us with a vengeful fury. His wicked perversity is beyond the scope of anything we can imagine.

Think of it. Delivery of the Word, prayer, and worship are the central components of the gatherings of believers. And Satan was originally involved deeply in the heart of God's fellowship with His creation. It stands to reason, then, that Satan's chief objective in his fallen state is to denigrate the true fellowship of humanity's personal relationship with Yahweh.

That leads us to the next chapter. In Isaiah 14, why is Satan often given the moniker "Lucifer"? The answer will help to more fully round out our understanding of who Satan really is and why he's such a formidable foe.

Never doubt: "Lucifer" is the false light. He masquerades as an angel or messenger of light. He fancies himself to be the master hunter of human souls. He also thinks of himself as an undefeatable warrior. And, he is forever trying to cover up what he really is.

29

THE ANGEL OF LIGHT

The Latin word *lucifer* is not a name for Satan.

W hat we will look at now is a portrayal of Satan's vilest character trait. It is a description that God Himself hangs around the fallen guardian cherub's neck. Satan hates it when this truth is exposed, so he desperately tries to cover it up. He's humiliated because of it. He hides this attribute behind the veil of language and translation nuances. However, we're going to reveal his secret before the world, like Yahweh intends.[101]

LUCIFER

The English translations of the Old Testament were, of course, first written in Hebrew. Those Hebrew versions were later—several hundred years before Jesus' appearance on earth—translated into Greek and/or Latin, then finally into English. This process has sometimes caused translation and interpretation confusion. That's exactly what happened with the apparent name of Satan—*Lucifer*—found in Isaiah 14.

We've already documented that many biblical scholars understand

Isaiah 14:12–17 as a compound reference to Satan. The translation problem happens in the first verse of that passage:

> How art thou fallen from heaven, **O Lucifer**, son of the morning.
> (Isaiah 14:12, KJV; emphasis added)

In a list of the twenty-eight most popular modern translations of the
Bible, the designation of this fallen one is translated as "Lucifer" nine
times. However, in the remaining versions, we find the following terms:
"morning star," "shining star," "day star," "shining morning star," "bright
morning star," and "shining one."[102]

Why so many different translations of one word? Why do some versions render it as a name and others as a title? And why is each translation
incorrect according to the original Hebrew language and context? In this
chapter and the next, we'll explore a couple of major considerations that
will precisely answer our questions.

A PROPER NAME?

In the nine translations that use "Lucifer," the term is always capitalized
in the English, suggesting that it is a proper noun—an alternative name
for Satan. But the word "Lucifer" isn't used as a name for Satan anywhere
else in the Bible, and it isn't in the original Hebrew text of Isaiah 14, either.
That's because *lucifer* is a Latin word that made its way into later English translations of the original Hebrew texts that had been translated into
Greek and Latin simply by being restated in its literal Latin form. However,
the Latin word *lucifer* simply is not a *name* for Satan; it is a *description*.

HELEL AND HALAL

Now, let's look at the exact Hebrew words used in Isaiah 14:12 that are
often rendered as the "bright morning star" or something similar. That
portion of the text reads *helel ben shachar*.[103]

Actually, this phrase most accurately translates to "the shining worship leader, the son of dawn." This is in spite of the fact that practically none of the English versions are translated this way, or even come close to this description. This revelation might be startling, but it is the correct *Hebrew* understanding of the phrase. In the next chapter, I'll have much more to share about this correct and pre-fallen position of Satan.

But for now, let's focus on the word *helel*, a noun used to convey an *attribute* of the subject. It's never used as a proper name, as it is often misused in modern Christendom. *Helel*, in its simplest Hebrew understanding, first translates to "shining one."[104]

But there's more. The word *helel* comes from the Hebrew verb *halal.*[105] *Keil & Delitzsch Commentary on the Old Testament*:

[Helel]…from *hâlal*, to shine, resolved from *Hillel* [Hebrew, to **praise or to worship**][106] (Emphasis added)

Now we are beginning to see something important. *Halal* is the verb form of *helel*, and it means "to shine." It is also connected to *worship!* Thus, instead of using the Latin *lucifer*, most translations translate *helel* as "the shining one." That is a pretty fair English rendering of this text, thus far, but it's still not in its complete context, as you will soon discover.

However, for now, think of *helel* like this: The association between *helel* and *halal* would be similar to our English noun "fisherman" and its verb form "to fish." One word, the noun, defines something *about* a person: He is a *fisherman*. The other word, the verb, speaks of the specific *action* of that person: He loves to *fish*. But the person's *name* is not "Fisherman," nor is his name "To Fish."

The link between *helel* and *halal* is important because of the context of Isaiah 14:12–17. Satan is not *named*; rather, he is *described*…and not in a positive manner at all.

Moreover, this label of disdain is given to Satan by Yahweh Himself. This is very important, because it doesn't matter one iota what the translators "think" this phrase means, what it "ought" to mean, or even what it "seems" to mean. What matters is what Yahweh is actually declaring about Satan.

The next two chapters will show us exactly what God is portraying about the evil one, the one some mistakenly call *Lucifer* as though that word is a title of honor or even his proper name. An accurate understanding of the Hebrew language will demonstrate none of that is true.

30

THE ANGEL OF DAWN

What a big difference the translation of one word makes!

At the beginning of this book, I emphasized that my native language is Hebrew, which allows me to understand the nuances of Hebrew words as they're used in various contexts. Those shades of meaning can completely change the appropriate translation. This advantage will prove important as we dig further into the Old Testament (and even the New Testament) declarations of who Satan really was and now *is*.

HELEL BEN SHACHAR

As presented in the preceding chapter, Isaiah 14:12's Hebrew *helel ben shachar* is often translated into English as something like: "Lucifer, son of the morning," the "shining one (or day star)" or "son of the morning (or of the dawn)." But those descriptions don't correctly deliver the intent of the actual Hebrew words based on their deepest context.

The first word, *helel,* is always used as "shiny" and/or "worship," which are sometimes used together and mean in English something like "glorious worship, or praise," or more specifically, "worship or praise that reflects God's brilliant glory." For example, *helel* is the word from which we get the English "hallelujah!"

The final two words of the phrase, *ben shachar,* is a coupling that *always* translates as "son of the dawn." It is never translated as "day star" or "morning star" except in English translations of Isaiah 14. This fact alone ought to be the first clue that we're dealing with a translation difficulty in this passage.

Shachar doesn't even mean "morning" or "day" in Hebrew. The Hebrew word for "morning" is *boqer*[107] and for "day" is *yom.*[108]

Why make such a big deal of the distinction between day, morning, and dawn? The word "dawn" is a specific part of the morning, the moment when the rising sun first begins to lighten the sky. *Shachar* can only mean "dawn" in the same way the English word "dawn" can only mean that specific moment at the beginning of the morning. This distinction gives Isaiah 14:12 its clearest meaning.

STAR

Surprisingly, the word "star" is found nowhere in Isaiah 14:12. So how did it find its way into so many translations?

The word "star" was inserted apparently in an effort to make sense of the full phrase *helel ben shachar.* Most likely the translators assumed that, since *helel* can mean "shining" and *shachar* means "dawn" (or, as often mistranslated *shachar* "day" or "morning"), the rendering must be something like the "shining star, son of the morning."

As previously revealed, the phrase *helel ben shachar* properly translates in English to something like, "O shining worship leader of Heaven's first moment of praise, which begins at dawn." This more precise translation is made even more apparent when considering all that we've discussed in the previous chapters concerning Satan's unquestionable and former position as Heaven's chief worship leader.

PSALM 108

Following is an interesting tidbit that sheds even more light on the subject. Notice the words we've just been studying in Psalm 108:1–5:

My heart, O God, is steadfast; I will sing and make music with all my soul. Awake, harp and lyre! **I will awaken the dawn.** I will **praise you,** Lord, among the nations; I will sing of you among the peoples. For great is your love, higher than the heavens; your faithfulness reaches to the skies. **Be exalted, O God, above the heavens;** let **your glory** be over all the earth. (Emphasis added)

There it is! The worship of Heaven itself *begins at dawn*—not simply sometime "in the morning"! Nor is dawn just a random time during the "day." The heavenly worship of Yahweh's glory is to begin precisely *at dawn.* The Hebrew word for "dawn" used in Psalm 108 is *shachar,* the same as in Isaiah. Soon we'll look at why the use of this word in Isaiah 14:12 is so important.

NUMBERS 24:17

In Numbers 24:17, we see an amazing prophecy of the eventual coming of Yeshua—Jesus Christ—and here He is genuinely called the "Star" *(kokab)*. Remember, the word "star" is not in the text of Isaiah 14, therefore it can't accurately be used there to describe Satan.[109]

I shall see Him, but not now: I shall behold Him, but not nigh: **there shall come a Star** out of Jacob, and a Scepter shall rise out of Israel. (KJV; emphasis added)

AN ILLUSTRATION

Here's a story that will help illustrate the difficulty concerning the Hebrew words we're exploring.

Once, when I was on a media tour around the United States with Pastor Carl Gallups, we were passing through a small town in rural, southern Alabama. When I asked about the town, Carl replied, "This is a lazy little town in Alabama, typical of many towns in the region."

Because Hebrew is my first language, I often *think* in Hebrew first—before my mind translates words into English. When Carl said the town was "lazy," I immediately formulated a vision wherein I believed that, in this town, no one actually worked for a living!

When I asked Carl about it, he laughed when he realized the translation difficulty. He went on to explain that the word "lazy" in that English context is not a disparaging word, but rather a compliment, of sorts. He explained that it could mean "quaint," "unique," and even "slow-paced in a way that enables its inhabitants to more thoroughly enjoy life." Wow! That was nothing like what I had understood it to mean.

This is exactly what we're dealing with in Isaiah 14:12: translation difficulties that only someone who *thinks* in Hebrew and speaks it as a first language could understand without difficulty. The true language and meaning of Isaiah 14:12 comes just as natural to me as it does to Pastor Carl, when he was speaking and thinking in English and talking about that "lazy little town." What a big difference the proper translation of one word can make!

31

THE REAL STAR OF HEAVEN

There is no problem with the original Hebrew text. The problem
lies within the nuanced translation of certain Hebrew words.

As we continue to unwrap this package of surprises in our search for the true identity of Satan, first recall the amazing—and related— declaration of Revelation 22:16:

> I, Jesus, have sent my angel to give you this testimony for the churches. I am the Root and the Offspring of David, and the bright Morning Star.

There it is again! This sounds a lot like the wording in the English translations of Isaiah 14:12. But how can this be? In Isaiah, *Satan* is the object of discussion. Here, in Revelation 22, *Jesus* is the subject. Would God's Word call both Satan and Jesus the "bright morning star"? Of course not! Well then, what's going on?

Let's first have a look at the Hebrew translation of this New Testament passage, where we find the words *kokab nega ha shachar,* a phrase most accurately stated as "the bright star of the dawn."

Note the appearance of the word *shachar* again. That term is another way of saying that Jesus Christ is "*the focal point* of Heaven's praise—divinely pointed worship—that *begins at dawn.*" It is Jesus who's being adored!

Yet, in Isaiah 14:12, the English translators seem to come close to interpreting the verse to mean that *Satan* is that focus. But the Hebrew of Isaiah is actually saying that Satan, the guardian cherub,[110] was the *leader* of that heavenly worship scene *before* he was expelled from Heaven. And, in that passage, Yahweh is lamenting how far Satan had fallen from his previously exalted position.

Think of it: In Isaiah 14, we do not find the word "star" (*kokab*), nor do we find the words "morning" (*boqer*) or "day" (*yom*). What we do find, as noted earlier, are the words *helel* ("shining"/"worship") and *ben shachar* ("son of the dawn"). Yet almost every English translation uses the words "star," "morning," or "day"—words that are not even in the Hebrew text.

2 PETER

Here's another illustration of the truths we're revealing. Take a look at 2 Peter 1:19. Again, note two of the concepts we've been studying.

> We also have the prophetic message as something completely reliable, and you will do well to pay attention to it, as to a light shining in a dark place, until **the day dawns** and the **morning star** rises in your hearts. (Emphasis added)

In the Hebrew version of this passage, we find the words *shachar* ("dawn") and *kokab* ("star") yet again. And, once again, they speak of none other than Jesus Christ.[111]

SON OF DAWN

Everything we've been studying thus far has been building up to our next discovery, which just might make you want to shout "hallelujah." Look at the following passages from each of the New Testament books of the Gospel. Again, note the emphasized words.

> After the Sabbath, at **dawn** on the first day of the week, Mary Magdalene and the other Mary went to look at the tomb. (Matthew 28:1; emphasis added)

> But on the first day of the week, at **early dawn**, they went to the tomb, taking the spices they had prepared. (Luke 24:1, ESV; emphasis added)

> **Very early** on the first day of the week, **just after sunrise** [see endnote], they were on their way to the tomb. (Mark 16:2; emphasis added)[112]

> **Early** on the first day of the week, **while it was still dark** [see endnote], Mary Magdalene went to the tomb and saw that the stone had been removed from the entrance. (John 20:1; emphasis added)[113]

Now we see it! Jesus is the Son of Dawn, the *object* of Heaven's worship. Satan was the *former* worship leader of Heaven; he was in charge of leading that heavenly orchestrated, dawn-time worship of Yahweh. Then, Satan fell and stole the earthly realm in his fall. Jesus has reclaimed the fallen realm through the cross and the resurrection. And that resurrection was first discovered by His disciples. . .*at dawn.* They might not have known it at the time, but all of Heaven was rejoicing with them—at dawn!

That dawn resurrection worship service was a divine signal to Satan that Jesus had won the battle and was the prophesied "seed" that would "crush" his head (Genesis 3:15). We might even say that this was when it finally "dawned" on Satan that he had been defeated!

Always remember, when reading Isaiah 14 in the English texts, Yahweh gave those words to the prophet by His Holy Spirit. Yahweh would never exalt Satan to any position of equality with Jesus. That is not what Isaiah 14 is supposed to convey.

To be clear, in summary: There is no problem whatsoever with the original Hebrew text of Isaiah 14. The problem lies within the nuanced translation of certain Hebrew words. It's much like describing a quaint, easy-going, small town in Alabama as "lazy"—context is everything!

I am convinced, as you probably know by now, that these translation "difficulties" were most likely influenced and moved along by the Chaldean spirit. This is not hard to believe. After all, in Isaiah 14, God is chewing Satan out; He isn't exalting him. Wouldn't Satan be embarrassed by that, and want to hide that fact? Of course! But that's why it's so important that we get it right.

32

THE HOWLING ANGEL

In this very evil sense he is the true Lucifer.

As stated earlier, the noun *helel* and the verb form *halal* are also the Hebrew words from which we derive the term "hallelujah."

That verb translates to "praise unto the Lord." In its most literal sense, we are proclaiming "Cry out! Shine the light of praise upon the Lord!" However, the term can also be used as the slightly more dramatic "howl."

This is another big clue for us. Here's what a few well-known scholars note:

Albert Barnes:

Helel—(hēylēl, from hâlal, "to shine"). **The word in Hebrew occurs as a noun nowhere else.** In two other places, Ezekiel 21:12; Zechariah 11:2, it is **used as a verb** in the imperative mood of Hiphil, and **is translated "howl"** from the verb yālal, **"to howl" or "cry."**[114] (Emphasis added)

Adam Clarke:

Heilel, comes **from yalal, yell, howl, or shriek, and should be translated, "Howl, son of the morning;"** and so the Syriac [translation] has understood it.[115] (Emphasis added)

A couple of the more literal Hebrew-to-English Bible versions bring additional light to our understanding as well:

How you have fallen from Heaven. **Wail at dawn.** You are fallen into the ground, **Infamous One** of the nations. (Isaiah 14:12, Peshitta Holy Bible Translated; emphasis added)[116]

How are you fallen from heaven. **Howl in the morning.** For you have fallen down to the ground, **O reviler of the nations.** (Isaiah 14:12, Lamsa Bible; emphasis added)[117]

SHINE THE LIGHT ON ME

As we draw ever closer to the genuine meaning of this verse, think about this next truth. In its negative sense, which would be determined by the context, *halal* can also mean to "shine one's own light" or "to boast. Especially in an extremely arrogant manner."[118]

For example, we might describe a haughty person by saying, "He's always shining the light on himself" or "He always wants to put himself in the limelight."

The word can also be used in a more westernized, urban sense, like this: "He's always shining somebody on." In that usage, the word means that the "shiner" is one who falsely compliments others or is deceptively charming. Does that sound like anybody you know from the Bible—maybe from the Garden of Eden?

So, in Isaiah 14, the context is that Satan is boasting about how he *will* "take" the throne of God. In fact, as we've already noted, five different times Satan proclaims, "I will ascend to the highest place in heaven." He is taunting Yahweh and shining the light of his intended goals upon himself.

God is basically saying to Satan, "You are a contemptable, conceited, flattering, and deceitful bigmouth. You, who howls and cries out to the heavens shaking your fist in *my* face—shining your arrogance throughout the realms and proclaiming that *you* will be their rightful ruler. *This* is who you *really* are."

While describing Satan's degenerate character, Isaiah 14:12 also includes a play on words. Satan was indeed originally created in light and splendor. As we've already seen, Ezekiel 28 says this:

> Your heart became proud **on account of your beauty**, and you corrupted your wisdom **because of your splendor**. (Ezekiel 28:17; emphasis added)

The Hebrew word for "splendor" is *yiphah,* which means "brightness"[119] and is directly related to the verb form *yapha,* meaning "to shine out or forth, to send out beams, to cause to shine."[120]

MASQUERADE

The ability to disguise his appearance is one of Satan's most hideous, lying wonders. In luring us away from God, he hides behind a mask of innocence and light.

His name is not *Lucifer.* He is no longer the "shining one" of Heaven. And he certainly isn't innocent. He is the destroyer of innocence. He is not an angel of light, either, although Scripture states that he still prefers to masquerade as one.

The Apostle Paul was trying to warn the church at Corinth about false teachers, who were really just doing the work of Satan, their real master. In so doing, Paul cautioned us about Satan's nature of hiding behind *light.* It is in this very evil sense that he is the true *Lucifer.*

> For such people [the false teachers] are false apostles, deceitful workers, masquerading as apostles of Christ. And no wonder, for

Satan himself masquerades as an angel of light. It is not surprising, then, if his servants also masquerade as servants of righteousness. Their end will be what their actions deserve. (1 Corinthians 11:13–15; emphasis added)

Before I close this chapter, have a look at classical biblical commentator Matthew Henry's words. Notice what he says about the king of Babylon and the tie to the very last days. It's just what we've been saying in our previous chapters.

The king of Babylon having the absolute command of so much wealth, by the help of it *ruled the nations*.... And it filled up the measure of the king of Babylon's sins. Tyrants sacrifice their true interest to their lusts and passions. ...it is sinful ambition to aim to be like the Most High....

The devil thus drew our first parents to sin.... He should be slain, and go down to the grave; this is the common fate of tyrants.

Learn from all this, that the seed of evil-doers shall never be renowned. The royal city is to be ruined and forsaken. **Thus the utter destruction of the New Testament Babylon is illustrated,** Revelation 18:2.[121] (Emphasis added)

To get to the throne of God, Satan will stop at nothing and will destroy everything in his path. He will mark out the territory he wants and seek to completely bring it under his command in order to capture it. And, when I say he will destroy everything in his path, I mean *everything*: You. Me. Nations. Homes. Families. Marriages. Children. Babies in the womb. Loved ones and friends. The Church. Israel. Jerusalem. The Temple Mount. Fallen nations and empires. *Everything.*

This is the *spirit of the Chaldeans/Babylonians*. This is the spirit that emanates from the very heart and soul of Satan. It is the nature of his howling, shrieking, bragging, and *shining-on* character.

33

PROPERLY CLOTHED

What makes these people, arrayed in the whole and proper armor of God, genuine "experts in war?"

Now that we know more about who we are battling, let's take a closer look at something else the enemy is trying to hide.

When we talk about spiritual warfare, almost every Bible reader is familiar with the Ephesians 6:10–14 passage in which the Apostle Paul describes "the whole armor of God." It tells us that if we wear the *true* armor of God, only then will we be properly equipped to "take our stand" against the evil one, especially against the flood of his wickedness in the very last days. This promise of being able to "stand" in those ominous days is repeated four times in Ephesians 6.

> Put on the full armor of God, so that you can **take your stand** against the devil's schemes. (Ephesians 6:11; emphasis added)

> Therefore put on the full armor of God, so that when the day of evil comes, you may be **able to stand your ground**, and after you have done everything, **to stand. Stand firm then**, with the belt

of truth buckled around your waist, with the breastplate of righteousness in place. (Ephesians 6:13–14; emphasis added)

What is the armor Paul is talking about? Many commentators insist that he must have been describing the armor of a Roman soldier. But what is described in the verses has nothing to do with the battle clothing of a Roman soldier. Notice the passage says we are to suit up "in the armor of God," not "in the armor of a Roman soldier." This is not an insignificant distinction.

Remember, the Roman soldiers were not greatly admired among the early Christians, and for obvious reasons. This was especially true among the Jewish believers in Yeshua. So why would Paul, or the various congregations of the early church, want to compare the apparel of someone fighting a spiritual battle as being metaphorically equivalent to wearing Roman armor? The short answer is: *They wouldn't have.*

However, if you really want to fight spiritual warfare and be victorious, you need to understand what the full armor is—in the physical as well as the spiritual understanding of that imagery. A huge part of that armor is *truth*.

So, let's begin here. As noted in an earlier chapter, the Bible says all who are born again are also priests and servants of the Most High. We have been called out of the darkness of the Chaldean spirit and into the light of Yeshua.

But you are a chosen race, a royal priesthood, a holy nation, a people for his own possession, that you may proclaim the praises of him who **called you out of darkness into his marvelous light**. (1 Peter 2:9; emphasis added)

With this in mind, we'll explore two key passages that perfectly shape up our complete answer to the question: Exactly what "armor" was Paul talking about in Ephesians 6?

WARRIOR PRIESTS

As priests of the gospel of Yeshua, we are called to be prepared in the daily matters of spiritual warfare. Consider the following passage from the book of Numbers. Notice that the men who were to serve as priests among God's people were given a specific calling, a mission defined with the use of a precise phrase.

> From thirty years old and upward until fifty years old shalt thou number them; all that enter in **to perform the service**, to do the work in the tabernacle of the congregation. (Numbers 4:23, KJV; emphasis added)

The Hebrew word translated "to perform" is *tsaba*, the verb form of the root. The *Hebrew Lexicon* is clear: The term, within the context of this passage, carries the meaning of *the performance* of spiritual service… in *military style.*[122]

But that's not all. The word "service," in the Hebrew lexicon, is the noun form of the root word. It means "service in the army, war, or within the physical act of warfare."[123] Therefore, this passage literally translates as: "All who are able must come to wage war in the army of the tent of meeting." In other words, the priests were to enter the tabernacle prepared for spiritual battle. They understood that, in the performance of their duties and as priests who were standing in the gap between the people of God and the demonic realm, they would be waging war against the "gods" (demonic realm). These are the same "gods" of the first two Commandments, and they are the same "gods" we fight daily.

Let's have a reminding look at those first two "shall nots" in the Ten Commandments given by God at Mt. Sinai.

[1] You shall have **no other gods** before me.
[2] **You shall not make for yourself an image** in the form of anything in heaven above or on the earth beneath or in the waters

below. **You shall not bow down to them or worship them;** for I, the Lord your God, am a jealous God, **punishing the children for the sin of the parents to the third and fourth generation of those who hate me,** but showing love to a thousand generations of those **who love me and keep my commandments.** (Exodus 20:3–6; emphasis added)

The priests had to be properly prepared and dressed for that battle, and their clothing was not that of a Roman soldier. The Jewish part of the early Christian church would have known fully well what Paul meant by "putting on the armor of God." Sadly, today's Westernized church has pretty much missed the point entirely. Guess who's behind that deception? You've got it. It's Satan's employment of the spirit of the Chaldeans.

How do we battle against an invisible enemy? Obviously, the armor has to be supernatural, designed for offense and defense. It has to be worn and wielded in faith beyond anything we can humanly comprehend. As we wear it, we stand with the King.

The Song of Solomon—speaking of warrior-priests—says all are experts in, of all things, *war.*

> ...**all of them wearing swords** and expert in war, each with his sword at his thigh, against terror by night. (Song of Solomon 3:8; emphasis added)

Benson's Commentary addresses the duty of these "warriors":

He alludes to Solomon's guard, whereby he designs all those creatures, whether angels, princes, ministers, or others, whose ministry God uses **for the protection of his church.** Every man **hath his sword**—is prepared and ready to fight, to prevent those dangers which are frequent in the night season.[124] (Emphasis added)

The *Pulpit Commentary* sees the guards, metaphorically, as the guardians of the bride. They are arriving with the bridegroom. This, then, becomes an allusion to the book of Revelation, which gives an account of Jesus returning for His bride, accompanied by the heavenly host of warriors ready to do battle on behalf of the bride's defense.

> **The long journey through the wilderness** [perhaps symbolic of our journey through this sin-stained world, and Egypt's sojourn in the wilderness] is implied in the mention of the bodyguard (cf. Isaiah 4:6; Isaiah 25:4). **The intention evidently is to show how dear the bride was to Solomon. His mighty men were chosen to defend her. So the Church is surrounded with armies of guardian attendants.** Her Lord is the Lord of hosts.[125] (Emphasis added)

The writers of the *Jamieson-Fausset-Brown Bible Commentary* see this passage similarly:

> In Solomon 3:6 **the wilderness** character **of the Church is portrayed;** Jesus Christ is seen dwelling in believers, who are His "chariot" and "body." …His body, **literally, guarded by a definite number of angels,** threescore, or sixty (Mt 26:53), from the wilderness (Mt 4:1, 11), and continually (Lu 2:13; 22:43; Ac 1:10, 11); **just as six hundred thousand of Israel guarded the Lord's tabernacle.**[126] (Emphasis added)

The book of Revelation also warns us about not having on the proper garments as we walk life's journey in a fallen creation.

> Yet you have still a few names in Sardis, people **who have not soiled their garments,** and they will walk with me in white, **for they are worthy.** (Revelation 3:4; emphasis added)

Notice the attendants, angels, priests, and warriors—spoken of in Numbers, Song of Solomon, and Revelation—are not wearing Roman soldier outfits. They're wearing priestly garments, and they are, therefore, prepared for spiritual warfare of the fiercest nature. They have on the proper, unsoiled garments.

The book of Exodus provides the first description of the appropriate attire for the priests of the tabernacle. These mirror the garments that we also are to wear, in the *spiritual* sense of Ephesians 6:

> You shall bring forward your brother Aaron, with his sons, from among the Israelites, to serve Me as priests…. **Make sacral vestments** for your brother Aaron, for dignity and adornment…. **These are the vestments** they are to make: **a breastpiece, an ephod, a robe, a fringed tunic, a headdress, and a sash.** They shall make those sacral vestments for your brother Aaron and his sons, **for priestly service** to Me. (Exodus 28:1–4; emphasis added)

What makes these people arrayed in the whole and proper armor of God "experts in war?" Ephesians 6 says nothing about them being physically young, strong, or in the military elite of an earthly society—usual prerequisites for going into battle. The only requirements that are listed are trust, faith in God, and being dressed in the proper gear—*God's gear.* The correct armor enables us to endure His calling, fight with courage, and walk through even the hottest flames of adversity, knowing that the Son of God will be in the flames with us as we go (Daniel 6).

34

THIS IS WAR

*God's people are not to sit idly by and allow
the enemy to advance on all fronts.*

A second passage in the Old Testament sheds magnificent light upon our topic. In it, Yahweh declares that He is adorning Himself with certain articles of armor for a specific purpose. He's preparing to engage in a righteous battle.

GOD PUTS ON HIS ARMOR

This passage from Isaiah had to have been where Paul, a former Pharisee and Jewish rabbi, obtained the metaphor for the early church's identification of the proper spiritual armor.

> **The Lord** looked and was displeased that there was no justice. He saw that there was no one, he was appalled that there was no one to intervene; **so his own arm achieved salvation** for him, and **his own righteousness** sustained him.

He [the Lord] **put on righteousness as his breastplate**, and **the helmet of salvation** on his head; he **put on the garments of vengeance and wrapped himself in zeal** as in a cloak. (Isaiah 59:15–20; emphasis added)

This is literally the armor of God, what He "puts on" when He engages in righteous, spiritual battle. It really can't get much clearer. We are to put on the spiritual armor of God Himself. He is the Lord of truth, righteousness, the Word, integrity, salvation, and the Gospel. When we stand in *His armor*, we stand in supernatural strength and protection. That's much different than what we hear preached in most churches today. Again, this is because of the work of the Chaldean spirits in our midst.

Many classical commentators clearly saw the same truths about Isaiah 59 in relation to Paul's instructions in Ephesians 6 as we are uncovering here.[127] (I have listed in the endnotes five additional commentaries on this topic.)[128]

Lange's Commentary:

[Isaiah 59] **is the original source** of the Apostle Paul's extended description of the spiritual armor, Ephesians 6:14; Ephesians 6:17. Also in 1 Thessalonians 5:8 there **underlies the same representation of the equipment required by Christians.**[129] (Emphasis added)

Ellicott's Commentary:

The close parallelism [of Isaiah 59] with…Ephesians 6:14–17 suggests a **new significance** for St. Paul's **"whole armor of God."**[130] (Emphasis added)

We're in a deadly, winner-takes-all battle. This is warfare at its ugliest and darkest—*spiritual warfare* that's often played out in the physical realm. It's a cosmic conflict between the Chaldean spirits and the throne of Heaven: a fight for our homes, marriages, families, children, babies in the womb, futures, legacies, and freedom. The dark spirits want to steal all of these.

Satan wants to enslave us. But Jesus has come to set us free and restore the original Paradise existence lost in the Garden. So the battle rages, until that soon-coming day when Jesus Christ puts an end to it all, to the glory of His name.

35

OUR STRENGTH

The Levite priests were not a bunch of pacifist hippies.

Let's do a quick biblical survey of our Spirit-empowered equipment, the armor of true spiritual warfare.

The breastplate is the breast piece of the High Priest, His righteousness or right standing with God. When we are in correct standing with God, our spines are aligned with His Spirit—straight and strong—through faith in Him.

He put on righteousness like a breastplate. (Isaiah 59:17, NASB)

You shall make a breastpiece of judgment, the work of a skillful workman.... Aaron shall carry the names of the sons of Israel in the breastpiece of judgment over his heart when he enters the holy place, for a memorial before the LORD continually. (Exodus 28:15–29, NASB)

The helmet is the headdress the priest wears, which signifies bearing the sins of the people and now indicates salvation through the blood of

Yeshua. The only headdress worn by our High Priest, Yeshua Jesus, was the crown of thorns, the ultimate helmet of sacrifice. Our helmet of salvation is not designed to protect the flesh, but it denotes a willingness to lay down our lives for the gospel. It is the crown of sacrifice through love and faith.

> And a helmet of salvation on His head; and He put on garments of vengeance for clothing and wrapped Himself with zeal as a mantle. (Isaiah 59:17, NASB)

The footwear: The Bible says Yeshua is coming back, and that His nail-pierced feet will land on the Mount of Olives. He won't be wearing Roman boots when that happens. When priests go into the Temple for service, they take off their shoes and thoroughly wash their feet.[131] Moses was instructed to remove his sandals before he approached the burning bush.[132] This is the same reason Joshua was also told to take off his shoes when in the presence of the Lord.[133] In the spiritual realm, we're priests with the feet of soldier/servants—we're not a Roman-ish military. We're called to walk sacrificially as we advance into spiritual battle, and to go forth in the Lord's work having cleansed ourselves of the corruption of this world that has dirtied our "feet" as we walk through it.

> How lovely on the mountains **are the feet of him who brings good news** [gospel], who **announces peace** and **brings good news** of happiness, who **announces salvation** [Hebrew for "salvation" is Yeshua/Jesus], and says to Zion, "Your God reigns." (Isaiah 52:7, NASB; emphasis added)

This is the verse upon which Paul was basing the need to have our feet "fitted with the readiness that comes from the gospel of peace."
Cambridge Bible for Schools and Colleges:

Isaiah 52:7; Nahum 1:15; and the quotation, Romans 10:15. Those passages are closely linked to [Ephesians 6:15] by the concurrence in them of the words "feet" and "message of peace." But in them the imagery distinctly suggests movement, message-bearing; in this, as distinctly, steadfastness in personal spiritual warfare.[134] (Emphasis added)

The belt of truth is the sash that commissions us and symbolizes the authority we're given in the name of Yeshua and through His blood. It's a sash of purity.

Also righteousness will be the belt about His loins, and faithfulness the belt about His waist. (Isaiah 11:5, NASB)

The shield, dazzling with the pure light of God, is the faith in Yeshua that protects us from the lies of the vile Chaldean spirit—the most wicked depths of the demonic realm—and the fiery arrows of the enemy. It enables us to see the way forward.

The LORD **is my strength and my shield**; My heart trusts in Him, and I am helped; Therefore my heart exults, And with my song I shall thank Him. (Psalm 28:7, NASB; emphasis added)

Every word of God is tested; **He is a shield** to those who take refuge in Him. (Proverbs 30:5, NASB; emphasis added)

The sword is the Word of God. The sword of Ephesians 6 is the only weapon of offense…and it is the Word of God, just as the power of that Word was wielded by Jesus in His own wilderness temptation (Matthew 4, Luke 4).

For the word of God is living and active, sharper than any two-edged sword, piercing to the division of soul and of spirit, of joints and of marrow, and discerning the thoughts and intentions of the heart. (Hebrews 4:12, NASB 1995)

In His right hand He held seven stars, and out of His mouth came a sharp two-edged sword; and His face was like the sun shining in its strength. (Revelation 1:16, NASB)

Therefore repent; or else I am coming to you quickly, and I will make war against them with the sword of My mouth. (Revelation 2:16, NASB)

Then I saw heaven opened, and behold, a white horse. The one sitting on it is called Faithful and True, and in righteousness he judges and makes war…. From his mouth comes a sharp sword with which to strike down the nations, and he will rule them with a rod of iron. (Revelation 19:11–16, NASB)

VIRTUOUS BATTLE

Never forget: The Levite priests were not a bunch of pacifist hippies. God used these priests—always armed, trained for physical war, and *zealous for the righteousness of God*—to engage in virtuous battle.

Moses saw that the people were running wild and that Aaron had let them get out of control and so become a laughingstock to their enemies. …

Then he said to them, "This is what the Lord, the God of Israel, says: '**Each man** [the context is the Levite priests] **strap a sword to his side.** Go back and forth through the camp from one end to the other, each killing his brother and friend and neighbor.'" **The Levites did as Moses commanded**, and that day about three thousand of the people died. Then Moses said, "**You have been set apart to the Lord** today, for you were against your own sons and brothers, **and he has blessed you this day.**" (Exodus 32:25–29; emphasis added).

These passages paint a picture of our High Priest, Yeshua, dressed in his priestly garments—*the whole armor of God*—going forth to war, physically and spiritually. He is our model; He is our template. His armor is the genuine armor "of God." He is God in the flesh. He is the Word that was with God and that was God, and that became flesh and dwelt among us (John 1:1–3, 14).

This is God, who wears the armor of the Great High Priest; and this is why Paul tells the Church: "Put on the armor of God."

On that day, we will follow Him, dressed in "fine linen, white and pure." No Roman armor is required. We have armor that is much more powerful and eternal. It is God's armor, and it's consistently spoken about throughout the Bible. There really shouldn't be any confusion within the true Body of Christ regarding this truth.

WARRIOR PRIESTS

We are not controlled by the Chaldean spirits. We need to know how to walk in spiritual warfare as a Kingdom of warrior priests. How do we fight the deadly spiritual battle that Paul talks about? We have to walk like priests—not as Episcopal, Lutheran, Roman Catholic, or Jewish Orthodox priests, but as followers of Yeshua, anointed priests before His throne. We are ambassadors for His soon-coming Kingdom.

How do we engage in spiritual warfare? In the same way the priests of Israel battled when the walls of Jericho tumbled down. We minister in the *power of God*, dressed in His spiritually represented armor. Then He fights *for us*. That's how.

In closing this chapter, consider once again words from the Apostle Paul:

I beg you that when I come I may not have to be as bold as I expect to be toward some people who think that we live by **the standards of this world** [invented by the Chaldean spirits].

For though we live in the world, we do not wage war as the world does. **The weapons we fight with are not the weapons of the world** [like Roman weapons and armor.].

On the contrary, [our weapons] have **divine power to demolish strongholds. We demolish arguments and every pretension that sets itself up against the knowledge of God,** and we take captive every thought to make it obedient to Christ. (2 Corinthians 10:2–5)

━◆━

We've scratched away an awful lot of surface sand from the first layers of our spiritual archeological "dig." Now, we're prepared to go much deeper. We'll have to be extremely cautious as we reach this next layer, since we might be upsetting some old, deceptive artifacts, long-buried and falsely revered by generations past.

When we dig up these next finds from amongst the rubble of Satan's deception, we may find they are not what most of today's church was expecting. And, some will not be happy that we found them at all.

But, the journey we will take next will reveal things that can forever change your perspective on Jesus' birth, crucifixion, and resurrection in a way that will cause your heart to burst with joy at the new depth of the life understanding and biblical perspective you'll gain.

Get your trowels ready.

PART VI

FROM JACOB'S LADDER TO BETHLEHEM

And you, O **Tower of the Flock**, hill of the daughter of Zion, **to you shall it come**, the former dominion shall come, kingship for the daughter of Jerusalem.

~Micah 4:8

36

LOCATION, LOCATION, LOCATION

For six and a half years, I've been doing private research in
Area C of Israel to find the real birthplace of Yeshua.

The starry skies over Bethlehem's fields suddenly came alive with a vast choir of angels proclaiming praises to *God in the Highest* as the shepherds, witnesses of their divine glory, quaked in fear. This account certainly is one of the most powerful images in the New Testament narrative.

The shepherds had been going about their daily routines, quietly guarding the sheep—animals that had been carefully selected and prepared for Temple sacrifice.[135] Like the sheep of their fields, these were not run-of-the-mill shepherds, either. But now, with no warning at all, those set-apart shepherds were given the most monumental news ever delivered to mankind.

> And the angel said to them, "Fear not, for behold, I bring you
> good news of great joy that will be for all the people. For unto you
> is born this day in the city of David a Savior, who is Christ the

Lord. And this will be a sign for you: you will find a baby wrapped in swaddling cloths and lying in the manger." (Luke 2:10–12)

It was a message of hope for Israel, the fulfillment of the promise of a Savior for humanity. But the power of that account has been watered down through the deception of the ages, which has cloaked the majesty of the moment in an unfortunate misunderstanding.

To find the purposes and plans of the God of the universe, we must dare to shake off long-held tradition and throw off the camouflage of secondhand language; only then are we able to uncover the pure, unvarnished Hebrew in which the gospels were originally written.

We can be sure the evil one has done everything possible to hide the truth presented in these next pages. But correctly understanding the original Hebrew language and customs brings God's Word to life in a way that might fill you with a new sense of awe and majesty—just as the birth narrative of our Savior was intended to inspire.

THE DETAILS

First, let's explore some details. For starters, the manger was not "a" manger, as in a randomly selected one. Rather, it was "the" manger, as in a place very specific, chosen by God Himself, and prophesied *by name* in the Scriptures. We'll discuss the powerful significance of this seemingly slight difference in translation shortly, but, on our spiritual archeological excursion, we must begin by carefully brushing the sand away from this artifact.

While most English translations of Matthew 2:7 render the verse as Mary laying her newborn son in "a" manger, *Young's Literal Translation* of that passage brings the ultimate, oft-hidden truth to its fullest understanding:

And she brought forth her son—the first-born, and wrapped him up, **and laid him down in** THE **manger**, because there was not for them a place in the guest-chamber.[136] (Emphasis added)

The *Literal Standard Version* makes the same distinction. By the way, note that both of these translations are described as "literal."

> And she brought forth her Son—the firstborn, and wrapped Him up, **and laid Him down in THE manger**, because there was not a place for them in the guest-chamber.[137] (Emphasis added)

What's the big deal if it's "a" manger, as in any old manger, *or* "the" manger, indicating a very specific one? Hang in there. We're about to dig up a gem.

IN SEARCH OF THE CRIB

Let's now sink our trowels into the treasures of Area C.

Area C is an Oslo II[138] administrative division in the land of Israel that now encompasses a little more than 60 percent of the West Bank region. Excluding East Jerusalem, this parcel of land is home to 385,900 Israeli settlers and approximately 300,000 Palestinians.[139]

As you might imagine, Area C is a disputed region, both internationally and politically. The reason isn't simply political; it's deeply spiritual and biblically important.

For six and a half years, I've been doing private research in Area C to find the real birthplace of Yeshua. As already noted, both Israel and the Arab authorities occupy the region. This fact is spiritually significant, because Yeshua always preached about the "one new man"—meaning believers, whether Hebrew or Gentile.

Isn't it just like Yeshua to enter this world disguised as a newborn child in a place currently occupied by both people groups? Yeshua Messiah is for *all* people who will believe, not just for the Jews. For this reason, I believe the area will remain occupied by both Jews and Gentiles until He returns. That area is a picture of the one new man for all who will believe.

In persistently searching this area, I visited practically every relevant mountain and combed through all the ancient ruins I could find. One would think the easiest place on earth to identify would be the birthplace of the Savior of the world, but the precise location has been lost under layers of misinformation and confusion, and, of course, it has been obscured because of the Roman Catholic "holy places."

However, I am convinced that Yeshua was not born in the Church of the Nativity, in the downtown area currently defined as Bethlehem, where everybody goes with the tour groups. Those who are particularly sensitive to the Spirit of God can often sense the Chaldean spirit there, as many have told me this over the years. The reason is because *this is not where Jesus was born.*

The Bible is clear: Jesus was laid in a unique and holy place, surrounded by a certain "class" of people for an exclusive purpose. Its location makes perfect sense and makes the entire plan of God's salvation through Yeshua sparkle throughout the Scriptures.

Most importantly, it is a place that is specifically named in the Old Testament prophecies.

37

THE TOWER OF THE FLOCK

The Jews deny any place *to be the authentic*
birthplace of Messiah because they don't believe He was,
or will be, born *anywhere.*

I am convinced that a scripturally identified location known as the Tower of the Flock is where Jesus was born in Bethlehem. As you will discover, this location fits all the important biblical descriptions and connects with eternally significant prophecy.

Many people have never even heard of the Tower of the Flock. Yet, along with the prophecies of the Bethlehem birth of the Messiah (Micah 5) also came a clearly stated prophecy about the location in that village where the child would be born (Micah 4):

And you, **O Tower of the Flock,** hill of the daughter of Zion, **to you shall it come, the former dominion shall come, kingship** for the daughter of Jerusalem. (Micah 4:8, ESV; emphasis added)

APPEARANCE VS. BIRTH

I am aware of one Israeli rabbi, Chuckie Rice, a non-Messianic Israeli scholar, who knows where the Tower of the Flock is and teaches that the "Messiah"—the one the Jews are still waiting on—needs to appear there. Rabbi Rice doesn't say Messiah needs to be *born* there, because the Jews don't believe He will be born of a virgin. They're still blind to that piece of the puzzle. At least the rabbi has part of the truth correct. However, the Jews deny *any place* to be the authentic *birthplace* of Messiah because they don't believe He was, or will be, *born* anywhere. Even so, it certainly appears that Rabbi Rice, who's not even a believer, is somewhere in the middle of the truth of the matter.

TWO NAMES, SAME SITE

Most Orthodox Jewish people in Israel have heard of the Tower of the Flock, but when asked if they know where it is, they simply say it's a settlement in Area C, somewhere near Ephrathah. They usually don't say it's near Bethlehem because they've separated Ephrathah from Bethlehem—but the Bible doesn't do that; it says: "For you Ephrathah (or Ephrath) Bethlehem" (Micah 5:2).

And, from Genesis, we also know that Ephrathah and Bethlehem are the same:

> As I was returning from Paddan, to my sorrow **Rachel died** in the land of Canaan while we were still on the way, **a little distance from Ephrath. So I buried her there beside the road to Ephrath (that is, Bethlehem).** (Genesis 48:7; parenthesis in original)

Fortunately, Rabbi Rice is revealing his findings to the public and teaching his students the details about the Tower of the Flock (*Migdal Eder*) and how their Messiah must appear there.[140]

Many Jews in Israel are becoming increasingly aware of the significance of this location, and even how it should be more correctly connected with the Christian claims of the birth of Jesus. Regardless of the fact that the Jewish people don't believe Yeshua has anything to do with the real Messiah, they do indeed think that if the Christians believe He was born in Bethlehem, they could at least read the Old Testament and get the exact location correct.

A TOUR-GROUP QUESTION

On the issue of where Jesus was actually born, I'll never forget the time I spoke to a Brazilian group visiting Israel. It wasn't a tour I was personally conducting, but the travelers had graciously asked me to teach and then participate in a question-and-answer time with them.

One gentleman raised his hand. "What real difference does it make if I go to a site here in Bethlehem and it's not the authentic site of the birth of Jesus?" he asked. "If I am able to experience something similar to what the Bible says and my heart is focused on Yeshua, what does it matter if the location isn't exactly right?"

I answered that it really could make a difference in our biblical understanding and faith. First, I said that we are walking in the territory of the enemy, so we must be continually be aware that he will try to lead us away from any biblical truth that he can. Second, I explained that we might become a stumbling block to the people in Israel if we don't know the truth. I added to the second part of my answer by pointing out that so many people come to Israel to tour the "Christian" sites that, when they are here, they're being watched by the unbelievers, most of them Jews. As long as tourists are flocking to the wrong places, they truly are stumbling blocks to genuine belief in Yeshua. The unbelievers are mocking and belittling them behind their backs...and Satan loves it.

Yet another consequence, I said, is that we may well miss something monumental regarding the depths of the true message of the birth of Yeshua, as well as the prophetic significance of the biblical account. I told him that we would be missing all the Old Testament connections, those

Scriptures that open up the New Testament into a brand new light and life.

So, to say it doesn't make a difference if I don't know something (something that I *could* know, if I only searched it out) is like saying, "What difference does it make if I never read and try to understand the Old Testament, as long as I occasionally read the New Testament?"

I believe that as the cords of deception regarding Yeshua's birthplace untangle and Christians begin to recognize the significance of the Tower of the Flock, acknowledging that Yeshua Jesus was born there, the more the Jews will begin to give them respect. Then, some might even attach more credence to the New Testament account of Messiah Yeshua and eventually turn to Him for salvation. They know with a certainty that the site of the Church of the Nativity is false, and they privately joke about the tourists who naively follow the tour guides. (I know this because I used to be one of the mockers.)

As long as Christians congregate at the fake sites, they continue to close the door to reception of the gospel by the Jews, and thus block their own blessings from Yahweh. I would say this is pretty important, wouldn't you?

But this is how Satan operates. He's the master of deception. The only way to overcome deception is through the power of the Holy Spirit, who leads us into all truth.

It is the glory of God to conceal a matter; to search out a matter is the glory of kings. (Proverbs 25:2)

Now, let's continue with this spiritual excavation. Over the next several chapters, you'll discover why I, earlier, made such a big deal about Jesus being laid in *the* manger, not just in *a* manger.

38

CAESAR'S DECREE

He thought he was merely devising a way to bring in more money.

Using Caesar Augustus' agenda as the human mechanism, it was God Himself who led Joseph and Mary to the prophesied birthplace of Yeshua.

> In those days, a decree went out from Caesar Augustus that all the world should be registered. (Luke 2:1)

Some translations read "taxed" in this verse rather than "registered." Caesar wasn't interested in numbers as much as he was in money, but the people had to be registered in order for the taxation system to work. That meant citizens had to go to the city of their birth to be counted properly. Joseph and Mary were living in the region of Galilee, but had to travel from there to Bethlehem, Joseph's hometown.

Remember that Jesus spent most of His ministry in the Galilee area, but Messiah had to come from the house and lineage of David. He had to be born in Bethlehem, according to prophecy. And, biblical lineage always traces through the line of the father's side.[141]

> But as for you, **Bethlehem Ephrathah**,[142] Too little to be among the clans of Judah, from you **One will come forth** for Me to be ruler in Israel. **His times of coming forth** are from long ago, **from the days of eternity.** (Micah 5:2, NASB; emphasis added)

Alfred Edersheim (7 March 1825–16 March 1889) was a Jewish convert to Christianity—*a Messianic Jew*—and a renowned biblical scholar[143] especially known for his book, *The Life and Times of Jesus the Messiah*, written in the late nineteenth century. Here is what Edersheim had to say about Caesar's decree in relation to the lineage requirements:

> To Bethlehem as the birthplace of Messiah, not only Old Testament prediction, but the testimony of Rabbinic teaching, unhesitatingly pointed. Yet nothing could be imagined more directly contrary to Jewish thoughts and feelings—and hence nothing less likely to suggest itself to Jewish invention—than the circumstances which, according to the Gospel-narrative, brought about the birth of the Messiah in Bethlehem.[144]

Had Joseph not been compelled to go to Bethlehem to pay his taxes, he most likely wouldn't have taken Mary there, where Jesus had to be born—especially when she was so near her time for delivery. Obviously, Joseph had family lineage there and was from the line of David. Of course we know that Joseph was not the biological father of Jesus, but because he was the adoptive father, he, too, had to be a descendant of David.

> **So we already see God's master plan** moving in the birth narrative found in the Scriptures. Joseph had to register with Mary because he was betrothed to her. **And it had to be done in Bethlehem Ephrathah.**[145] (Emphasis added)

CONNECTIONS

Jerusalem and Bethlehem are only a few short miles from each other; the two cities almost join. However, access between them is limited by the fact that Bethlehem is currently under Palestinian control. Entrance to Bethlehem today, even for tourists, involves crossing a border checkpoint.[146]

Jerusalem and Bethlehem share the name "City of David" because David was born in Bethlehem, then later ruled there as king just a few short miles from his own birthplace. In David's day, that part of the cities of Jerusalem and Bethlehem were linked by roads, residences, and businesses. In addition, the City of David is the place where Jesus will reign in the future. The final chapters of the Bible describe a New Jerusalem where God's people will rule forever, marking the earthly city with an eternal honor.

There are deep prophetic connections among the birth of Yeshua, King David, and the coming Kingdom of God on earth. For starters, consider a few biblical/spiritual ties between King David and Jesus Christ, the *Son* of David (Matthew 1:1).

- Both were born in Bethlehem.
- Both died in Jerusalem.
- Both came from practical anonymity, yet rose, by the hand of Yahweh, to become kings.
- Both were identified as "shepherds."
- Both took on the role of priest.
- Jesus was a descendant of David (Revelation 22:16), from the tribe of Judah, the region where David first reigned as king.

While Caesar's registration of the population was a strictly secular event, God's master spiritual plan was behind it from the beginning. God uses circumstances and events of the world to carry out His grand design. If we don't know the details of the events, we can't understand the depths of God's plan.

BETROTHAL

Prior to the trip to Bethlehem, Joseph had received the news of Mary's pregnancy. At first, it was a terrible shock because, although he and Mary had given each other public and binding vows, they had not yet lived together as husband and wife. The obvious conclusion would have been that Mary had committed adultery with another man. Under Mosaic Law, adultery was punishable by a death sentence—stoning. Matthew 1:19 reveals that, even though Joseph respected the law, he was unwilling to expose Mary to shame, so decided to divorce her quietly…until an angel appeared to him in a dream and told him not to be afraid to take Mary into his home, because the child she was carrying was not a product of adultery but had been conceived by the power of the Holy Spirit. That heavenly message changed everything, and Joseph took her into his home as initially planned.

THE BRIDE OF CHRIST

Note the parallels between the account of Mary and Joseph and our own personal betrothal to Christ, but much more is happening in that description. The engagement of Joseph and Mary explains why we, the *remnant*,[147] are called the "Bride of Christ" even before the wedding takes place.

While the Marriage Feast of the Lamb is a future event, we have made vows to Yeshua, and He has made vows to us. These constitute the permanency of our "marriage" relationship. The marriage has not yet been consummated. The consummation will be an eternal one, when we will finally be reunited with our own Creator in Paradise, like we were in the Garden of Eden.

However, right now, we are in stage one—the process of betrothal. Now we have to make it to the end and take part in the heavenly ceremony of eternal marriage. The great Marriage Feast of the Lamb will be the wedding of the ages (see Revelation 19:6–9).

Now, let's go back to the Tower of the Flock, where our next treasure awaits discovery.

39

THE SHEPHERD PRIESTS

God was going to reveal His glory from Migdal Eder.

How often have you envisioned simple, everyday shepherds whiling away the hours in a Bethlehem field when a glorious heavenly host suddenly splits the starry skies and delivers the most dazzling message ever told? Much has been made of the supposition that the angelic announcement came to *ordinary* shepherds, rather than to the political rulers or the halls of the esteemed religious elite. And that is largely true.

In fact, shepherds, in general, were basically near the bottom rung of the ladder in ancient biblical society. But on that night, these were not merely the simple shepherds we have often imagined, the ones who were the most common among the pasturelands of ancient Israel. No, the men guarding the flocks that evening were the ones sanctioned by the Temple priests for a specific purpose. For this reason, sometimes they are referred to as "shepherd priests" to describe their official duties.[148]

This special class of shepherds was responsible for the sacrificial system of Temple worship. They served the Mosaic covenant by looking after the sheep that would be given as offerings, and they were specialists in raising and preparing lambs for the ongoing rituals. It was the specific duty for which they had been trained, and they were held strictly accountable.

I will now refer to the ancient Jewish writings of the earliest rabbis—not because I'm appealing to their specific theology (I never do that), but because the historical and cultural facts they record lend insight into our current spiritual archeological excursion.[149]

There *were shepherds* who were from the priestly families according to the Mishnah Bekhorot 5:4.[150] Could the *shepherds* of Luke 2:8 be priests?

> **Migdal Eder** is also mentioned by name again in the **Mishnah**[151] regarding lambs who were found in the vicinity being accepted **as Passover offerings**, making it very likely that this area was a common grazing place **for Priestly-Shepherds….Mishnah, Shekalim 7:4.**[152] (Emphasis added)

If anyone in that culture besides the priests themselves truly understood the requirements for the Temple sacrifice, it would have been these shepherd priests in the field on that holy night. Had these men been ordinary shepherds, they would never have been allowed in the Temple. While it's true that God uses the simplest things to confound the wise, and He certainly uses simple people for His purposes (1 Corinthians 1:27), these men, again, did not fit the common idea of shepherds.

THE SHEPHERD'S FIELDS

History records that the Bethlehem fields were a consecrated place because the sheep and cattle used for sacrifice in the Temple were raised in this area surrounding Jerusalem. Eusebius, the church historian, records the location of these fields as *Migdal Eder*, a unique biblical location.[153]

Notice that the writers of the classic *Pulpit Commentary* wrote of these truths many decades ago, right down to the specific tower where Messiah was born.

And thou, O **tower of the flock** (**Migdal Edar**). There was a village **with a tower** so-called **near Bethlehem** (Genesis 35:21), and it is thought that Micah refers to it as the home of David.[154] (Emphasis added)

Gill's Exposition of the Entire Bible:

And thou, **O tower of the flock.**... The words "Migdal Eder" are left by some untranslated, and think that place to be intended so called, which **was near to Bethlehem**, Genesis 35:19...**about a mile** from Bethlehem: this is supposed to be **near the place where the shepherds were watching over their flocks at the time of Christ's birth**, the tidings of which were first brought to them here.[155] (Emphasis added)

E. W. Bullinger's Companion Bible Notes:

Tower of the flock. Hebrew tower of "Eder." Used here of Bethlehem (compare Genesis 35:19 with Micah 5:2); coupled here with "Ophel" in next clause, "David's birth-place" and "David's city."[156] (Emphasis added)

International Standard Bible Encyclopedia:

This "tower of the flock," which may have been only a tower and no town, must therefore be looked for **between Bethlehem and Hebron.** Jerome says that it was **one Roman mile from Bethlehem.** In the Septuagint, however, Ge 35:16 and Ge 21:1–34 are transposed, which suggests that there may have been a tradition that **Migdal Eder was between Bethel and Bethlehem.**[157] (Emphasis added)

Strong's Concordance, NAS Exhaustive Concordance, Brown-Driver-Briggs, and *Strong's Exhaustive Concordance* all record that Migdal-Eder speaks specifically of a "flock tower" *at Bethlehem.*[158]

Migdal Eder was actually in the northern part of Bethlehem, on the road to Jerusalem. In Jesus' day, the city of the Temple of God was less than an hour's journey by foot. The shepherd priests would make the same trip every day, taking the specially chosen lambs to *the* manger—a specific one—*where they prepared the lambs for Temple sacrifice.*[159]

And you, O Tower of the Flock, hill of the daughter of Zion, **to you shall it come,** the former **dominion shall come,** kingship for the daughter of Jerusalem. (Micah 4:8, ESV; emphasis added)

Following are what a couple of commentaries appealing to early Jewish scholars say about that passage.

Pulpit Commentary:

There was a village **with a tower so called near Bethlehem** (Genesis 35:21), and it is thought that Micah refers to it as the home of David and as destined to be **the birthplace of Messiah.**[160] (Emphasis added)

Barnes' Notes on the Bible:

And thou, O **tower of the flock**—"'Tower of Eder,' which is interpreted 'tower of the flock,' about **1000 paces (a mile) from Bethlehem,"** says Jerome who lived there, "and foresignifying (in its very name) by a sort of prophecy the shepherds **at the Birth of the Lord."**...The Jews inferred from this place that the Messiah should be revealed there.[161] (Emphasis added)

And this, from *Gary Everett's Study Notes on the Holy Scripture,*[162] found at Studylight.org:

[Several scholars] believe that phrase [Migdal Eder] refers to a place in Israel called the "Tower of Eder," which is located just outside of the city of Bethlehem. It is believed to be indicative of the **birthplace** of David, **as well as that of the Messiah, as Micah later indicates** in his prophecies (Micah 5:2).[163] (Emphasis added)

When once again appealing to the work of Albert Edersheim's *Nativity of Jesus the Messiah*, we find the emphatic declaration that the Jewish expectation of the place where the Messiah of Israel would be "revealed" was known as the Tower of the Flock—Migdal Eder.

That the **Messiah was to be born in Bethlehem, was a settled conviction. Equally so** was the belief, that **He was to be revealed from Migdal Eder**, "the tower of the flock." [From: *Targum Pseudo-Jon.* On Gen. xxxv. 21. Edersheim's endnotes]....

Thus, **Jewish tradition**...apprehended **the first revelation** of the Messiah from that Migdal Eder [tower of the flock], where shepherds watched the Temple-flocks all the year round. Of the deep symbolic significance of such a coincidence, it is needless to speak.[164] (Emphasis added)

It appears to be a sound conclusion that God was going to reveal Messiah from Migdal Eder, close to where the shepherds would be camped in Bethlehem that night. All of this was foretold more than four hundred years before it happened.

40

THE TAMID SACRIFICE

This is why Jesus cried out, "It is finished."

Every day, the shepherd priests took two lambs from the Bethlehem fields up to the Temple for the *tamid* sacrifice, the perpetual morning and evening practice. Hundreds of lambs were used for these sacrifices each year—and that number climbed to tens of thousands for the special feasts of the Lord. This monumental responsibility was, understandably, the dominating force in the lives of those shepherd priests.

PERFECT SACRIFICE

Leviticus 22 speaks of the unblemished lambs that were to be brought every day and offered with a sacrifice of flour, oil, and wine. (See also Numbers 28:1–8; Exodus 29:38–42.)

> You must present a male without defect from the cattle, sheep or goats in order that it may be accepted on your behalf. Do not bring anything with a defect, because it will not be accepted on

your behalf. When anyone brings from the herd or flock a fellow-ship offering to the LORD to fulfill a special vow or as a freewill offering, it must be without defect or blemish to be acceptable. (Leviticus 22:19–21)

When we remember Yeshua through communion, the bread and the wine remind us that He fulfilled every prophecy and was born to die for us—the perfect sacrifice—the Lamb of God, the Lamb of lambs.

FINISHED

When Jesus died, at approximately 3 p.m.—the ninth hour—it was the same time that the Jewish *tamid* sacrifice was coming to its conclusion in the Temple in Jerusalem.[165] This is why Jesus cried out, "It is finished."

So on that night, these blessed shepherd priests were being told by an angelic host that the ultimate once-and-for-all sacrifice, which would carry away the sins of the world, had just been born. And He was born in a specific place, the one Micah had prophesied—the Tower of the Flock. Furthermore, just thirty-three years from that day, there would be no further need to sacrifice animals. It would be *finished*.

While prophecy concerning the coming Messiah had been read from the scrolls for many years, that holy night was the first declaration of the genuine gospel—the *good news*.

And there were shepherds in the same region, lodging in the field and keeping the night-watches over their flock, and behold, a messenger of the LORD stood over them, and the glory of the LORD shone around them, and they feared [with] a great fear.

And the messenger said to them, "Do not fear, for behold, **I bring you good news** of great joy that will be to all the people, because today in the city of David a Savior was born to you, who is Christ the LORD. And this [is] the sign to you: you will find a baby wrapped up, **lying in the manger.**"

And suddenly there came with the messenger a multitude of the heavenly host, praising God, and saying, "Glory in the highest to God, and on earth peace, among men—good will." (Luke 2:8–14, Literal Standard Version;[166] emphasis added)

The kingdom of Israel—under the lordship of *Yeshua Ha Mashiach*—was destined to first be revealed in the area of Migdal Eder, very near the actual birth spot. And, the divine revelation would first be given to anything but simple shepherds of the Bethlehem fields. It was given to the *shepherd priests* of God's Temple service. They knew exactly what to do next, and exactly where to go.

41

NO ROOM IN THE INN

The use of swaddling bands was a
custom among the ancient Jews.

Following is another important finding in our search, one that's also connected to the Tower of the Flock.

Most translations simply get right to the point in describing Mary and Joseph's arrival in Bethlehem and why they would eventually end up with their firstborn son lying in *the manger*.

> And she brought forth her Son—the firstborn, and wrapped Him up, and **laid Him down in the manger,** because there was not a place for them in the guest-chamber. (Luke 2:7, Literal Standard Version; emphasis added)

> And she brought forth her first-born son, and wrapped him in swathing-clothes, and **laid him in the stable,** because there was no place for them in the inn. (Luke 2:7, Anderson New Testament; emphasis added)

> And she brought forth her first-born son, and wrapped him up in swaddling-clothes and **laid him in the manger**, because there was no room for them in the inn. (Luke 2:7, Darby Bible Translation; emphasis added)

> And she brought forth her son—the first-born, and wrapped him up, and **laid him down in the manger**, because there was not for them a place in the guest-chamber. (Luke 2:7, Young's Literal Translation; emphasis added)

NO VACANCY

However, there's a reason there was no room in the inn. In those days, in compliance with the law, a woman who was about to give birth was—to the Jews—considered unclean, like a woman who had an issue of blood (was menstruating). Therefore, she wasn't supposed to be around people; she was to remain secluded. So, the "no vacancy" notice from the inn-keeper probably wasn't given because there was literally no room in the inn; rather, it was given because there was no mistaking her condition. She was about to give birth.

> And the LORD spoke unto Moses, saying, Speak unto the children of Israel, saying, if a woman have conceived seed, and borne a male child: then shall she be unclean seven days, even as in the days of the separation for her infirmity shall she be unclean.[167] (Leviticus 12:1–5, KJV)

The spiritual connection to this living metaphor is striking. We who are pregnant with the Word of God, covered in the blood of the Lamb, and bringing the message of God's salvation also experience this kind of rejection from the worldly system. There is *no room* for us, either—with our message of the soon-coming Yeshua—in a fallen and thoroughly secular society. We are often considered *unclean*. We are made to feel as though we don't belong. We don't fit with the worldly, demonic, and anti-Christ narrative.

Again, it's an *issue of blood*—the blood of Yeshua that covers us. And again, it's a spiritual thing. People don't see the blood that covers the remnant, but it's evident in the spiritual realm, and it makes the evil ones hate us. The Chaldean demons try to take everything from us that should be ours. As we have discovered, that is *mission number one* in the Chaldean spirit's job description.

BIRTHING ROOMS

Something else is important about the watchtowers that were in the sheep fields of Bethlehem. Jerusalem is located on a series of mountainous ridges overlooking the Valley of Blessing.[168] That valley, which extends from Jerusalem to the Dead Sea, is about a mile wide just south of Jerusalem and is the area known as the "Shepherds' Field." About a dozen shepherds' towers are scattered throughout the valley. It was from these towers that the shepherds were able to scout for predators.

The bottom level of each tower was also used for *birthing rooms*—specialized stables for the lambs. These lambs were cared for with the utmost concern because they needed to be spotless—without blemish. Allowing them to be born naturally out in the field would have put them at risk of injury. By placing them in a manger/stall off the rough ground, protecting them within the walls of the observation towers, and wrapping them in special cloth bands called swaddling bands (more on this in the next chapter), the shepherds were able to ensure the animals' perfection.[169]

Yeshua was born in the Tower of the Flock because He came to be the ultimate sacrificial Lamb. It made perfect prophetic sense that the Lamb of God would be born in the same place as the lambs for Temple sacrifice. How could it be otherwise?

More importantly, it's exactly where the fourth chapter of Malachi proclaimed He would arrive.

42

SWADDLING BANDS

Jesus was fulfilling prophecy before He
was cooing in His mother's arms.

Before we read about the swaddling bands—the material in which Jesus was wrapped—we will first examine a metaphor in the book of Ezekiel about the "birthing" of Jerusalem. In that passage, notice the emphasis upon the *absence* of the swaddling strips, or bands[170] that would have ordinarily enfolded Jerusalem when it was "born." This juxtaposition is an important one.[171]

> Again the word of the Lord came to me: "Son of man, make known to Jerusalem her abominations, and say, Thus says the Lord God to Jerusalem: ...on the day you were born your cord was not cut, nor were you washed with water to cleanse you, nor rubbed with salt, **nor wrapped in swaddling cloths.** (Ezekiel 16:1–4; emphasis added)

The implications of this passage are prophetic for two reasons. First, Yeshua can metaphorically represent Israel in the Scriptures.[172] And second, it foreshadows Yeshua being wrapped in swaddling strips/bands, as opposed to the fact that Israel was not. One was born in perfection; the other was born in imperfection.

SYMBOL OF PERFECTION

The use of swaddling bands was a custom among the ancient Jews and has been practiced among various cultures until the most recent times. Ezekiel 16 points to the fact that while Israel/Jerusalem was not created in "perfection," Jesus, the perfect Lamb of God was, indeed, divinely created to be the perfect Lamb. Therefore, our Messiah and Savior *was* swaddled in the proper bands. It would be in Jerusalem, where the "perfection" would be crucified for the sins of the "imperfection."

However, when we come to the birth of Yeshua, we see a very different picture of those swaddling bands.

And she gave birth to her first child, a son. She wrapped him **in strips of cloth.** (Luke 2:7, ISV; emphasis added)

She brought forth her firstborn son, and she wrapped him **in bands of cloth.** (Luke 2:7, Word English Bible; emphasis added)

The word used for "swaddling strips"/"bands," which is found here in Luke, as well as in Ezekiel, also appears in in the book of Job. In chapter 38 of that book, God asks Job about his knowledge of the origin of the cosmos. In so doing, God presents Job with the well-known imagery from human childbirth.[173]

Who shut in the sea with doors **when it burst out from the womb,** when I made clouds its garment and thick darkness its **swaddling band?** (Job 38:8–9, ESV; emphasis added).

The detail of the swaddling bands in Luke 2 ties to those Old Testament foreshadowings because that same detail involves not only the physical realm, but also the spiritual. These passages, taken together, represent all of those who are under the blood—*the Bride of Jesus,* those who are wrapped in His swaddling bands.

COVERING

This means, in the deepest spiritual sense, that Yeshua *covers* us. We are also *overshadowed by, swaddled in,* and *wrapped in* the eternally protective blood of the Lamb. In this way, we are spiritually "clothed" with Christ just as He was clothed when He made His grand entrance into this earthly realm. In baptism, we are "spiritually swaddled" and enveloped in the bands of perfection like the infant Yeshua.

> **So in Christ Jesus you are all children of God** through faith, for all of you who were baptized into Christ **have clothed yourselves with Christ.** (Galatians 3:26–27; emphasis added)

The particular "clothing" in which we are "swaddled" ensures our safe and unblemished arrival into Paradise, just as the lambs were swaddled to ensure their purity and perfection before they were taken to the Temple to become a sacrifice for sin. It's a beautiful and prophetic picture.

Those who read Ezekiel without understanding the swaddling bands of the universe, as well as the absence of the swaddling bands of Jerusalem—along with the Tower of the Flock, the most likely place of Yeshua's birth—are bound to miss the central prophetic significance of the entire birth narrative of Luke 2 and its link to our own walk with Him. But now we see it more clearly. Satan can't hide it from *you* any longer.

This "holy child" was to be Heaven's perfect sacrificial Lamb, the one who would also be our Great High Priest, as well as our Good Shepherd. All of these prophecies had to converge into one person, born in *one* uniquely destined place, and handled in one specific manner. And everything had to be witnessed by a certain class of priestly shepherds who would do the "first sacrificial inspection" of Heaven's newborn Lamb of God.

Now, we can see why the demonic realm has worked overtime through the millennia to try to thoroughly muddle the understanding of what happened that night in Bethlehem.

43

INTIMATE KNOWLEDGE

These shepherds knew where the lambs to be sacrificed were placed before being taken to the Temple.

Have you ever noticed, within the scriptural birth narrative, that the shepherd priests who received the pronouncement from the heavenly host never asked exactly *where* Jesus would be found? They didn't say to the angels: "How do we know *which* manger in Bethlehem? It'll take us all night to find Him."

The angels simply said: "You will find him lying in **the** birthing room [manger],[174] swaddled [like a sacrificial lamb]." And the shepherds took off, racing toward Bethlehem, because they knew precisely where He would be—not in "a" manger, but in "the" manger. There was only one place in Bethlehem that met the specifications of that place.

> So **they hurried off** and found Mary and Joseph, and the baby, who was lying in **the manger**. (Luke 2:15; emphasis added)

A FAMILIAR PLACE

The recipients of this proclamation knew they would find the baby in a birthing stall because, again, as the shepherd priests, they understood the significance of what they were about to see and then tell of as earth's first witnesses. They also knew exactly where that manger was located, because they knew the prophecy of Malachi 4.

Luke's original audience would have picked up on the significance of this as well. They would have recognized the "the" manger in reference to where these Temple shepherds took care of the lambs chosen for sacred sacrifices.[175]

The "stable" was not, as generations have supposed, a place shared by oxen, donkeys, and cats. It would have been kept very clean, befitting the perfect lambs chosen by the shepherd priests. That glorious night, after the angelic pronouncement, the shepherd priests said to each other:

> Let us go up to Bethlehem and see this thing that happened, that was **made known** to us. (Luke 2:15; emphasis added)

Then they gathered their robes around their waists and dashed off to the birthing room of the Tower of the Flock.

The phrase, "made known," in the Hebrew text of the Greek New Testament derives from the Hebrew word *yada* in Genesis 4:6 stating that Adam "knew" his wife.[176] The Greek word is *ginóskó*.[177] Both indicate a knowledge found in intimacy.

Yada doesn't always have to indicate conjugal intimacy, but it always means "beyond regular knowledge" and denotes a personal, immediate, and fond understanding. There was intimacy in Heaven's angelic revelation of the Messiah as it was delivered to those shepherds.

I will again appeal to the work of Alfred Edersheim in his *Life and Times of Jesus the Messiah* for further comment:

This **Migdal Eder** was **not the watchtower for the ordinary flocks** which pastured on the barren sheepground beyond Bethlehem, but **lay close to the town**, on the road to Jerusalem.

A passage in the Mishnah (Shek. vii. 4) leads to the conclusion, that the flocks, which pastured there, were destined for Temple-sacrifices, and, accordingly, that the **shepherds, who watched over them, were not ordinary shepherds.**

In fact the Mishnah (Baba K. vii. 7) expressly forbids the keeping of flocks throughout the land of Israel, except in the wilderness—and **the only flocks otherwise kept, would be those for the Temple-services (Baba K. 80 a).**[178] (Emphasis added)

That's the message of the New Testament. God wants us to "know" who He is, intimately. He wants to personally reveal His glory to us so we can have a special and loving relationship with Him. Here are a couple examples of how that same nuanced meaning of the word is used by Jesus, in both the positive and negative senses:

My sheep listen to my voice; I **know** them, and they follow me. (John 10:27; emphasis added)

Then I will tell them plainly, "I never **knew** you. Away from me, you evildoers." (Matthew 7:23; emphasis added)

This is why it's so important for us to understand the birth narrative in the way we are discerning it through these last several chapters. God wants us to *know* it, so that we might *know* Him and His Word in a more intimate sense—as workmen handling the Word of God accurately.[179]

Part VII

From Ancient Pictures to New Testament Realization

And all these things happened to those persons as types, and they were written for our admonition, to whom the end of the ages came.

~1 Corinthians 10:11, Literal Standard Version

44

TWO NAMES, ONE MESSIAH

The two names of Benjamin, the son of Jacob and Rachel,
foreshadow the crucifixion and resurrection of Jesus.

The first time we hear of *Migdal Eder* is in the story of Rachel, who died while giving birth to Jacob's youngest son, Benjamin (Genesis 35:16–21). Before his marriage to Rachel, Jacob had a dream about a ladder reaching to the heavenly realm. He recognized it as a portal[180] to Heaven, and said:

> This is none other than the house of God, and this is the gate of Heaven. (Genesis 28:17b).

It was there, later, in the place Jacob called Beth-el, meaning "in the House of God," that God changed Jacob's name to "Israel," meaning "to overcome or to prevail" in the House of God.[181]

We know that spiritual Israel—*the Church*[182]—is going to be victorious, through the power of the Lord of Heaven, until it finally has *overcome the world* forever in the New Jerusalem (Revelation 22). So it's not just that Jacob wrestled with God, but it's also that *God* prevailed, because He is always in full control. Although Satan is the temporary prince of this world, God is still on His throne.

ONGOING SPIRITUAL WARFARE

"Israel" also means "victory—to triumph with God."[183] All those who are covered by the blood of Yeshua Jesus, who are grafted into Israel, have spiritual victory through Messiah Yeshua. Wherever there is anything to do with Israel, there will always be spiritual warfare. The Chaldean spirit is always operating behind the scenes and even within the name "Israel."

For example, when God named Israel "to *persevere* with God'"—and He did this in a place called the *House of God*—Satan said, "Oh yeah? I'm going to smear Israel's name. I'm going to wipe it out."

> O God, do not keep silence; do not hold your peace or be still, O God. For behold, **your enemies make an uproar; those who hate you** have raised their heads. **They lay crafty plans against your people**; they consult together against your treasured ones. They say, "Come, **let us wipe them out** as a nation; **let the name of Israel be remembered no more.**" (Psalm 83:1–4; emphasis added)

We see this continually raging spiritual battle in Israel as the world and God's enemies—both physical and spiritual—try to occupy territory that doesn't belong to them. Sometimes they even try to *change the name* of Israel,[184] which is, spiritually speaking, the true and complete body of Yeshua (Romans 11; Ephesians 2).

Jacob's journey moved from Bethel—and his heavenly vision of the ladder—to Migdal Eder, the Tower of the Flock. This happened because *the ladder to Heaven* had to ultimately go through Jesus. He is the only way for anyone to get into Heaven/Paradise (John 14:6). This is one of those pearls of revelation found only through the excavation techniques of spiritual archaeology. What an amazing find.

Rachel was pregnant at Bethel, and it was there that she went into labor. The foreshadowing happened with the birth of the youngest child of Jacob. She died in childbirth, but before she died, Rachel named the baby *Benoni*, "Son of Sorrows" (Isaiah 53:3). However, Jacob renamed him "Benjamin," meaning "Son of My Right Hand" (Genesis 35:18).

> **Then they journeyed from Bethel.** When they were still some distance from Ephrath, Rachel went into labor, and she had hard labor. And when her labor was at its hardest, the midwife said to her,
> "Do not fear, for you have another son." And as her soul was departing (for she was dying), **she called his name *Benoni*; but his father called him Benjamin.**
> **So Rachel died, and she was buried on the way to Ephrathah (that is, Bethlehem),** and Jacob set up a pillar over her tomb. It is the pillar of Rachel's tomb, which is there to this day. Israel [Jacob] journeyed on and pitched his tent beyond **the tower of Eder** [the Tower of the Flock]. (Genesis 35:16–21; emphasis added, parenthesis in original)

MIGDAL EDER = BETHLEHEM

This passage pinpoints the location of Migdal Eder as being near the north, to what is present-day Bethlehem, establishing that Migdal Eder, the Tower of the Flock, was in Bethlehem in Bible times. Today, almost every scholar and archeologist agree that Rachel's grave is located in Bethlehem, but in Rachel's day, even the place from where Jacob had come was also known as the area of Bethlehem.

As we have established, according to Genesis 35, Ephrathah and Bethlehem are the same place. If you look at a biblical map, you'll see that Bethlehem overlooks the Valley of Blessing. Today's Bethlehem is very small, but in biblical times, it expanded all the way to Ephrathah, beyond Rachel's grave, which would make sense. Rachel's grave is located in Bethel, near *Migdal Eder*.

FORESHADOWS

The two names of Benjamin, the son of Jacob and Rachel, foreshadow the crucifixion and resurrection of Jesus. Benjamin, "Son of my Right Hand," was born in the same place as Jesus. And Yeshua was born to sit at the "right hand of God." Also, Yeshua, the "Son of Sorrows," was led like a lamb to sorrow.

> Looking to Jesus, the founder and perfecter of our faith, who for the joy that was set before him endured the cross, despising the shame, and **is seated at the right hand of the throne of God.** (Hebrews 12:2, ESV; emphasis added)

> He was despised and **rejected by men, a man of sorrows** and acquainted with grief; and as one from whom men hide their faces he was despised, and we esteemed him not. (Isaiah 53:3, ESV; emphasis added)

All those who are grafted into spiritual Israel comprise the House of God (Romans 11). That House of God is us; our bodies are clearly declared as the Temple of God (1 Corinthians 6; Romans 12).

The true Temple of God of the last days is *spiritual* Israel, which is made up of both Jews and Gentiles under the blood of Jesus—the genuine Church (Ephesians 2). And Israel (through Jacob) was born in the House of God (Beth-el), the place where Jacob's name was changed to Israel.

God is giving us intimate knowledge through the birth narrative of Yeshua. He's pouring out His *yada* of the precious and deep treasures of His Word and His ways for all who have the "eyes" to see.

45

THE VALLEY OF BLESSING

On the fourth day, when the people were finished
gathering the plunder, they assembled in the Valley of Blessing
and blessed the Lord for delivering them.

Before Jesus was born, God gave us a picture of how He would fight and win our battles for us. The demonstration of that picture played out in the very location of the birth of Messiah. The drama was so powerful that its significance is undeniable.

Over a half century before the birth of Messiah, God prepared the location of His birth with victory over the Chaldean spirit. The narrative of the happenings at the Tower of the Flock (Migdal Eder) and in the Valley of Blessing is recorded in 2 Chronicles 20:23. It's the account of Jehoshaphat, king of Judah, whose name means "judgment," and God's deliverance of the tribe of Judah from the Chaldean spirit. It all unfolds in the place where the greatest blessing to mankind was introduced to the world.

The Battle

After God delivered Jehoshaphat from the deception of the king of Israel, he returned in safety to his house in Jerusalem and sought to bring his people back to the Lord. He appointed judges and attempted to set everything in order, admonishing the people to live in the fear of the Lord and the knowledge that God would not tolerate injustice.

But the unseen realm of demonic manipulation rose up in fury against the godly order, stirring the Moabites, Ammonites, and Meunites against Jehoshaphat in a war to remove peace and take Judah for themselves. Some of Jehoshaphat's men ran to him warning of a great multitude coming against him. The enemy was already in Ein Gedi.[185]

Jehoshaphat was afraid and sought God with prayer and fasting. He stood in the assembly of Judah and Jerusalem and reasoned with God, reminding Him that He had driven out the inhabitants of the land and given it as an inheritance to the descendants of Abraham, and that they had cried out to Him, believing He would hear and save them. In his impassioned plea, Jehoshaphat asked God to execute judgment on the evil hordes because the people of Judah had no chance against them. Their only chance of survival lay in the faithfulness of God and His great power.

The historian of Chronicles paints a powerful picture of the entire tribe of Judah gathered before the Lord with their families. Everyone knew they had no chance without the supernatural intervention of God's mercy. They heard their king crying out to God in humble recognition of their terrifying situation. If God did not hear them, the men faced gruesome deaths, and the women and children would be raped and taken as slaves, ripped from the love and safety of their families. Their only security was to be found in Yahweh, the Creator of everything.

Satan was determined to use this opportunity to devour the people of Judah and steal their inheritance. But his earthly emissaries were no match for the God of the Universe. His Spirit came upon Jahaziel, a Levite in the assembly who stood before the people and said:

Listen, King Jehoshaphat and all who live in Judah and Jerusalem. This is what the Lord says to you: "Do not be afraid or discouraged because of this vast army. For the battle is not yours, but God's. Tomorrow march down against them. They will be climbing up by the Pass of Ziz, and you will find them at the end of the gorge in the Desert of Jeruel.

"You will not have to fight this battle. Take up your positions; stand firm and see the deliverance the Lord will give you, Judah and Jerusalem. Do not be afraid; do not be discouraged. Go out to face them tomorrow, and the Lord will be with you." (2 Chronicles 20:15–17)

Everyone fell on their faces before God in thanksgiving and worshiped Him in brokenness. The next morning, they went into the wilderness, and Jehoshaphat reminded them to believe in God and His prophets so that they would succeed. God, not Judah, would do the fighting for Israel.

While the people would have to confront the enemy, it would be as spectators of what God was about to do—not as combatants. Rather than sending them out with carnal weapons, Jehoshaphat appointed people to sing praises to the Lord. As they stood and sang praises, God set an ambush against the men of Ammon, Moab, and Mount Seir, and turned them against each other.

THE VICTORY: VALLEY OF BLESSING

When the tribe of Judah reached the watchtower, the Tower of the Flock, all they could see in the valley below were dead bodies on the ground. This was the Valley of Beracah, *the Valley of Blessing*. It became the Valley of Blessing only when God defeated the demonic realm there. What better blessing could there be than the salvation of mankind through Jesus Christ, who would come into the world in this exact locale?

When Jehoshaphat and his people came to take their spoil, they found among them, in great numbers, goods, clothing, and precious things, which they took for themselves until they could carry no more. They were three days in taking the spoil, it was so much. (2 Chronicles 20:25)

It took *three days* to gather all the jewelry, equipment, and precious belongings of the dead enemies. So, on *the third day*, the battle had been indisputably won, and the "strong man's house" had been plundered as a result of the victory.

On the fourth day, when the people were finished gathering the plunder, they assembled in the Valley of Blessing and praised the Lord for delivering them. They returned to Jerusalem with joy, and the fear of the Lord came on all the kingdoms that surrounded them when they heard that the Lord had fought against the enemies of Israel. So the realm of Jehoshaphat was quiet, and God gave him rest all around.

What a beautiful picture of God fighting our battles for us and defeating our enemies. Just as with Jehoshaphat, we may have to face the enemy, but God will fight for us. We are shown what was, what is, and what is to come.

THE SPOILS

The picture of the tribe of Judah plundering the evil forces is reminiscent of the Israelites being released from Egypt with all the spoils God gave them from the Egyptians as they left. If you're under the blood of Jesus, serving the Lord, He will take the riches of the world and bring them into your coffers to enable you to take the gospel back to Jerusalem. He will bless you with more than you can take away.

Isaiah 45:3 speaks of the riches of darkness—God giving us the treasures of this world. It's not a "prosperity" message; it means that if you are under the blood of Jesus, He will enable you to take the gospel back to Jerusalem.

But as for you, you will be called priests of the LORD, and you will be named ministers of our God. You will feed on the wealth of the nations, and you will boast about their riches. (Isaiah 61:6, ISV; emphasis added)

In the Valley of Blessing—also known as the Shepherds' Fields of Bethlehem—God overcame Satan through Jehoshaphat. The demonic army was, once again, defeated by the birth of Jesus at the Tower of the Flock.

It's a foreshadowing of Yeshua crushing Satan on the cross.

I will gather all nations, and will bring them down into the **valley of Jehoshaphat; and I will execute judgment on them** there for my people, and for my heritage, Israel, whom they have scattered among the nations. They have divided my land. (Joel 3:2; emphasis added)

Let the nations arouse themselves, and come up to the **valley of Jehoshaphat; for there will I sit to judge** all the surrounding nations. (Joel 3:12; emphasis added)

Everything God does is according to His design of the ages; He blends time, circumstances, names, locations, and supernatural purposes until they converge into a fuller revelation of *Yeshua Ha Mashiach*. It's all about Jesus. It always has been. *Every* word of God's Word points to Him.

And beginning with Moses and all the Prophets, **he explained to them** what was said in **all the Scriptures** concerning himself. (Luke 24:27; emphasis added)

When finally discovered, these are the kinds of treasures in which spiritual archeologists take true delight.

Jesus said to them, "Therefore every teacher of the law who has become a disciple in the kingdom of heaven is like the owner of a house who brings out of his storeroom new treasures as well as old." (Matthew 13:52)

Now that we've discovered these amazing truths about Yeshua's birth, let's go a couple layers deeper to a nugget of information in the Scriptures that is often misunderstood by the modern, westernized church. It consists of a handful of divine clues that tell us exactly where Jesus was crucified and resurrected.

More importantly, the clues tell us why it all took place at yet another specific, prophesied location. And, as you've just discovered, locations are very important to Yahweh. They should be to us as well. They tell a story. They fill in the blanks. For those patient enough to never grow weary of digging, they reveal God's plan of the ages like never before.

They are also the kinds of discoveries that Satan hopes we'll never see—especially this next one.

PART VIII

FROM COSMIC WAR TO ETERNAL VICTORY

But David continued up the Mount of Olives, weeping as he went; his head was covered and he was barefoot. All the people with him covered their heads too and were weeping as they went up. Now David had been told, "Ahithophel is among the conspirators with Absalom." So David prayed, "O Lord, turn Ahithophel's counsel into foolishness." When David arrived at the summit, where people used to worship God.

~2 Samuel 15:30–32

46

THE HOLY HILL

*King David was ascending the hillside carrying the
burden of that guilt and heartbreak, and the whole
kingdom looked on—and they wept with him.*

Other than the First Coming of Messiah, the greatest gifts ever given
to mankind were His death and resurrection. Yet, all the Bible
appears to say about where those events took place is that He was taken to
Golgotha (the "place of a skull"), where He was crucified, then buried in
a nearby garden tomb (Matthew 27:33; Mark 15:22; John 19:17; Luke
23:33). But, you'll soon find out that's certainly not all the Word of God
has to say about the matter.

A specific location in Jerusalem is central to understanding what God's
been up to since the Garden Fall. It is biblically, historically, and archeo-
logically connected to that seemingly enigmatic Golgotha better than any
other place in Jerusalem. That place is the Mount of Olives.

Like the revelation regarding the Tower of the Flock in the previous section, you'll soon grasp why a look at the Mount of Olives is so
important to the larger biblical understanding of God's intricate plan of

217

salvation. You'll also understand why Satan and his demonic horde so desperately want to hide this disclosure as well.

FIRST ASSOCIATED WITH DAVID

The Mount of Olives, as it turns out, is *first* biblically connected to King David. Later in the Old Testament, it's again connected to the place where Messiah will eventually rule and reign over the entire earth (Zechariah 14).

However, as a number of readers know, that hillside shows up again several times in the New Testament, and in those instances, it's connected to Jesus Christ and His last week on earth, just before He is crucified.

THE HILL OF GRIEF

Our first look at the Mount of Olives is in the book of 2 Samuel in an account involving King David's ascent of that well-known hill while he was in the midst of great personal suffering. He had been horribly betrayed by his son Absalom and his fellow conspirators. The betrayal was initially brought about by David's own heinous sin. So the king ascended that famous mountain road carrying the burden of guilt and personal heartbreak, and practically the whole kingdom looked on as he did. They wept with him all the way up the trail.

In the same heartrending passage of 2 Samuel, we also learn that the hillside upon which David trod was, in fact, the ancient Mount of Olives, and on it was a specific place where "people used to worship God." A little later, you'll see why this is important.

But David continued up the Mount of Olives, weeping as he went; his head was covered and he was barefoot. All the people with him covered their heads too and were **weeping as they went up.** Now David had been told, "Ahithophel is among the conspirators with Absalom." So David prayed, "O Lord, turn

Ahithophel's counsel into foolishness." When David arrived **at the summit, where people used to worship God.** (2 Samuel 15:30–32; emphasis added)

Scholars haven't missed the connections of this passage with a similar situation in Jesus' earthly ministry.
Benson's Commentary:

The reader will perhaps think it worth his notice, that Josephus should tell us, that **David wept and viewed the city** in the **same spot** from which, the evangelist informs us, **our blessed Saviour wept** over it.[186] (Emphasis added)

Gill's Exposition of the Entire Bible:

And David went up by the ascent of Mount Olivet, So called from the olive trees that grew upon it, which is often mentioned in the New Testament, and where **our Lord Jesus Christ, the antitype of David, often was, in his state of humiliation,** Matthew 26:30, and from whence he ascended to heaven after his resurrection, Acts 1:12; it was about a mile from Jerusalem, to the east of it: and [David] wept as he went up; thinking perhaps of the wickedness and rebellion of his son, of his own hard case, to be obliged to quit his metropolis and palace, and make his flight afoot; and perhaps also of his own sins, which were the cause of his calamities.[187] (Emphasis added)

David has often been presented as a biblical "type" of Yeshua—and, in this case, as Gill noted, as an "anti-type." Myriad commentaries, articles, and books have highlighted the numerous, striking parallels between David and Yeshua.[188]

We must also remember that Messiah Himself is called the "Son of David" throughout the Scriptures. This was the very title the crowds bestowed upon Him during His triumphal entry, just before His own brutal journey of death to a place known only in the Scriptures as Golgotha. He began that prophetic entry into Jerusalem by passing through the Eastern Gate of the Temple Mount area. Jesus had just come into the city *directly from the Mount of Olives,* where He had recently been staying with His disciples.

THE HILL OF VICTORY

As already mentioned, it is also on the Mount of Olives where we learn that the Lord Himself will victoriously descend at His Second Coming, and from where He will rule the nations at the culmination of all things. The prophet Zechariah tells us about that event:

> Then the Lord will go out and fight against those nations, as he fights in the day of battle. **On that day his feet will stand on the Mount of Olives**, east of Jerusalem, and the **Mount of Olives** will be split in two from east to west, forming a great valley, with half of the mountain moving north and half moving south. (Zechariah 14:3–4; emphasis added)

The New Testament affirms this as well:

> After [Jesus] said this, **he was taken up before their very eyes**, and a cloud hid him from their sight. They were looking intently up into the sky as he was going, when suddenly two men dressed in white stood beside them. "Men of Galilee," they said, "**why do you stand here** looking into the sky? **This same Jesus, who has been taken from you into heaven, will come back in the same way you have seen him go into heaven.**" Then they returned to Jerusalem **from the hill called the Mount of Olives**, a Sabbath day's walk from the city. (Acts 1:9–12; emphasis added)

Again, scholars have long seen the predictive connection between the prophecy of Zechariah 14 and what the angels announced in Acts 1. *Ellicott's Commentary for English Readers* (on Acts 1:11):

Those who do not shrink from taking the words of prophecy in **their most literal sense**, have seen in **Zechariah 14:4**, an intimation that…the feet of **the Judge shall stand upon the Mount of Olives, from which He had ascended into heaven.**[189] (Emphasis added)

Bengal's Gnomen:

[Jesus Christ] shall come, in a visible manner, in a cloud, with a trumpet, with an attendant train, and perhaps in the **same place**, Acts 1:12, "the mount called Olivet." Add Zechariah 14:4, "**His feet shall stand in that day** upon the Mount of Olives, which is before Jerusalem on the east." Comp…Matthew 24:27, "As the lightning cometh out of the East, so shall the coming of the Son of man be" [It is probable that Christ's coming will be from the east].

Now those who saw Him ascending are said to be about to see Him when He shall come. Between His Ascension and His Coming in glory **no event intervenes equal in importance to each of these two events: therefore these two are joined together.**[190] (Emphasis added)

Gill's Exposition of the Entire Bible:

[Jesus] **shall descend himself in person, as he now ascended in person**; and as he went up with a shout, and with the **sound of a trumpet**, see Psalm 47:5 so he shall descend with a shout, with the voice of the archangel, and the trump of God; and, **it may be, he** shall descend upon the very spot from whence he ascended; see Zechariah 14:4.[191] (Emphasis added)

It would appear, in many ways, that the Mount of Olives is probably the most specific place on the planet that is the literal epicenter of demonic warfare. There's a reason for this.

47

THE MOUNT OF COSMIC WAR

The Mount of Olives very centrally figures into God's
unfolding story of the restitution of all things.

O f all places, it was the Mount of Olives that King Solomon
utterly desecrated, playing right into Satan's long-range agenda of
deception.

The demonic outrage happened when Solomon built pagan altars on
the mountain in order to appease his Moabite and Ammonite concubines.
In so doing, he plainly established the Mount of Olives as the place where
the first two Commandments of God were made into a vile sacrilege. It
was right there where the cosmic war of the *gods*—that had started in the
Garden of Eden—was put on full display. It's also important to note that
the Mount of Olives was the highest point in Jerusalem. It actually looked
down on the Temple Mount. Solomon built his pagan altars in a place
and position where they could "look down" upon Yahweh's altar.

> On **a hill east of Jerusalem**, Solomon built a high place for Che-
> mosh the detestable god of Moab, and for Molek the detestable
> god of the Ammonites. (1 Kings 11:7–8; emphasis added)

The Cambridge Bible for Schools and Colleges (on 1 Kings 11:7–8) assures us that the "hill east of Jerusalem" is, in fact, the famed Mount of Olives.

> **The hill** facing Jerusalem **is the Mount of Olives.** It is described in **Ezekiel 11:23** as "the mountain which is on the **east side of the city**," and in **Zechariah 14:4** as "the **Mount of Olives**, which is before Jerusalem **on the east**."[192] (Emphasis added)

Subsequently, this site on the Mount of Olives infamously became used for idol worship throughout the First Temple period, until Josiah, the boy king of Judah, finally destroyed "the high places that were before Jerusalem, to the right of *Har HaMashchit*" (2 Kings 23:13, KJV). To this day, that part of the Mount of Olives is still known as the Mount of Corruption, or *Har HaMashchit.*

THE HILL OF GOD'S GLORY

Another striking foreshadowing in the Old Testament concerning the Mount of Olives, its direct connection to the eventual First Coming, and then to the return of Yeshua the Messiah is found in the book of Ezekiel 11. The prophet Ezekiel is ministering to his fellow Jews, who have been taken captive under the Babylonian/Chaldean empire. *There's that spirit of the Chaldeans again.*

In that passage, Ezekiel has a vision of the very last days. Not only does that vision involve the Mount of Olives, but it also includes something specific that happens there. It is something that we now know was perfectly fulfilled in the final passion of Jesus Himself and will reach its ultimate culmination in His Second Coming.

> Then did the cherubims lift up their wings, and the wheels beside them; and the **glory of the God** of Israel was over them above. **And the glory of the LORD went up from the midst of the city,**

and **stood upon the mountain** which is on the **east side** of the city. Afterwards the spirit took me up, and brought me in a vision by the Spirit of God into Chaldea, to them of the captivity. So the vision that I had seen went up from me. Then I spake unto them of the captivity all the things that the LORD had shewed me. (Ezekiel 11:22–25, KJV; emphasis added)

Ellicott's Commentary for English Readers states the following about that passage:

Stood upon the mountain.—This Mountain, on the east of the city, is that which was **afterwards known as the Mount of Olives.** It is considerably higher than the city, and commands a view over its entire extent. **Here the Divine glory rested after taking its departure from the Temple** and the city in the vision of the prophet. Here, in the vision of a later prophet (Zechariah 14:4), **the Lord is represented as standing in the day of final judgment.**

Here, not in vision, **the incarnate Son of God** proclaimed the second destruction of the obdurate city (Matthew 24; Luke 21:20); and **from the same mountain** He made His visible ascension into heaven (Luke 24:50-51; Acts 1:11-12).

The vision is now closed, and **the prophet is transported in spirit back into Chaldea,** to declare what he had seen to his fellow-captives, and show them the vanity of their trust in the preservation of the guilty city.[193] (Emphasis added)

This is only the foundation of our next discovery; the biblical dots are about to connect.

48

THE TOMBS

It's not just a curious spot on the map, chosen at random.
There's something very holy about this hill.

There's yet another connection with Jesus and the Mount of Olives, as well as the crucifixion and resurrection narrative of the New Testament. That holy hill has been used as a Jewish cemetery for over three thousand years, making it the most prominently known among all Jewish cemeteries on the planet.[194]

The desire among many Jews, especially those of great importance and wealth, to be buried on the Mount of Olives stems from an ancient Jewish tradition originating from the promise in Zechariah 14:4. That passage declares that when Messiah comes, the resurrection of the dead will begin in that very spot. That's why this graveyard is the holiest place in the world for those in the Jewish faith to be laid to rest.[195]

And in that day His feet will stand on the Mount of Olives, which faces Jerusalem on the east. And the Mount of Olives shall be split in two, from east to west, making a very large valley; half of the mountain shall move toward the north and half of it toward the south.... **Thus the Lord my God will come, and all the saints with You.** (Zechariah 14:1–5; emphasis added).

The graveyard on the southern ridge, the location of the modern village of Silwan, was the burial place of Jerusalem's most important citizens in the period of the biblical kings. An estimated 150,000 graves are on the mount, including tombs traditionally associated with the prophet Zechariah, the prophets Haggai and Malachi, and David's son, Absalom. On the upper slope, there are also the tombs of notable rabbis and others interred there from the fifteenth century until now.[196]

CENTRAL TO JESUS' LIFE AND MINISTRY

One cannot escape the centrality of this sacred mount. Have a look at the following connections:

- The Mount of Olives is mentioned several times in the New Testament (Matthew 21:1, 26:30, etc.) as part of the route from Jerusalem to Bethany.
- As previously noted, the site is also where Jesus stood when He wept over Jerusalem (Luke 19:28–41).
- Jesus spent a lot of time on the Mount of Olives teaching and prophesying to His disciples (Matthew 24–25), presenting sermons that included the Olivet Discourse (Luke 21:37; John 8:1).
- From the Mount of Olives, Jesus entered Jerusalem at the beginning of the last week of His life (Matthew 21:1; Mark 11:1).
- Two days before His crucifixion, as He was sitting on that hillside with His disciples, Jesus foretold the destruction of Jerusalem and the end of the world (Matthew 24–25; Mark 13; Luke 21).
- At the foot of the Mount of Olives lies the Garden of Gethsemane. The New Testament states that Jesus and His disciples sang together after eating the last Passover meal, then they went out to the Mount of Olives (Matthew 26:30). This is where Jesus

prayed just before He was betrayed by Judas Iscariot and arrested by the Temple guard (Matthew 26; Mark 14).

- Finally, of course, Jesus ascended to Heaven from the Mount of Olives, according to Acts 1:9–12. Luke mentions that Jesus' ascension took place at an Olivet location very near the village of Bethany (Luke 24:50–51).[197]

Think of the amazing Mount of Olives links we've uncovered so far.

The connecting dots culminate with the glory of the Lord—none other than Yeshua Himself—"leaving" the city of Jerusalem, going up from the Temple courts in His last week of ministry, then during His very last hours being taken "outside" the city to a specific place to be crucified. And the Mount of Olives was where He would literally depart from this earthly realm after His resurrection. It is also the spot He has promised to return to at His Second Coming.

There can be no doubt: The Mount of Olives is the focal point of God's unfolding story of the restitution of all things. It's not just a spot on the map, chosen at random. There's something very holy about this hill.

49

THE DECEPTION OF TRADITION

*The traditional sites simply do not pass all the historical,
scriptural, cultural, and archeological tests.*

As we continue to head toward the Mount of Olives as the crucifixion and burial site of Yeshua, please understand that I'm not undertaking this journey lightly; it's not a wild theory that I've plucked out of my back pocket.

The biblical connections to this journey are almost indisputable. A number of acclaimed scholars, archeologists, theology professors, biblical researchers, and teachers of the Word of God have also arrived at this conclusion. You'll read some important excerpts from their works in the next few pages. Plus, I've done some personal investigation into this matter—*on location*—and have made some shocking discoveries along the way. More on that later.

THREE LEADING CONTENDERS

First, let's examine the three most popular sites currently considered the sites of Yeshua's crucifixion and nearby burial.[198]

231

Because it was the Jewish day of Preparation and **since the tomb
was nearby**, they laid Jesus there. (John 19:42; emphasis added)

Site 1: The Talpiot Family Tomb. This first proposed site is so ridiculous I'd rather not mention it at all. However, since the secular media has made such a big deal out of it, we'll briefly examine—*and eliminate*—it as a possibility.

The Talpiot Family Tomb was discovered in 1980 and was made famous by James Cameron in his Discovery Channel movie, *The Lost Tomb of Jesus.* It is located about two miles south of Old Jerusalem. Ossuaries[199] bearing the names of several main characters of the family of Jesus were found there, including one inscribed "Jesus, son of Joseph."

Another ossuary was inscribed "Mariamene," and yet another "Jude, son of Jesu." These findings led to all types of unbiblical theories that Jesus might have been married to Mary Magdalene and had a son named Jude. Numerous scholars have been forthright in downplaying the outlandish assumptions. Most call attention to the fact that all of the names on the ossuaries were popular Hebrew names in the first century. Therefore, there's no reason to accept Cameron's inferences. To add to the confusion, all but one of the scholars interviewed for that documentary have since claimed their statements were misrepresented.[200]

Questions like why Jesus' family, from Galilee, would have a rock-cut tomb in Jerusalem point to the strong *improbability* of this being the burial place of Yeshua/Jesus. But, the documentary certainly made for great theological controversy, of course aiding the work of the ever-active realm of demonic deception.

Site 2. The Church of the Holy Sepulcher. A typical Roman Catholic edifice, this is the oldest site said to be the burial place of Jesus. Stations 10 to 14 of the Stations of the Cross are located within the Church—the places where Jesus supposedly was stripped of His garments, was nailed to the cross, died on the cross, and finally was taken down and laid in the tomb. Eusebius, author of *Life of Constantine*, details the "official" identification of the tomb and Constantine's order to honor it by building a church over it.

While it has been authenticated as a Jewish burial site in the same time frame as Jesus' crucifixion, there simply is no proof that it had anything at all to do with the burial of Yeshua. Even the writer of a very pro-Church of the Holy Sepulcher news article, published in 2017—claiming to have new evidence to support it as the true site—had to admit the following:

> There is **currently no proof** that Jesus was buried at the Church of the Holy Sepulcher.[201] (Emphasis added)

So, exactly what was the "new proof" to support the Church of the Holy Sepulcher as being the burial site of Jesus? Have a look for yourself:

> New scientific testing adds credence to the long-held belief that the Church of the Holy Sepulcher in Jerusalem is the final resting place of Jesus Christ. But **the tomb is about 700 years older than previously thought**, built in the year 300, according to research from the National Technical University of Athens. This **aligns with historical belief** that the Romans constructed a shrine on the site around the year 325 to mark the place of Jesus's burial.[202] (Emphasis added)

In other words, the only real "proof" is that the Romans constructed this site in AD 300—almost three hundred years after Jesus' burial. To put this in perspective, that's longer than the United States has been a nation.

So the Romans built this structure and declared it to be the location. How in the world does that prove this must be correct? It doesn't. Thus, the final admission of the article: "There is currently no proof." I believe there will never be any real proof at all. The place simply doesn't fit the major biblical or historical requirements.

Even by April 2020, the Biblical Archeological Society was still insisting that the Gospels make it fairly clear that Jesus was crucified outside the city walls (Mark 15:20; Matthew 27:31ff, John 19:17ff). And to this day, there has *been no archeological find* of an ancient city wall that would place the Church of the Holy Sepulcher outside the Jerusalem of Jesus' day. This popular tourist destination simply cannot be verified as the site of the crucifixion.

> Eminent scholars Conrad Schick and Louis-Hugues Vincent **thought they had found the Second Wall in 1893** when a wall was uncovered during the construction of the Church of the Redeemer just south of the Church of the Holy Sepulcher. **For almost a century this seemed to solve the problem of authenticity—the Church of the Holy Sepulcher was located at Golgotha....**
>
> **But in the 1970s,** German archaeologist Ute Wagner-Lux of the German Protestant Institute of Archaeology in Jerusalem excavated under the Church of the Redeemer and **determined that this wall could not have been the Second Wall.** Why? "This wall was only five feet thick—far too narrow to be a city wall," say Serr and Vieweger. **So the search began anew.**[203] (Emphasis added)

Now we're left with the third most culturally popular option. This is certainly *the most popular* tourist site among evangelical Christians.

Site 3. The Garden Tomb (or Gordon's Tomb)[204] was made popular in 1883 by General Charles Gordon.[205] "In 1842 Otto Thenius[206]—a German theologian and biblical scholar—advanced the theory that Golgotha was a rocky hill about 250 yards northeast of the Damascus Gate. He based his opinion on assertions that it had been a Jewish place of stoning, it was outside the city wall, and—in the eyes of a great number of people—it was shaped like a skull.[207]

Later, Gordon also advocated for this spot, and it has since come to be known in many circles as "Gordon's Calvary." It is now owned by evangelical Christians and is accepted by a large number of Jerusalem pilgrims as the location. Because of this, the site is found on the schedules of most tourist expeditions.

However, the tomb there has since been reliably determined to be an Iron Age tomb of the seventh or eighth century BC; therefore, it simply does not fit the description of being a "new tomb in which no one had yet been laid" (John 19:41).[208] Furthermore, the organization maintaining the Garden Tomb doesn't even insist that this is indeed the tomb of Jesus. Instead, it simply emphasizes "similarities" with the spot described in the Bible. (I do appreciate their honesty in this matter.)

Zondervan Academic:

> Gordon's Calvary, to the north of the present-day Damascus Gate, with the nearby Garden Tomb…. Although this site lies outside the ancient as well as the present-day city wall and is quite amenable to certain types of piety, **there is no compelling reason to think that this is either Calvary and/or the tomb**; in fact, **the tomb may date back to the Iron Age (1000–586 BC) and thus would not have been a tomb** "in which no one had yet been laid" (Luke 23:53).[209] (Emphasis added)

Biblicalarcheology.org:

> Currently, the most popular alternative site to traditional Golgotha, located in the Church of the Holy Sepulcher, Jerusalem, is the area of Gordon's Calvary, with the so-called 'Garden Tomb,' but **scholarly endorsement of this locality has never been very strong**. Generally, the current consensus holds that Golgotha was located in the vicinity of the **traditional site**, somewhere north of the first wall of Jerusalem at the time of Jesus, and west of the second wall, **though specificity is impossible**.[210] (Emphasis added)

One of the most well-known archaeological studies of the area of Gordon's Calvary is the investigation conducted by Dr. Gabriel Barkay, professor of biblical archaeology at the Hebrew University of Jerusalem and at Bar-Ilan University during the late 1900s.

Here are Barkay's four main conclusions, published in *Biblical Archeology Review*:

1. **The tomb is far too old to be the tomb of Jesus**, as it is **typical of the 8th–7th centuries BCE**, showing a configuration which fell out of use after that period. It fits well into a wider necropolis **dating to the First Temple period** which also includes the nearby tombs on the grounds of the Basilica of St Stephen.
2. The groove was a water trough, **built by the 11th-century Crusaders** for donkeys/mules.
3. The cistern was built as part of the same stable complex as the groove.
4. The waterproofing on the cistern is of **the type used by the Crusaders**, and the cistern must date to that era.[211] (Emphasis added)

So, while Gordon's Calvary is a serene setting where countless groups have shared communion and meditated on the events of the crucifixion and resurrection, in my opinion—as well as that of a number of reputable scholars—it simply cannot be the genuine location. It's a great tourist stop, but it's still not the place we're looking for.

NONE PASS THE TESTS

The traditional sites simply do not pass all the historical, scriptural, cultural, and archeological tests necessary to declare that any of these was the original location of Jesus' crucifixion and burial.

Ellicott's Commentary for English Readers:

All the first three Gospels dwell on the fact of its not being, as so many graves were, a natural cavern, **but cut,** and, as St. Luke's word implies. To some extent, smoothed and polished. Like almost all Eastern graves, it was **an opening made in the vertical face of the rock. Neither of the two localities** which have been identified with the sepulcher [Gordon's Calvary or the Church of the Holy Sepulcher] presents this feature.[212] (Emphasis added)

Here's what we're left with. The Talpiot Family Tomb as the burial site is undoubtedly a sham and makes a mockery of the entire biblical text and message. And, neither Gordon's Calvary nor the Church of the Holy Sepulcher offers hardcore evidence to lay absolute claim to the site of Jesus' crucifixion and nearby burial. So the three most commonly named sites are, at best, historically dubious, and, at worst, simply not anywhere near the truth.

At this point, you might be asking whether there are any reliable biblical, historical, and archeological clues that might put us much closer to the valid location. Indeed, there are *solid* clues, and, they all point to the same place.

PART IX

FROM GOLYATH
TO GOLGOTHA

They came to a place called Golgotha (which means "the place of the skull"). There they offered Jesus wine to drink, mixed with gall; but after tasting it, he refused to drink it. When they had crucified him, they divided up his clothes by casting lots. And sitting down, they kept watch over him there. Above his head they placed the written charge against him: THIS IS JESUS, THE KING OF THE JEWS.

~Matthew 27:33–37

50

THE KEYS

*Joseph's tomb most likely would have been someplace
highly desirable for a person of his deeply
Orthodox and prominent standing.*

Let's begin this newest of our excursions of spiritual archeology by
dealing with the most visible textual keys that help us unlock the
mystery of the location of Jesus' crucifixion and burial.

The contemplations upon these clues are not without various interpretations, critics, and cynics, but they are central clues within the biblical
text itself. We will start by examining them from their contextual and
historical foundations.

GOLGOTHA

First, we are told that Jesus was crucified at a place called Golgotha (Matthew 27:33; Mark 15:22; John 19:17). This will be our starting point.

In most English translations, Luke 22:33 calls the place where they took Jesus to crucify Him "the Skull." However, both the King James Version and the Douay-Rheims Bible give the name of the place in Luke 22 as "Calvary," an English word that comes from the Latin *calvaria*—simply meaning "the skull." In Matthew, Mark, and John, the word "Golgotha" is defined in the original text as meaning "the place of *the* skull" or "the place of *a* skull."

Of course, we also know from the Gospel texts that the burial was very near the crucifixion scene.

> **At the place where Jesus was crucified**, there was a garden, and **in the garden a new tomb**, in which no one had ever been laid. (John 19:41; emphasis added)

The Greek phrasing of that English-translated verse doesn't necessarily mean the tomb was at the *exact spot* of the crucifixion, but rather in the same general area—yet apparently very close by.

Expositor's Greek Testament:

> "There was in the place," i.e., in that neighborhood.[213]

Bengel's Gnomen:

> John 19:41. (In the place) the cross itself was not in the garden.[214]

THE EDEN CONNECTION

Several scholars do acknowledge the likely connections to the garden of Joseph of Arimathea's tomb and the location of Golgotha's cross—as well as the Garden of Eden[215]—with the Mount of Olives. Following are examples of this exciting potential association.

The Pulpit Commentary:

John alone tells us of the "garden;" and he clearly saw the **significance of the resemblance** to the "garden" **where Christ agonized** unto death, and **was betrayed with a kiss**, and **also to the garden where the first Adam** fell from the high estate of posse non peccare.[216] (Emphasis added)

Dr. Ernest L. Martin (PhD), who wrote *Secrets of Golgotha, the Lost History of Jesus' Crucifixion*, states:

Using **the Land of Eden** in its symbolic fashion, this meant the [place of Jesus' sacrifice] was situated "without **the Land of Eden**" and on **its east side.** Where was this altar situated in **relationship to the Temple?** In the time of Jesus, Jewish records show that this outer altar was **located near the southern summit of the Mount of Olives** directly east of the Temple. It was also positioned just "outside the Camp" of Israel, **which made it to be analogous to being just "outside the Land of Eden."** This was the same type of altar on which the sacrifice for Cain mentioned in Genesis 4:7 was to be offered at the **eastern entrance (door) to Eden.**[217] (Emphasis added)

Biblical scholar and researcher Peter A. Michas also believes that the Golgotha crucifixion was located at the Mount of Olives, and that this area is also connected to the Garden of Eden:

Scripture records the existence of a miraculous rod that budded, producing blossoms and ripe almonds (Numbers 17:8). This same rod was used by Moses to part the Red Sea and by David in battle against Goliath. Hebraic sources link this miraculous rod to the Tree of Life in the Garden of Eden. From the **Tree of Life in the Garden of Eden to the Crucifixion Tree on the Mount of Olives.**[218] (Emphasis added)

JOSEPH'S TOMB

Additionally, we are told the tomb was that of the family of Joseph of Arimathea. We also know from the Scriptures that Joseph was a well-to-do and renowned member of the Sanhedrin Council.

> So as evening approached, Joseph of Arimathea, **a prominent member of the Council**, who was himself waiting for the kingdom of God, **went boldly to Pilate and asked for Jesus' body.** Pilate was surprised to hear that he was already dead. Summoning the centurion, he asked him if Jesus had already died. When he learned from the centurion that it was so, [Pilate] **gave the body to Joseph.**
>
> So Joseph bought some linen cloth, took down the body, wrapped it in the linen, and **placed it in a tomb cut out of rock.** Then he **rolled a stone against the entrance** of the tomb. Mary Magdalene and Mary the mother of Joseph saw where he was laid. (Mark 15:42–47; emphasis added)

Joseph of Arimathea's tomb, most likely, would have been someplace highly desirable for a person of his deeply Orthodox and prominent standing. His position in society was so well respected that he obviously enjoyed a direct audience with Governor Pilate.

Joseph's request to have charge of burying the body of Jesus was granted without question. Somewhere on or near the Mount of Olives, among the other tombs of Israel's elite, would certainly be a reasonable place to assume Joseph's tomb might have been located. It meets the biblical, archeological, and historical criteria as a logical hypothesis.

So, this premise would be an entirely logical and scholastic one, unless the Scriptures clearly indicate that it was definitely *not* located there. However, they make no such distinction.

51

THE SKULL PLACE

Golgotha means the "place of a/the skull."

Considering all we've uncovered in the last several chapters, we already have quite a bit of information that, at least circumstantially, points us toward the Mount of Olives as the region of Jesus' crucifixion and burial.

But what do we do with the crucifixion site as being biblically designated as "Golgotha"—"the place of a skull"? Is this referring to a geological location that might look like a skull? Is it referring to a little knoll or simply a small, specific spot?

Vincent's Word Studies:

Golgotha: An Aramaic word, Gulgoltha = the Hebrew, Gulgoleth and translated skull in Judges 9:53; 2 Kings 9:35. The word Calvary comes through the Latin *calvaria*, meaning skull, and used in the Vulgate. The New Testament narrative **does not mention a mount or hill.** The place was **probably a rounded elevation.** The **meaning is not, as Tyndall, a place of dead men's skulls,** but simply [a/the] **skull.**[219] (Emphasis added)

245

Vincent's correctly notes that the New Testament doesn't directly state that the place known as Golgotha, in biblical times, is a mount or hill. I would argue, however, if the place were already a well-known mount, hill, or any such larger and specific region, the biblical text would not *have* to describe any other particular distinction about it. That hill or region would simply have been commonly known—in the AD 30s—by its apparent nickname as "the place of a/the skull."

LIVINGSTON'S RESEARCH

The late Dr. David Livingston (1925–2013), who held a PhD in archaeology from Andrews University, was a renowned biblical researcher, archeologist, and founder of the website Biblicalarcheology.org. He published a lengthy article that lends several clues as to what we might be looking for regarding the location of Golgotha.

> In the Bible, a skull might be referred to as "gulgolet" (cf. 2 Kgs 9:35), presumably because it could roll along if it was dropped. Figuratively, however, it could refer to a "head" count: in Nm 1:16, men are counted "according to their skulls/heads": *laggul-gelotam* (Brown, et. al.: 166). Indeed, in modem Hebrew, *gulgolet* **may mean "head," in this way, like "rosh."**
>
> It is often pointed out that the Arabic equivalent to **rosh, can be used for a hill, rising up or sticking out of the ground like a** "head." However, this need not at all imply that what we should be looking for at Golgotha is a **little knoll**: the "hill of Calvary" is a traditional understanding **not found** in the New Testament.
>
> [However] In Hebrew also, **rosh can mean the "top" of a mountain, or a hill** (2 Samuel 15:32).[220] (Emphasis added)

Though Dr. Livingston's lengthy examination *does not* focus upon the Mount of Olives as the place of Golgotha, it does offer detailed geographical and biblical information that could very well point to that location *spe-*

cifically, especially when we consider what we will examine in the next few chapters. Here are several of Dr. Livingston's most important observations.

> But are we talking about **a general vicinity, or else a definite "spot"** on the ground? Some scholars have the "spot" understanding....
>
> **However, the Gospel of John** gives us the clear impression that Golgotha **was not a small, specific locality,** associated only with the death of Jesus, but **a much larger region.** Here we are informed that Jesus was crucified in **the topos** named Golgotha (John 19:17–18), but then....
>
> "In (en) the place (topos/Golgotha) where He was crucified there was a garden (kapos), and in the garden there was a new tomb in which no one had been laid." (John 19:41).
>
> Here the author gives us a visual image that may be shown pictorially **as circles,** the **largest of which is Golgotha as a topos, a place or region.** Jesus was both crucified and buried here **in two different spots** that **need not be side by side;** the maximum distance between these two locations will depend on how large an area Golgotha was in the first place. No source tells us that the tomb and the place of the crucifixion were very close to one another.
>
> The early Church tended also to [believe] that **Golgotha was a region rather than a specific, small place.**[221] (emphasis added)

Here's what we have before us thus far. Golgotha means the "place of a/the skull." In the next chapter, we'll examine a very real biblical possibility that might define the specific "skull"— a skull that was so renowned as to become the actual nickname for a specific region or *topos.*

ANOTHER FAMOUS PERSON BURIED THERE?

Interestingly, Dr. James Tabor points out that ancient Roman history locates the burial of *another famous person* in "the place of the skull." The location got that name because the skull of a famous king had been found there. Since this is the case, it would make sense that Jesus' crucifixion site was also where a literal and famous skull had been located, a place the people of His day would have known about. Apparently, it was a spot that could simply be called "the place of the skull" without further description—just as the Scriptures designate.

Dr. Tabor states:

> **Julius Caesar was also buried at a "place of the skull,"** according to Appian, Civil Wars-Book 2: "The people returned to Caesar's bier and bore it as a consecrated thing to the Capitol." The word capitol (Capiolium) is derived from the Latin word CAPUT which means dead man's head or SKULL
>
> Supposedly an Etruscan king, Olus (i.e. Aulus Vulcentanus) was killed and buried there, and that the Capitoline temple and **hill in Rome received its name after his skull was later found:** "the head of Olus"—caput Oli—Capitolium…**place of the skull.** So Julius Caesar's murdered body was also carried to the Place of the Skull.[222] (Emphasis added, ALL CAPS in the original)

Also, we've already discovered that the crucifixion site of Yeshua was most likely a sizable area—perhaps consisting of a large hill or mount—that was commonly known as Golgotha in Jesus' day and that would have needed no additional illumination. The Gospel of Luke uses the word *topos,* meaning a local region or a "common place."[223] Even Dr. Livingston confirms, as we've seen, that the early church understood it to be a larger, well-known region rather than an obscure knoll or spot.

It would then most likely be a prominent hill or mount, a place that would encompass not only the site of the crucifixion but also a relatively nearby garden, which also contained a family tomb and maybe part of a larger cemetery complex, as well as belonged to a prominent member of the Sanhedrin.

What "skull" could be so famous among the Jewish people that it would actually *define* the region by that name—the place of the Skull?[224]

52

A Skull and a Sword

When young David was on the run from an insanely
jealous King Saul, he ended up back on the Mount of Olives.

From an earlier chapter, we already know the Mount of Olives was an
ancient place of the worship of Yahweh in David's time, even before
he was King of Israel.

Let's revisit that Scripture noted earlier from 2 Samuel. The context
of the passage is situated during the time when David was king of Israel.
His son, Absalom, had instigated a coup against him. In his grief, David
went up the Mount of Olives in mourning. He went to a specific place
of the long-held tradition of Hebrew worship. Remember that we also
noted several scholars who have compared David's ascent up the Mount
with that of Jesus' life—specifically, the centrality of the Mount of Olives
to His last forty days on the earth.

> **But David continued up the Mount of Olives, weeping as he
> went; his head was covered and he was barefoot.** All the peo-
> ple with him covered their heads too and were **weeping as they
> went up.** Now David had been told, "Ahithophel is among the

conspirators with Absalom." So David prayed, "O Lord, turn
Ahithophel's counsel into foolishness." When David arrived **at
the summit, where people used to worship God…** (2 Samuel
15:30–32; emphasis added)

THE SKULL

The historical context of that passage is found in 1 Samuel, during the time
when David was still a young man who would relatively soon become the
king of Israel. After he killed a certain giant—*Goliath*—he did something
interesting that relates directly to our study.

David took the Philistine's head and brought it to Jerusalem; he
put the Philistine's weapons in his own tent. (1 Samuel 17:5)

Right there in the Word of God, we are told that, in David's early
days, just after he killed Goliath (a metaphorical picture of the defeat of
Satan by Yeshua),[225] he brought Goliath's head (skull) to Jerusalem. Of
course, the Mount of Olives was a prominent region of Jerusalem. As
we've seen from the Scriptures, that mount was *the most ancient place of
Jerusalem's worship.*

Exactly where did David take Goliath's skull? The Bible doesn't say
with specificity; however, it does state where the giant's sword ended up.
Remember, David also brought Goliath's *armor* to "Jerusalem," on *the
same day* he brought the skull. So, it makes sense that, most likely, David
took the skull to the same place he took the armor and the giant's sword.

Sometime *after* David had killed Goliath and taken his head and
armor to Jerusalem—when young David was on the run from an insanely
jealous King Saul—he ended up back on the Mount of Olives. And he
didn't go to just any old place on it; he went back to Nob, the central
"head" of the mount, right to the ancient place of worship…at the *rosh*
of the *topos*.

Cambridge Bible for Schools and Colleges:

Nob: **The northern summit of Mount Olivet,** the **place of worship** which David passed in his flight from Absalom (2 Samuel 15:31).[226] (Emphasis added)

Jamieson-Fausset-Brown Bible Commentary:

Then *came David to Nob* to Ahimelech—*Nob*, a city of the priests (1Sa 22:19), was in the neighborhood of Jerusalem, on the **Mount of Olives**—a little north of the top, and on the northeast of the city.[227] (Emphasis added)

Encyclopedia.com:

The term **"Mount of Olives"** refers most properly to the southernmost of **the ridge's three sections.** The northernmost section is known as Mt. Scopus. **The middle section is probably the site of the Old Testament Nob** (1 Sm 21.1).[228] (Emphasis added)

THE SWORD

While David was at Nob, at the place of worship, he retrieved a piece of Goliath's battle gear: *his sword.* It was the weapon David had used to cut off Goliath's head.

Cambridge Bible for Schools and Colleges:

[The sword] was probably **dedicated as a memorial of the victory** on the conclusion of the Philistine war.[229] (Emphasis added)

Keil and Delitzsch Biblical Commentary on the Old Testament:

The priest replied, that there was **only the sword of Goliath,** whom David slew in the terebinth valley (1 Samuel 17:2), wrapped up in a cloth hanging behind the ephod (the high priest's shoulder-dress), —a sign of the great worth attached **to this dedicatory offering.**

David accepted it, as a weapon of greater value to him than any other, because **he had not only taken this sword as booty from the Philistine, but had cut off the head of Goliath with it** (see 1 Samuel 17:51).[230] (Emphasis added)

Now, look at that passage from 1 Samuel:

David went to Nob, to Ahimelech the priest. Ahimelech trembled when he met him, and asked, "Why are you alone? Why is no one with you?"....

David asked Ahimelech, **"Don't you have a spear or a sword here?** I haven't brought my sword or any other weapon, because the king's mission was urgent."

The priest replied, **"The sword of Goliath the Philistine, whom you killed in the Valley of Elah, is here**; it is wrapped in a cloth behind the ephod. If you want it, take it; there is no sword here but that one."

David said, **"There is none like it**; give it to me." (1 Samuel 21:1, 8–9; emphasis added)

Obviously, that's where David had previously left Goliath's armor when he brought it to Jerusalem after his victory over the gigantic arch-enemy of Israel. Therefore, it's not a far stretch at all to believe this locale is exactly where Goliath's skull was left by David as well. Why would the sword be in one place and the skull in another, when the Scripture says David brought them to Jerusalem *together*, at the same time?

David would have brought the head there as an offering at the altar in that revered place of worship as a "trophy" used in the process of thanking Yahweh for his miraculous victory over the giant. The sword used to cut off the giant's head would also have been brought to that altar.

And, indeed, that's exactly where David retrieved it—at the same place the giant's skull would have been: Golgotha, the place of "the" skull.

We're now getting much closer to being able to almost definitely identify the region or the hill of the Mount of Olives as *the place of the Skull.* We've established the Mount of Olives as the most probable location for the resting place of the famous skull. And that's not to mention that, to this very day, it is also the location of the most famous Jewish cemetery in the world, dating back to the time of Jesus and before. Many tombs there are those of "rich" people.

Think of it: The *place of the skull* and a *tomb of a prominent man* located *nearby.* Only one place in Jerusalem meets both criteria—the Mount of Olives.

> So the soldiers took charge of Jesus. Carrying his own cross, **he went out to the place of the Skull** (which in Aramaic is called **Golgotha**). **There they crucified him**, and with him two others— one on each side and Jesus in the middle.
>
> **At the place where Jesus was crucified**, there was a garden, and **in the garden a new tomb**, in which no one had ever been laid. Because it was the Jewish day of Preparation and **since the tomb was nearby**, they laid Jesus there. (Matthew 27:16–18, 41–42; emphasis added)

53

WHAT'S IN A NAME?

This would explain why the "place of the skull"
is oddly named "Golgotha."[231]

Note the following Old Testament passages that use the Hebrew words *Gath* and *skull* for "Goliath":

A champion named **Goliath** [Heb. Golyath], who was from **Gath**, came out of the Philistine camp. (1 Samuel 17:4; emphasis added)

A woman dropped an upper millstone on his head and cracked **his skull** [Heb. *gulgōleth*]. (Judges 9:53; emphasis added)

SIMILAR WORDS

The word for "skull" in Hebrew is *gulgōleth*, but the word used for the place of the crucifixion is the Koine Greek *Golgotha*. That reflects the Syriac *gāgūltā*. Now add to the mix the Hebrew for Goliath, *Golyath*, along with the Hebrew word for skull, *gulgōleṯh*. All these words are similar in appearance and sound. We can see how the Greek word "Golgotha" sounds an awful lot like the Hebrew for "Goliath's skull."

Dr. Rick Shenk, who holds a PhD in systematic theology from the University of Wales, Lampeter, taught as an adjunct professor in Bethlehem College and Seminary's Master of Divinity program until he was invited to serve full-time in 2017.[232] Dr. Shenk also believes the name "Golgotha" is not a mere coincidence:

> David took the severed skull to Jerusalem. Odd, because Jerusalem was not David's capital, but a city of God's enemies. What did he do with the giant-head, the head of the Bronze Serpent? Perhaps, he impaled it on a hill outside of the city, visible to all.
>
> Hundreds of years later, Jesus was crucified at the "place of the skull" outside of Jerusalem. But why was that place called *Golgotha* in Jesus' day? The text does not tell us, but it is intriguing that this place name sounds very much like Goliath.[233]

BIBLICAL SIGNIFICANCE

Dr. Taylor Marshall, with a PhD in philosophy from the University of Dallas, is a prominent theologian and author. Even though he doesn't arrive at a specific location for the site of the crucifixion, he definitely sees the deep biblical significance of the identification of the place of Jesus' crucifixion as the place of Goliath's skull.

> So Golgotha is the "place of the skull." But if you've ever studied Hebrew, you may have realized a difficulty with the Bible's claim. **Golgotha doesn't mean anything close to "skull" in Hebrew, Aramaic, or any other language.**
>
> The "place of the skull" is where King David buried the head of the decapitated giant Goliath of Gath. The Bible teaches that

after David slew Goliath, he cut off his head and brought the skull to Jerusalem.

This would explain why the "place of the skull" is oddly named "Golgotha."

The term is a corruption of Hebrew for "Goliath Gath": Goliath Gath > GoliGath > GolGath > **GolGatha.**

The slaying of Goliath by David was one of the most important events in "Israelite history." [In Jesus day] The location of the giant's head **would have been known by all.** Hence, "Golgotha" is likely **the place of not just any old skull, but the place of the skull of Goliath** of Gath.[234] (Emphasis added)

54

NOB, SATAN, AND GOLGOTHA

Spiritually speaking, do you think the location
Sennacherib chose is mere coincidence?

We discover yet another stunning connection of Golgotha with the Mount of Olives in the book of Isaiah. Remember, Isaiah is the prophet who gave us Messianic foreshadowings in Isaiah chapters 7, 9, and 53.

> Therefore the Lord himself will give you a sign: The virgin will conceive and give birth to a son, and will call him Immanuel. (Isaiah 7:14)

> For to us a child is born, to us a son is given, and the government will be on his shoulders. And he will be called Wonderful Counselor, Mighty God, Everlasting Father, and Prince of Peace. (Isaiah 9:6)

> But he was pierced for our transgressions, he was crushed for our iniquities; the punishment that brought us peace was on him, and by his wounds we are healed. (Isaiah 53:5)

It was this prophet who, in the tenth chapter of Isaiah, warned those living in Judah and Jerusalem of the approaching, dreaded Assyrian commander Sennacherib. Sennacherib had on his mind the total possession of Jerusalem as his own. He wanted the wealth of the Temple's riches, and its people—the people of God—as his servants and subjects. He took his overwhelming army of several hundred thousand to the outskirts of Jerusalem, both to survey his plan of attack from a high vantage point, as well as to make certain he would be clearly seen by Jerusalem's inhabitants. He wanted to strike fear into their hearts and render them paralyzed in terror.

Where did Sennacherib go to accomplish these tactics? He went to the Mount of Olives, overlooking Jerusalem. Not only that, but he went to Nob. As we've already noted, this was the place David had stood and where he had taken Goliath's skull and armor. It was also where God's people had one of their very first national altars of worship.

Spiritually speaking, do you think the location Sennacherib chose is mere coincidence? Or do you think it might have been directed by Heaven's throne? You'll soon see what Yahweh Himself had to say about that.

Right now, have a look at these portions of Isaiah 10 that succinctly relate the context.

> Therefore this is what the Lord, the Lord Almighty, says: "My people who live in Zion, **do not be afraid of the Assyrians**, who beat you with a rod and lift up a club against you, as Egypt did.
>
> Very soon my anger against you will end and my wrath will be directed to their destruction."...
>
> This day they **will halt at Nob**; they will **shake their fist** at the mount of Daughter Zion, at the hill of Jerusalem." (Isaiah 10:24–25, 32; emphasis added)

The Hebrew word *Nob* means to be "high, elevated, or prominent."[235] It is the highest peak on the Mount of Olives—2,700 feet—and from it, the entire landscape of the Old City can be observed.[236] Nob is a full two hundred feet higher than mount Zion, the next highest Jerusalem peak.

Here's what the scholars affirm concerning Sennacherib's location before his planned attack on Jerusalem.

Cambridge Bible for Schools and Colleges:

The most probable conjecture is that [Nob] **was on the height of Scopus overlooking the city** from the north.[237] (Emphasis added)

Gill's Exposition of the Entire Bible:

Nob was a city of the priests, 1 Samuel 22:19 and so it is called in the Targum here; it was **so near Jerusalem**, that, as Jarchi and Kimchi say, **it might be seen from hence**; wherefore here he stood, in **sight of** Jerusalem; **against the wall** of it.[238] (Emphasis added)

Jamieson-Fausset-Brown Bible Commentary:

At Nob; **northeast of Jerusalem on Olivet**; a town of the priests (Ne 11:32).[239] (Emphasis added)

Barnes' Notes on the Bible:

Nob must have been situated **somewhere upon the ridge of the Mount of Olives**, to the northeast of the city.[240] (Emphasis added)

Dr. Richard T. Ritenbaugh, *Forerunner Commentary*:

Nob, known as a dwelling place for priests, **is a city located on the eastern slopes of Mount Scopus**[241] **opposite the Mount of Olives** and just a mile or so northeast of Jerusalem.[242] (Emphasis added)

Smith's Bible Dictionary:

There is Old Testament evidence that **there was a "high place" here.** In the account of David's flight mention is made of **the spot on the summit** "where he was wont to worship God" (2 Sam 15:32 margin). **This is certainly a reference to a sanctuary, and there are strong reasons for believing that this place may have been Nob** (which see) (see 1 Samuel 21:1; 22:9, 11, 19; Nehemiah 11:32; **but especially Isaiah 10:32).**[243] (Emphasis added)

Isaiah 10 closes with Yahweh's promise that He will bring about the defeat of Assyria and ultimately deliver His chosen people from their hands. But that's not the end of Isaiah's prophecy.

It turns out the entire foretelling is a *compound prophecy.*[244] You'll remember we spoke of this biblical literary feature several chapters earlier. A compound prophecy first speaks to the matter at hand, usually within the lifetime events of the prophet himself. Then, it morphs into a metaphor for something else—something usually dealing with the end times, before or at the return of Yeshua's reclamation of the fallen world. It often speaks of God's restoration of Paradise, saving His people from Satan's[245] clutches and finally bringing about the restitution of all things.

ISAIAH 11

That's exactly what happens in the next chapter—Isaiah 11. It's as though God is making it clear that Isaiah 10 and 11 go together as one *compound prophecy.*

Look at several sections of Isaiah 11, beginning with verse 1. This begins the unbroken flow from the ending of Isaiah 10:

A shoot will come up from the stump of Jesse; from his roots a Branch will bear fruit.

The Spirit of the Lord will rest on him—the Spirit of wisdom and of understanding, the Spirit of counsel and of might, the Spirit of the knowledge and fear of the Lord....

but with righteousness he will judge the needy, with justice he will give decisions for the poor of the earth. He will strike the earth with the rod of his mouth; with the breath of his lips he will slay the wicked.

Righteousness will be his belt and faithfulness the sash around his waist....

In that day the Root of Jesse will stand as a banner for the peoples; the **nations will rally to him**, and his resting place will be glorious....

He will raise a banner for the nations and gather the exiles of Israel; he will assemble the scattered people of Judah **from the four quarters of the earth.** (Isaiah 11:1–2, 4–5, 10, 12; emphasis added)

Even the Apostle Paul quotes from Isaiah 11:10 in his letter to the Romans:

And again, Isaiah says, "The Root of Jesse will spring up,
     One who will arise to rule over the nations; the Gentiles will hope in him." (Romans 15:12)

This brings us to the imagery of that specific spot on the Mount of Olives.

55

THE PLACE OF SATAN'S DEFEAT

Isaiah 10:23 shows the metaphorical image of Satan
standing on a specific place on the Mount of Olives.

There can be no doubt that Isaiah 11—a compound prophecy—refers to God's deliverance through Jesus Christ in the very last days. Note what the scholars say concerning the compound nature of Isaiah 10 and 11.

Matthew Henry's Concise Commentary:

Some think [Isaiah 11] **looks to the deliverance of the Jews** out of their captivity....

And further yet, to the redemption of believers **from the tyranny of sin and Satan.** And this...**for the sake of the Messiah,** the Anointed of God.[246] (Emphasis added)

Maclaren's Exposition:

The prophecy is distinctly **that of One Person,** in whom the Davidic monarchy is concentrated, and all its decadence more than recovered. Isaiah **does not** bring **the rise of the Messiah** into

chronological connection with the fall of Assyria; for he contemplates a period of decay for the Israelite monarchy, and it was the very burden of his message as to Assyria that it should pass away without harming that monarchy.

The contrast is not intended to suggest continuity in time. The period of fulfilment is entirely undetermined.[247] (Emphasis added)

Cambridge Bible for Schools and Colleges:

The advent of the Messiah. Idea and figure correspond to those of Isaiah 6:13; as **a new Israel will spring up from the "stump" of the old, so the Messianic King will arise** from the decayed family of David. Some commentators find in the image **an intentional contrast to that of Isaiah 10:34....**

The precise relation of the Messiah to the reigning branch of the family is purposely left indefinite (cf. Micah 5:2). In its present setting the passage is no doubt intended as a sequel to Isaiah 10:5–34.[248] (Emphasis added)

Pulpit Commentary:

This chapter is closely connected with the preceding. The recovery is connected—or rather identified with the coming of Messiah, whose character is beautifully portrayed (verses 2–5). An elaborate description of Messiah's kingdom follows (verses 6–10).[249] (Emphasis added)

Barnes' Notes on the Bible:

"And a king shall proceed from the sons of Jesse, and the Messiah from his sons' sons shall arise;" **showing conclusively that the ancient Jews referred this to the Messiah.**[250] (Emphasis added)

In The New Testament

Now note what the Apostle Paul had to say about Isaiah 11. He is quoting from Isaiah 11:1, 10:

And again, Isaiah says, "The Root of Jesse will spring up, one who will arise to rule over the nations; in him the Gentiles will hope." (Romans 15:12)

The following is from the *Expositor's Greek New Testament* on Romans 15:12:

The words are meant to describe the Messianic kingdom and its Davidic head. It is a universal kingdom, and the nations set their hope in its King, and therefore **in the God of salvation whose representative He is.**[251] (Emphasis added)

Bengel's Gnomen:

Christ is elsewhere called the root of David, Revelation 22:16; but, if we compare **this passage taken from the passage in Isaiah,** He is called **the root of Jesse.... the Messiah, who was to descend from Jesse,** had been promised neither entirely to him, nor to the Gentiles: and yet **He was bestowed on both.**[252] (Emphasis added)

Gill's Exposition of the Entire Bible:

This prophecy is applied to the Messiah by the Jews, who say, "that when the King Messiah is revealed, there shall be gathered to him all the nations of the world, so that that Scripture shall be fulfilled which is written, 'There shall be a root of Jesse'."[253] (Emphasis added)

Since Isaiah 11 metaphorically represents Jesus the Messiah, then Isaiah 10:23 (the compound companion to chapter 11) shows the metaphorical image of *Satan* standing on a specific place on the Mount of Olives; he is represented in the immediate person of Sennacherib.[254]

Sennacherib's army would then be a figurative picture of Satan's demonic host. Here is a striking image of the ancient evil one surveying the city of Jerusalem below, desiring it as his own, and longing to make God's people his own slaves.[255]

But God makes it known that He will strike down Sennacherib/Satan on *this very spot* and will not let him prevail against God's people in that moment in Israel's history, and most assuredly not in the eternity that is to come. So, then, Satan's defeat—as he is using Sennacherib—would happen immediately, in Isaiah's day. And, it would happen again in about AD 33 when Jesus would be crucified at, or near, this very spot, thus securing Satan's ultimate defeat as declared in Revelation 20.

When the thousand years are over, **Satan will be released from his prison and will go out to deceive the nations** in the four corners of the earth—Gog and Magog—and to gather them for battle. In number they are like the sand on the seashore.

They marched across the breadth of the earth and **surrounded the camp of God's people, the city he loves.** But fire came down from heaven and devoured them.

And the devil, who deceived them, was thrown into the lake of burning sulfur, where the beast and the false prophet had been thrown. They will be tormented day and night for ever and ever. (Revelation 20:7–10; emphasis added)

So it is that Isaiah 11 opens with a compound tie-in, indicating that Messiah will be the one to defeat Satan, here, in this place, and the one to rule over the New Jerusalem of the final days. This place is the "high place" of Jerusalem, where Sennacherib/Satan stood and declared that he alone would possess it. And it is the same location from where Jesus hung on a cross and arose from a tomb declaring, "Oh no you won't."

STRIKING IMAGERY

All of this imagery takes place at Nob, on the Mount of Olives, where Goliath's sword was deposited. And it was most likely the very site where Goliath's skull had been displayed, then buried, and offered up to the Lord as a token of gratitude for David's victory.

Goliath, in that sense, was also a picture of Satan rising up against God's people, and David was a picture of Messiah, defeating the giant and cutting off his head—hearkening all the way back to the Garden of Eden, when Yahweh pronounced His curse of death upon Satan: "You will bruise His heel, but *He will crush your head*" (Genesis 3:15).

Over and over, we come to Nob—in the heart of the Mount of Olives—as the *head* of everything. It appears to be the cosmic *ground zero* for the final battle of the ages. And, it is the place where Yeshua will, once again, place His feet upon the earth's soil, but this time to rule and reign over the restored Paradise forever.

It is also where Jesus agonized in the Garden before the crucifixion, and it's where He was betrayed, then arrested. And, more than likely—being the only position that possesses the preponderance of biblical, historical, and archeological evidence—it is the very spot that would have been known, even in Jesus' day, as "the place of the skull."

PART X

FROM HEBREWS
TO THE
MOUNT OF OLIVES

We have an altar from which those who minister at the tabernacle have no right to eat. The high priest carries the blood of animals into the Most Holy Place as a sin offering, but the bodies are burned outside the camp. And so Jesus also suffered outside the city gate to make the people holy through his own blood. Let us, then, go to him outside the camp, bearing the disgrace he bore.

~Hebrews 13:10–13

56

THE HEBRAIC KEY

The writer of Hebrews very clearly says that Jesus was
crucified "outside the city gate"—but not just any city gate.

In an earlier chapter, I began with the words: "Yet, all the Bible appears to say about where the dual event took place is that He was taken to Golgotha (the 'place of a skull'), where He was crucified, then buried in a nearby garden tomb." However, in the wider scope, that statement wasn't entirely accurate, as we've already observed in previous chapters.

Still another place in the New Testament discloses a treasure trove of clues regarding the location of the crucifixion. Numerous scholars believe this passage actually *pinpoints* the Mount of Olives as the site.

That Scripture is not found in the Gospels; it's found in Hebrews 13:10–13. However, one would need an intricate understanding of the Old Testament sacrificial system (as many of the early church members who first read that book would have had) to glean the nuggets of truth from it:

> **We have an altar** from which those who minister at the tabernacle **have no right to eat.** The high priest carries the blood of animals into the Most Holy Place **as a sin offering,** but the bodies are

burned **outside the camp**. And so Jesus also suffered **outside the city gate** to make the people **holy through his own blood**. Let us, then, **go to him** outside the camp, bearing the disgrace he bore. (Hebrews 13:10–13; emphasis added)

The writer of Hebrews clearly says Jesus was crucified "outside the city gate" and "outside the camp." But this wasn't referring to just any city gate. He is identifying Jesus' place of sacrifice with a specific gate through which the sin offering was taken "outside the camp." There was only one gate, one place this would happen. The early church knew where it was.

Why are these precise words so important? They speak to Jesus' crucifixion site as being *east* of Jerusalem, not *west* of it, as are Gordon's Calvary and the Church of the Holy Sepulcher. This is a huge first clue.

For a more specific answer to this important question, we'll appeal to the writings of Rabbi Eliezer ben Hurcanus, one of the most prominent Hebrew sages of the first and second centuries within the Roman region of Judea and the sixth most-mentioned sage in the Mishnah. Rabbi Eliezer had actually seen the Second Temple before its destruction in AD 70.

This ancient rabbi was insistent that "outside the camp"—in its purest biblical context—meant nothing less than *to the east of Jerusalem*, and no place else.

It is said here [in Leviticus 4: 12]: Without the Camp, and it is said there [in Numbers 19:3]: Without the Camp. Just as here [in Leviticus] it means outside the three Camps [of the priests, of the Levites, and of the Israelites], so does it mean there [in Numbers] outside the three Camps; and just as there [Numbers 19:3–the burning of the Red Heifer Sacrifice] it means TO THE EAST OF JERUSALEM, so does it here [Leviticus 4:12] TO THE EAST OF JERUSALEM.[256]

We now must resolve at least three more important questions from the text in Hebrews 13:

1. What is the "altar" referred to in this passage?
2. What is the "ritual" the author of Hebrews is referencing?
3. Which "city gate" did this "ritual" involve?

THE EXPERTS SPEAK

Several noted biblical scholars—all of them holding doctorates and other academic distinctions—have taken a deep dive into this topic. Their studies have spanned from the mid-1800s to our own day. I'll cite several of those scholars, including the following, in the next several chapters:

- **Ernest L. Martin.**[257] His book, *Secrets of Golgotha*, has long been a go-to work on this topic because it explores the Hebrews 13 passage from about every angle one could imagine, using reliable ancient sources and the work of other modern scholars. (I certainly recommend it if you're interested in an exhaustive study of this topic.)
- **Dr. James D. Tabor**[258] and **Dr. Douglas Jacoby.**[259] Both of these modern-day scholars served as professors in major universities and have authored several books in addition to receiving numerous prestigious academic awards.
- **Dr. Nikos Kokkinos** (1955–).[260] University of Oxford professor and archeologist.
- **Dr. N. F. Hutchinson.**[261] Professor and archeologist whose writings date from the mid to late 1800s.
- **Dr. Helmut Heinrich Koester** (December 18, 1926–January 1, 2016). A German-born American scholar who specialized in the New Testament and early Christianity at Harvard Divinity School. Dr. Koester's research was focused on the arenas of New Testament interpretation, history of early Christianity, and archaeology of the early Christian period.[262]

THE THREE QUESTIONS ANSWERED

Before we look at some of the observations of these scholars, let me summarize what they say concerning the clues given in Hebrews 13. Their findings also tie to my own biblical exploration and discoveries, as well as to my firsthand understanding of the spoken and written Hebrew language—both modern and ancient—in addition to my personal knowledge. They are also in line with my formal yeshiva training in Jewish Orthodox customs and scriptural interpretation.

Succinctly, here are the answers to the questions proposed from the textual declarations found in Hebrews 13.

1. The "altar" is the ancient Miphkad[263] Altar on the Mount of Olives.
2. The "ritual" is the sacrifice of the Red Heifer.[264]
3. The "city gate" is the Eastern Gate,[265] the one through which Jesus entered Jerusalem the last week of His life. And, in coming into the city through that gate, He had just come from the Mount of Olives.

Now, let's look at what academicians have to say about all of this.

57

Appealing to the Scholars

Very few people pay attention to this important altar,
but it was a sacred piece of furniture associated
with the sacrificial services of the Temple.[266]

An exhaustive study of the implications of Hebrews 13 and the fact of Jesus being crucified and buried on the Mount of Olives would fill another entire book of several hundred pages. That task has already been accomplished by others. What I will do in the next couple of chapters is reproduce a portion of the relevant information from these scholars so you can see the evidence in an abbreviated format.

Dr. James Tabor:

The basic case for the Mount of Olives being the site of Jesus' crucifixion rests on several interrelated arguments The first, and in my view, the most weighty, is a passage in the New Testament book of Hebrews (13:10–13)[267] (Emphasis added)

Dr. Douglas Jacoby says of the Miphkad Altar:

There is substantial evidence in the Old Testament for a location "outside the camp" devoted to the incineration of the bodies of sacrificial animals, the Miphkad Altar (Leviticus 4:12, 6:11).

In Hebrews 13, the writer contrasts the holocausts at the Temple with those outside—namely, at the Miphkad Altar, mentioned in Numbers, Ezekiel, and the Mishnah.[268]

Jesus' death is symbolically connected with this altar outside the Temple. (Not to say that the crucifixion necessarily took place at this altar.) Where were the bodies of the sacrificial victims totally incinerated? The Miphkad Altar stood 2000 cubits from the Temple on the Mount of Olives, and although few Christians today—or Jews, for that matter—realize its true significance, this is arguably the most important of the three altars of the Temple. The three are: (1) the altar of burnt offering, (2) the incense altar, and (3) the Miphkad Altar (technically a pit, according to Parah 4:2[269]).[270] (Emphasis added)

Dr. Ernest L. Martin relates this altar to a specific location mentioned in the Old Testament and ties it to the known site of the altar in Jesus' day:

In the time of the later Sanctuaries, there was an altar associated with those Temples that...the prophet Ezekiel said was located east of the Temple and "without the sanctuary" (Ezekiel 43:21).

Very few people pay attention to this important altar, but it was a sacred piece of furniture associated with the sacrificial services of the Temple. On this particular altar some of the main sin offerings ordained by Moses were burnt to ashes. Indeed, the important sacrifice of the Red Heifer was performed at this eastern altar which was located as Ezekiel says "without the sanctuary."

Where was this altar situated in relationship to the Temple? In the time of Jesus, Jewish records show that this outer altar was located near the southern summit of the Mount of Olives

directly east of the Temple. It was also positioned just "outside the Camp" of Israel."[271] (Emphasis added)

THE RED HEIFER SACRIFICE AND THE EASTERN GATE

Dr. James Tabor deals with these two elements of the Hebrews 13 declaration:

> The author of the book of Hebrews makes use of this essential sacrificial practice, "outside the camp," to establish the legitimacy of Jesus being crucified "outside the gate." Rather than a gate on the north of the city, **the Eastern Gate is really the only one that would make sense in this passage.**
>
> This image of the **Red Heifer**, that had to be "without spot or blemish" was picked up by the early Christians as the most fitting allegorical image of Jesus' own cleansing sacrifice, with the "sprinkling" of his blood likened to that of the water prepared with the ashes of the **Red Heifer.**
>
> The writer of Hebrews, preserving pre-70 CE traditions, subsequently lost after the destruction of two Jewish Revolts and the establishment of Jerusalem as Aelia Capitolina by Hadrian, seems to be reflecting some actual take on the geography of Jerusalem and is able to make a very effective point to his readers based on Jesus being crucified east of the city, outside the gate, on the Mount of Olives.[272] (Emphasis added)

Dr. Douglas Jacoby says of the importance of the red heifer sacrifice:

> It is certainly not difficult to see how much richer the **symbolism and typology of death of Jesus** is if our "red heifer sacrifice" was "slaughtered" on the Mount of Olives, **in roughly the same location as the original Red Heifer sacrifice.**[273] (Emphasis added)

Once again, Dr. Martin provides another fascinating piece of information concerning the Temple ritual of the red heifer sacrifice.

> In the time of Jesus, there was a **double tiered arched bridge supporting a roadway** which led from this eastern gate of the Temple to the top of the Mount of Olives. That double tiered arched bridge was built by the priests to span the Kidron Ravine. This bridge was constructed by the priests for sacerdotal purposes and it was known as the **Bridge of the Red Heifer**[274] (Shekalim 4:2).[275] It connected the single gate in the eastern wall of the Court of the Gentiles with a **sanctified road that led up to a Third Altar of the Temple located near the summit of the Mount of Olives**. It is this altar referred to by the Book of Hebrews that was associated with the crucifixion of Jesus.[276] (Emphasis added)

Interestingly, even though Dr. Martin independently arrived at his observations concerning the crucifixion of Jesus as being on the Mount of Olives, he later discovered that Dr. Nikos Kokkinos, professor of ancient history at Oxford University, had also, earlier, arrived at the same conclusion—the crucifixion of Yeshua did indeed occur at the Mount of Olives.[277]

THE GARDEN OF GETHSEMANE

Dr. Kokkinos believed the crucifixion most likely would have taken place in the same general vicinity of Jesus' *arrest*—in the Garden of Gethsemane. He based this assessment upon his research of Roman law from the first century[278] when, apparently, this procedure of execution, whenever possible, was a fairly common practice, as explicitly stated in an apocryphal document titled the *Gospel of Nicodemus* (also known as the *Acts of Pilate*),[279] written in the middle of the fourth century.[280]

Here is that portion from the *Gospel of Nicodemus*:

Then Pilate commanded the veil to be drawn before the judgement-seat whereon he sat, and saith unto Jesus: Thy nation hath convicted thee (accused thee) as being a king: **therefore have I decreed** that thou shouldest **first be scourged** according to the law of the pious emperors, and **thereafter hanged upon the cross in the garden wherein thou wast taken:** and let Dysmas and Gestas the two malefactors be crucified with thee.[281] (Emphasis added)

John W. Ritenbaugh, a scholar, preacher, author, and Bible researcher, describes this manner of execution:

The Roman method, from their own history, says that the place of execution for capital crimes, in order to produce the maximum effect on the public, was this: (1) It was **done at the scene of the crime.** If they could do it right there, good. **Bang them up against a tree,** and that is the end. (2) If they could not do that, then it was **at the place where the person was arrested.** (3) It was to be **on an area of high ground** or at a busy place. Incidentally, it also remarks **that they frequently used a tree.**[282]

[Jesus] **started on the Mount of Olives. That was the starting place of the crimes that the Jews held against Him.** He went in and claimed Himself King, and the people said, "Yes. He is King of the Jews." The Romans (Pilate) could have charged Him with sedition, of overthrowing the Roman government....

Where does the action proceed from there? It went **back to the Mount of Olives** to the **Garden of Gethsemane.** Gethsemane was on the side of the Mount of Olives. What happened at Gethsemane? **That is where He was arrested.**

The scene of the crime was the Mount of Olives. Where He was arrested was on the Mount of Olives, and it was a high place where everybody could see what was going on. **The Mount of**

Olives fits every requirement of a Roman crucifixion: (1) the scene of the crime, (2) the place where He was arrested, and (3) a high place where everybody could see what was done.[283] (Emphasis added)

Since this location was the case in Jesus' arrest, it might have, therefore, placed the crucifixion in or near the Garden of Gethsemane, also located on the Mount of Olives. That garden was situated at the foot of the mount, close to a heavily trafficked area, near the Eastern Gate of the Temple Mount and the Mount of Olives cemetery.

I still believe, because of the other reasons we have discussed, that the crucifixion took place near the summit of the Mount of Olives. However, even if the Garden of Gethsemane area were to be discovered as the genuine location, we still have Jesus being crucified and resurrected at the *Mount of Olives—the place of the Skull.*[284] All of this correctly ties all of the prophecies and scriptural connections back to this one region. It seems we can't logically escape the biblical pointers toward the Mount of Olives.

At this point in our study, one thing is certain: the crucifixion and burial of Yeshua certainly *did not* take place at Gordon's Calvary or at the site of the Church of the Holy Sepulchre.

58

EAST OF JERUSALEM

The Mount of Olives crucifixion and resurrection
beautifully complete the entire biblical message and
faithfully illuminate the bigger picture of Satan's ultimate defeat.

Later in his life, Dr. Earnest L. Martin made yet another discovery concerning the site of Jesus' crucifixion and resurrection by calling attention to the views of Dr. N. F. Hutchinson. Hutchinson's work had been published as far back as 1870, in the *Palestine Exploration Quarterly* "Notes on our Lord's Tomb,"[285] and in an 1873 revision.[286]

EAST, NOT WEST

In those two publications, Dr. Martin noted that Dr. Hutchinson might have been one of the first, at least in relatively "modern" times, to have insisted that Jesus' crucifixion and resurrection would have taken place *east of Jerusalem*, rather than the commonly held *west-Jerusalem* view of his day. Lo and behold, Dr. Hutchinson arrived at his eastern-view theory by using Hebrews 13:11–12 as his basis.

Dr. James Tabor writes further:

Hutchinson puts forth a number of other arguments: that [the crucifixion scene] was on a "high road" visible to all, leading past gardens; that the scene could be witnessed "from afar off" by bystanders, and that it was on a main road upon which throngs of pilgrims arrived for the feast (from Jericho, through Bethany, to Jerusalem), **rather than from the south or west.**

Their first view of the city was when they crested the Mt of Olives and beheld the Temple in its splendor. Hutchinson asserts that **none of these descriptions fit the Western part of the city.**

In his subsequent note he observes that **according to Melito of Sardis,**[287] **Mary, the mother of Jesus, is also associated with the Mt of Olives in later tradition**, including her own tomb near that of her son, and that she "went out every day" to pray at the tomb of Christ and at Golgotha—which **implies close proximity to the Mt. of Olives.**[288] (Emphasis added)

Additionally, Dr. Douglas Jacoby notes a reference to our topic that is also found in the Jewish Mishnah.[289]

The Mishnah says clearly that the priests offering the sacrifice of the Red Heifer needed to be able to see the altar of burnt offering from their vantage point on the Mount of Olives:

"All the Temple walls were high, save only the eastern wall, because **the priest that burns the Heifer and stands on top of the Mount of Olives** should be able to **look directly into the entrance of the sanctuary** when the blood of the Red Heifer is sprinkled" (Middoth 2:4).

Since the Mount of Olives (Upper Mount Moriah) is taller than the Temple Mount (Lower Mount Moriah), the priests sacrificing at the third altar were able to look down on the Temple Mount and see (over the intentionally lowered wall) the altar of burnt offering. If Jesus' sacrificial death fulfills the sacrifice of the Red Heifer, as the Hebrew writer and early Christian tradition affirm, then the Son of God was almost certainly crucified on the Mount of Olives.[290] (Emphasis added)

THE OTHER "ALTAR"

What about those who might argue that the "altar" spoken of by the author of the book of Hebrews was simply referring to the "cross of Jesus" or the "Lord's Supper," as a number of the classical scholars argue?[291] Each of the scholars quoted in these chapters refutes the notion that the "altar" of Hebrews 13 is the cross itself. I believe as they do; however, I understand the additional symbolic meaning of the altar as being found through the cross, as well as in the Lord's Supper. But, the point I am interested in here is the *literal meaning* the writer of Hebrews was emphasizing. This is the *first* meaning that the early Jewish Christians would have clearly understood.

Dr. Helmut Koester, writing for the *Harvard Theological Review* in 1962, was adamant in insisting that the other "altar" mentioned in Hebrews 13 simply cannot be a symbol for the Lord's Supper. Nor was it, he said, a mere figure of speech for the "cross" of Jesus.

Koester was firm in his findings that the other "altar" of that passage was speaking of the literal "Third Altar" of the Temple—*the one associated with the sin offerings of the red heifer.* That altar, he correctly states, was located near the summit of the Mount of Olives. And, Dr. Koester says the location of Jesus' crucifixion according to Hebrews 13 is directly connected to that altar's general location.[292]

Dr. Martin agrees with Dr. Koester and quotes him in his classic book *Secrets of Golgotha*:

It has been shown by Helmut Koester...that the "altar" cannot be a symbol for the Lord's Supper nor is it a figure of speech for the "cross" of Jesus. ...because there was in fact a literal altar (the Third Altar) of the Temple associated with these sin offerings.

There can really be no doubt in this matter. The altar being discussed in the Book of Hebrews was the Third Altar of the Temple that the inhabitants of Jerusalem in the time of Jesus were well acquainted with. This altar was not shaped like the other two altars in the Temple. …It was the specific altar located outside the Camp of Israel that surrounded the city of Jerusalem where certain sin offerings were burnt to ashes.

This important Third Altar was located near the summit of the Mount of Olives where the Red Heifer was killed and burnt to ashes and where special sin offerings were burnt according to the Law of Moses (Leviticus 4: 12).[293] (Emphasis added)

Vincent's Word Studies nails down the matter as well:

It is a mistake to try to find in the Christian economy **some specific object** answering to altar—**either the cross, or the Eucharistic table, or Christ himself.** Rather the ideas of approach to God,—sacrifice, atonement, pardon and acceptance, salvation, —are gathered up and **generally represented in the figure of an altar, even as the Jewish altar was the point at which all these ideas converged.**

The foundation of the figure is the [established Jewish] sacrifice of [their day]. The writer is speaking **in the present tense, of institutions in operation** in his own time.[294] (Emphasis added)

Gill's Exposition of the Entire Bible also presents the larger, more literal meaning of Hebrews 13 in regard to the altar spoken of in that passage. That altar is "not" the cross, or the Lord's table, but Jesus Himself, offered as the ultimate fulfillment of the burnt sin offering of the red heifer sacrifice. That sacrifice was always pointing to its greater fulfillment in the crucifixion of Jesus Christ on the Mount of Olives.

We have an altar…By which is meant, **not the cross** of Christ, on which he was crucified; **nor the Lord's table,** where his flesh and blood are presented to faith, as food, though not offered; **but Christ himself**, who is altar, sacrifice, and priest.

He was typified by the altar of the burnt [i.e., the red heifer] **offering**, and the sacrifice that was offered upon it.[295] (Emphasis added)

Most of today's Christians have never even considered the possibility of Jesus being crucified and resurrected on the Mount of Olives. However, now we can see—with plenty of evidence—that this is what the Bible has been stating all along.

59

PUTTING THE EVIDENCE IN ORDER

The matter simply can't be made any clearer in regard
to the location of Golgotha and Jesus' resurrection.

For a quick summary of what we have learned thus far, here are the most important facts concerning the Mount of Olives as being the crucifixion and burial/resurrection site of Jesus:

1. The Mount of Olives is an integral site in Jesus' last week of ministry in Jerusalem, just before His crucifixion and resurrection.
2. It was the place of His ascension forty days *after* His resurrection.
3. It is the place to which He will return to begin His earthly rule and reign. This is supported by both the Old and New Testaments.
4. The Mount of Olives location for the crucifixion is supported by Hebrews 13, especially once the modern reader understands what the early church knew about that declaration and its relationship to the red heifer sacrifice.

5. The Mount of Olives fits the description of the "place of a skull" and is the most ancient altar of worship for the Jews of that area, as well as the most likely place where Goliath's head (skull) was brought, along with his armor. We know from the Old Testament that David retrieved Goliath's sword from this place after he brought the giant's armor "to Jerusalem."

6. The Mount of Olives crucifixion is supported by several historical documents written during the first several centuries.

7. Neither of the two traditional locations for the crucifixion and resurrection—Gordon's Calvary and the Church of the Holy Sepulcher—has *any* of the aforementioned evidence to support them; they have only the pronouncements of "authenticity" by the Roman Catholic Church and General Gordon. Even those locations have been disproven by modern archeological and scientific examination.

8. The Mount of Olives crucifixion and resurrection scenario beautifully completes the entire biblical message, and it faithfully illuminates the bigger picture of Satan's ultimate defeat through the sacrifice and resurrection of Jesus Christ—on the very spot where the battle of the *gods* (satanic and demonic forces) had taken place—and continues to transpire through the millennia.

TWO SITES

Here is what Dr. Douglas Jacoby has to say about the traditionally accepted Church of the Holy Sepulcher and the Via Dolorosa, tourist sites we've already examined and eliminated as being authentic.

> Simply stated, **traditional Christianity is probably mistaken in its identification** of the western site of the Church of the Holy Sepulcher as the location of Jesus' death and resurrection...

No need to follow the crowds. In addition, there will be **little need to "compete" with the "tour groups"** down the traditional Via Dolorosa and inside the Church of the Holy Sepulcher, since we recognize that **they are well over a kilometer** from the **true site** of the crucifixion, on the Mount of Olives.[296] (Emphasis added)

Dr. James Tabor agrees:

The problem with [the Church of the Holy Sepulcher], despite its overwhelming favor with both Christian believers and a score of scholars who have written on the subject, is **there is no connection of Jesus to the site before the early 4th century**—approximately **300 years after the time of Jesus.** Helena, the pious mother of Constantine, the Roman Emperor, is the first one to give it her stamp of approval and consecrate it as the location of Golgotha, but **it has little or no other basis in any of our historical records.**[297] (Emphasis added)

No Doubt

Dr. Martin is rather adamant. He asserts that the Mount of Olives as Jesus' crucifixion site should not even be doubted any longer. The evidence is in, especially in the book of Hebrews, and the details of that evidence have been confirmed over and over:

There is no longer any doubt. **Jesus was crucified near the summit of the Mount of Olives about half a mile east of the Temple Mount.** This fact is confirmed in the New Testament in a variety of ways.... In fact...the Book of Hebrews...[was to the early church] sufficient to pinpoint the region where the crucifixion of Jesus took place.[298] (Emphasis added)

At this point, the matter seems clear. However, there's still a bit more illumination we can shine upon what we've already discovered. We've burrowed deep and have found some stunning artifacts pointing to the truth of what really happened.

Now, let's dust off those finds.

60

THE RED HEIFER AND JESUS

They had seen Yeshua in many places,
but demanded an answer in this particular place.

Now that we've settled that the Mount of Olives is indeed the very best conclusion as to where Jesus' crucifixion and burial/resurrection took place, let's take a closer look at the Temple sacrifice that foreshadowed it. The altar of the rare and perfect *red heifer* points to the sacrifice of the sinless Messiah and the sanctifying power of that sacrifice for all who will come under that blood offering.

WHY THE RED HEIFER?

Just as the ashes of the red heifer sin offering were used to purify one from defilement, the sacrifice of Yeshua took away the sin of the world. His perfection qualified Him as the heavenly sacrifice for the sins of humanity.

The requirement for the red heifer to *have never borne a yoke* pointed to Yeshua never having borne the yoke of sin.

For we do not have a high priest who is unable to empathize with
our weaknesses, but we have one who has been tempted in every
way, just as we are—yet he did not sin. (Hebrews 4:15)

The ashes of the red heifer were all about cleansing and purifying the
impure. It was a foreshadowing of the ability to enter the perfect tabernacle—the Holy Spirit entering redeemed humanity, the "one new man."

We have this hope as an anchor for the soul, firm and secure. It
enters the inner sanctuary behind the curtain, where our forerunner, Jesus, has entered on our behalf. He has become a high priest
forever, in the order of Melchizedek. (Hebrews 6:19–20)

The sacrifice of the spotless Lamb was about *salvation*—deliverance
from the eternal penalty of sin. And, the sacrifice of the perfect red heifer
was about sanctification—setting a person apart unto God, in the righteousness of God, in order to be a fit representative of His glory in a fallen
world. The sacrifice of Yeshua our Messiah—as both the Lamb of God
and the Red Heifer offering—fulfilled both salvation and sanctification.

For our sake he **made him to be sin** who knew no sin, so that in
him we **might become the righteousness** of God. (2 Corinthians
5:21; emphasis added)

The Old Testament understanding of the location of the red heifer
sacrifice is significant because it proves the crucifixion and burial site of
Yeshua had to be on the Mount of Olives. He had to be taken to the
Mount of Atonement, the region in which the sacrifice took place. It
couldn't be anywhere else.

Now the Lord spoke to Moses and to Aaron, saying, "This is the
statute of the law that the Lord has commanded: Tell the people
of Israel to **bring you a red heifer without defect, in which there**

is no blemish, and on which a yoke has never come. And you shall give it to Eleazar the priest, and **it shall be taken outside the camp** and slaughtered before him. (Numbers 19:1–8, KJV; emphasis added)

The heifer had to be totally red and at least three years old. It was to be slaughtered and burned. The ashes were then kept to use for cleansing and purification of sin.

The other striking significance of the heifer was the fact that it is a young female cow that has not had any offspring. The physical body of Yeshua was conceived by the power of the Holy Spirit, but Genesis 3:15 speaks of the "seed of a woman." So the red heifer also foreshadowed the male seed, *born of a woman*—a virgin—brought forth at *just the right time* in humanity's history, being used by God to bring forth the Messiah.

But when the set time had fully come, God *sent his Son, born of a woman*, under the law, to redeem those under the law, that we might receive adoption to sonship.

Because you are his sons, God sent the Spirit of his Son into our hearts, the Spirit who calls out, "Abba, Father." So **you are no longer a slave, but God's child**; and since you are his child, **God has made you also an heir.** (Galatians 4:4–7; emphasis added)

Everything God does is for a reason.

The Pharisees were waiting and watching for the arrival of the Anointed One of God, and they wanted to know for sure if Jesus was the Messiah. So, when Yeshua Jesus walked into Solomon's Colonnade, in the Temple complex, the Pharisees surrounded Him, and in the course of the questioning, they asked Him who He was. Basically, they were saying, "If you're really the genuine Messiah, just tell us." His response was that He *had* told them over and over again, but they simply wouldn't believe.

Then came the Festival of Dedication [Hanukkah] at Jerusalem. It was winter, and Jesus was in the Temple courts walking in Solomon's Colonnade. The Jews who were there gathered around him, saying, "How long will you keep us in suspense? If you are the Messiah, tell us plainly." Jesus answered, "I did tell you, but you do not believe." (John 10:22–25)

Much of the significance of our study is wrapped in the reason for the Pharisees' question to Jesus, and why it was asked in that location. They had seen Yeshua in many places but demanded an answer in *this* place. Solomon's Porch *points eastward* to the Mount of Olives. Ezekiel says that the glory of the Lord "departed eastward," and must "return from the east" back to the Temple.

Then the glory of the Lord went out from the threshold of the house, and stood over the cherubim. And the cherubim lifted up their wings and mounted up from the earth before my eyes as they went out, with the wheels beside them. And they stood **at the entrance of the east gate of the house of the Lord,** and the glory of the God of Israel was over them. (Ezekiel 10:18, 19; emphasis added)

As the glory of the Lord **entered the temple by the gate facing east.** (Ezekiel 43:4; emphasis added)

The Pharisees and the crowd hailing Him as the Son of David knew the significance of Jesus' entry into Jerusalem through the Eastern Gate.

Rejoice greatly, **O daughter of Zion.** Shout aloud, O daughter of Jerusalem. **Behold, your king is coming to you;** righteous **and having salvation** [Hebrew for "salvation" is Yeshua] is he, **humble and mounted on a donkey,** on a colt, the foal of a donkey. (Zechariah 9:9, ESV; emphasis added)

The glory of the Lord must always come from the east. Jesus did. And, the Messiah of Israel was predicted to come riding on the back of a donkey. Jesus did this as well, from the east. For this reason, the Pharisees were confronting Him and demanding that He tell them plainly whether He was indeed the Messiah. He said, "I told you but you don't believe me."

Again Jesus spoke to them, saying, "I am the light of the world. Whoever follows me will not walk in darkness, but will have the light of life." (John 8:12)

Jesus said to them, "If God were your Father, you would love me, for I came from God and I am here. I came not of my own accord, but he sent me. Why do you not understand what I say? It is because you cannot bear to hear my word. You are of your father the devil, and your will is to do your father's desires. He was a murderer from the beginning, and does not stand in the truth, because there is no truth in him. When he lies, he speaks out of his own character, for he is a liar and the father of lies. But because I tell the truth, you do not believe me. (John 8:42–45)

PERSONAL DISCOVERY

As stated earlier, I did some personal research in exploring the Mount of Olives and looking for potential locations for the Garden Tomb. Now I will share that exploration with you; what I found was thrilling.

PART XI

FROM A HUNCH TO AN AMAZING FIND

Businessmen from the United States and Canada have recognized that there is a massive amount of tourism in Israel, and almost 100 percent of the tourists go up to the Mount of Olives. And yet there is nothing commercial there—no restaurants, no hotels, no shopping—nothing. I have long thought this was a very odd thing, especially for the Israeli tourism industry, one of the major backbones of our entire economy.

61

FINDING THE REAL GARDEN TOMB

*What really bothered me was knowing that
God never contradicts Himself in His Word.*

As I revealed in the opening chapters, when I first began my search for the genuine footsteps of Yeshua, I began by exploring all the established tourist locations. I shared what happened concerning our experiences at the Church of the Holy Sepulcher and at the 14 Stations of the Cross. There was a palpable, even visible presence of darkness there. You'll remember this is where my wife and I saw the vision of the "witch." That's when I knew that was not the correct place.

SPIRIT-DIRECTED RESEARCH

However, when I went to Gordon's Calvary for the first time—the Garden Tomb, as it's sometimes called—I felt the presence of the Holy Spirit, and I spoke with the owners, who were very gracious to me. I read through their pamphlets and pored over the Scriptures looking for references that might describe that location. I also searched out scholarly material and archeological discoveries concerning the location of Gordon's Calvary. Following is what I found.

Dr. Jerome Murphy-O'Connor (April 10, 1935—November 11, 2013) was professor of New Testament studies at the École Biblique in Jerusalem, a position that he held from 1967 until his death in Jerusalem. Dr. Murphy-O'Connor writes in his book, *The Holy Land: An Oxford Archaeological Guide*:

> **It is much easier to pray here** [at Gordon's Calvary] than in the Holy Sepulcher. Unfortunately **there is no possibility** that it is in fact the place where Christ was buried.[299] (Emphasis added)

Dr. W. Harold Mare also discussed this location in *Bible and Spade* (Vol. 3, No. 2), a respected archeological periodical. Dr. Mare commented regarding the "skull" feature of the small hill associated with the site:

> Although the side of the hill looks like the face of a skull, **this may be due to man-made cuttings in the hill**.... The nearby rock-hewn Garden Tomb, though aesthetically satisfying, is not of the first century A.D. It contains a Byzantine (fourth to sixth centuries A.D.) trough-type burial place, and two Byzantine crosses were found painted on one wall.[300]

Before I discovered these facts concerning the location, I was hoping this might be the place. At the conclusion of our first tour of Gordon's Calvary, when I went to the Place of the Skull, it was easy to see why people would liken the cliff face to a human skull, and I could see a garden, as well as a winepress, as mentioned in Scripture.

I thought, "Wow, this is the only major site on the tourist maps not owned and operated by the Roman Catholic Church. Maybe this really is the authentic site of the crucifixion and burial."

Also, the Garden Tomb is, in fact, *outside the gate*, as described in the Bible. And the site's representatives claimed it was where they took Jesus to be crucified. The distance between the area that looks like a skull and the supposed burial site is not far.

In the biblical account, we read that it was 3 p.m. when Jesus gave up His Spirit. That doesn't mean it was 3 p.m. when His body was taken down from the cross. All we know is that it was several hours before sundown when they removed His body from the cross and took it to the burial site, which didn't have to be in the immediate vicinity, but still was relatively nearby (John 19:42).

A TROUBLING SNAG

However, what really bothered me was knowing that God never contradicts Himself in His Word. He said we are not to have any other *gods* besides Him, and we certainly are not to worship idols (Exodus 20:3). That explicitly includes the use of carved images. If a carved image is supposed to be the evidence indicating where Jesus was crucified, wouldn't that violate one of the Ten Commandments? Would God allow a rocky knoll in the apparent image of a skull to commemorate the place of Jesus' sacrifice? That would be a flagrant contradiction to the Word of God. This troubling fact kept sticking in my soul.

The Bible tells us to "test the spirits" (1 John 4:1). In other words, if the Holy Spirit puts an uneasiness in our heart about something supposedly being from God, we should thoroughly check it out to make certain we stay on the right track. All the answers I received in the Spirit—and in the Scripture—added up to a big *no*. So that was the first red light telling me this could not be the place. It is a beautiful place, and the keepers of it were very kind to me and my wife, but I believed it simply was not the genuine location of Jesus' crucifixion and resurrection.

While I did sense the presence of the Holy Spirit there, that wasn't really surprising, because sincere believers were there almost every day of every week. Still, something was wrong with the Garden Tomb. I knew I had to dig deeper. This is why I immersed myself in years of subsequent research—digging through the piles of academic examination and doing feet-on-the-ground snooping, as well as talking a lot with regional authorities who had jurisdiction over the mountain area I was researching.

62

A CERTAIN SPOT

Years ago, there was a gate before the grave.
But that gate is not there now.

In a small, vacant lot near the top of the Mount of Olives is an Israeli flag. *Ninety-nine point nine* percent of that area is occupied by Arabs. The only place on the Mount of Olives where a small community of Jews live is in the vicinity of the flag. From that locale, one can look directly to Mount Moriah where Abraham built an altar to sacrifice Isaac, and it also looks right down upon the Eastern Gate to the Temple Mount—the gate through which Jesus entered Jerusalem in the last week of His earthly ministry and the one through which He will return.

BLOCKING BUSINESS

Businessmen from the United States and Canada have recognized that tourism is a big business in Israel, and almost all of the tourists go up to the Mount of Olives. Yet there is nothing commercial there—no restaurants, no hotels, and no shopping. I have long thought this was odd, especially for the Israeli tourism industry, a backbone of our economy.

305

The only commerce taking place in that area is a bunch of Arab people walking around with donkeys, trying to sell souvenirs to the Christians. Why is that? Business people have tried to build malls and all kinds of other relevant businesses and tourist attractions on this lot for many decades. They've long recognized the potential, but they simply can't build there. The reason they can't build has remained virtually unexplainable.

Believe me—I've lived here all my life. And, as I've already explained, I have deep connections in the rabbinical world, the Israeli military, and within the deepest halls of the Israeli government. It's usually not hard for me to find out the inner workings of important matters—to get answers to the tough questions of business, religion, and politics. But this one has completely stumped me.

I've spoken with the Canadian owners of several prominent malls in Tel Aviv and Haifa who have tried to build on the Mount of Olives, but they can't make it happen. No matter how much money they try to spend or how much influence they exert, they simply can't make any headway. And they can't explain it, either.

Even Jerusalem's city hall is hindered in its efforts to get commercial activity going at that spot. They can't say why. Additionally, the mayor of Jerusalem can't, or won't, state why he's not granting a permit for anyone to build up there. He just isn't. Everyone knows it would be great for the economy. But, the officials of Israel flatly refuse to let it happen.

I believe the problem is not a financial issue, it's a spiritual one. Somehow, God has thus far thwarted the plans for anyone to build tourist attractions there. I think this is because He won't allow His holy place to be desecrated. It would be hard for me to put into words that reasoning to business owners and potential builders, but I am almost certain that's why.

On that lot with the flag, there are two olive trees—that's all. Across the street from the lot is the ancient Church of the Pater Noster, built right next to the Byzantine ruins of the Church of Eleona. The original church was commissioned by Constantine and construction began under the direction of his mother, Helena, in the early fourth century to commemorate the Ascension of Jesus Christ. However, the structure, which Helena called the "Church of the Disciples," was never completed. Reconstruction began in 1915 by the French, but funds ran out in 1927, and it remains unfinished. It's the only place in Israel that was "captured" by the Roman Catholic Church but suddenly came to a complete halt, as far as building on the site. *The only place.*

At that site today, there are no idols, no statues of Mary, no candles, no incense, and no crucifixes. Obviously, if the Roman Catholic Church thought they could finish the structure, they would buy it from the French and complete the work, but God simply hasn't allowed it.

A CAVE AND A GRAVE

The unroofed Church of the Pater Noster features steps leading down into a cave. That cave was partially collapsed when it was discovered in 1910. Unbelievably, under the ruins of this unfinished church and partially collapsed cave is an empty tomb. Since its discovery, it has been rarely spoken of as anything of significance regarding the biblical narrative of Jesus' life. I suppose since the Chaldean spirits had done such a good job of leading the tourists to all the fake sites, few even considered this tomb.

Even though the church itself is a fourth-century Byzantine church, the tomb that cuts into that cave has been dated much earlier; it has been verified to be a *first-century* tomb.[301] That means the tomb would have been present in the time of Jesus. To this day, no one knows to whom the tomb belonged, but it meets all the descriptions of Joseph of Arimathea's tomb where Yeshua was buried. I'll explain this as we move forward.

When I first investigated the site years ago, there was a gate in front of the entrance to the grave. But that gate is not there now. Someone has also placed a picture of the Romanized representation of Jesus in the cave. Here, once again, the demonic Chaldean spirit is on display. Spiritual warfare is right before your eyes when you visit the place, especially now that you *know what you know* from reading this book.

Ever since about 2017, I've seen several indications that others are starting to recognize this spot as the place of Jesus' tomb. I occasionally see notes left there and other small indications of increased interest in the area—not only from amateur researchers, but from growing numbers of scholars who agree that the place of crucifixion and resurrection has to be the Mount of Olives.

However, as exciting as this possibility might be, I still couldn't proclaim this to be Jesus' tomb. I had to be certain.

63

RESURRECTION POWER

When I go to that spot on the Mount of Olives, I literally shake.

After going to the Church of the Pater Noster—*Church of the Disciples*—several times, Lian and I decided we would go there one more time, but this time with a special purpose: to go there *and just pray*. We wanted to see what the Lord might say to us. We agreed that if, after praying together at the site, and if we had no peace in our hearts, we would drop the idea that this was the genuine tomb of Yeshua. So we went. *And we prayed...*for two solid hours.

A HEARTFELT PLEA AND
A SUPERNATURAL SIGN

In our prayers, we asked the Lord of Hosts to show us whether this spot was indeed the place. We did not ask for a physical sign, only that the Lord would somehow confirm the truth to both of us, in the depths of our souls. In the midst of our fervent and sincere prayers, we received an amazing revelation. Just as God supernaturally showed us the demonic presence at the Church of the Nativity, He revealed His glory to us in this place, the most pivotal spiritual location on the face of the earth.

With all truthfulness, I can say that, as we opened our eyes, we both saw *a beam of light* coming out of that grave. It was an overwhelming spiritual experience. We had never seen such a thing before, nor have we seen anything like it since. The spectacle reminded me of that portion of Scripture from the New Testament book of Philippians, in which Paul writes: "I want to know Christ—yes, to know the power of his resurrection" (Philippians 3:10).

That powerful vision shook us to our core. The instantaneous revelation of that dazzling shaft of light was beyond description and appeared as a direct result of our praying together. We weren't sure what to do next. How would we explain such an experience to others? They weren't there. They would probably think we had lost our minds.

This must be what Paul felt like on the road to Damascus, or how Moses had felt after hearing God and experiencing a visible manifestation at the burning bush. Perhaps Mary was confronted with the same feelings and fears. Who would believe that an angel had visited her and told her the wondrous way she would be used in God's plan of salvation? Surely many other men and women of God struggle with these kinds of feelings and hesitations after they receive supernatural signs from the Lord of Hosts.

Please remember, I didn't rush into sharing my conclusions regarding the birthplace of Yeshua or the place of the crucifixion. The responsibility for handling and disseminating such discoveries of relatively concealed biblical truth is so huge that I had to be certain before I related them. But, this vision of that shaft of light—like that of the witch at the Church of the Holy Sepulcher—was so powerful and so intimate that it would require an extra measure of courage to convey my experience to the world. So, we had to overcome that hesitancy. God had not given us a spirit of fear. After all, hadn't we prayed that God would give us a sign or speak to us? We had. And in response, He did. So, we *had* to share it.

In the midst of that struggle, I was reminded by the Holy Spirit that the demonic realm hates it when a true believer begins to boldly shine the light of truth upon what was previously hidden through satanic deception. But it is our high calling to do so, regardless of who likes it or not.

> **For you were once darkness, but now you are light in the Lord.** Live as **children of light** (for the fruit of the light consists in all goodness, righteousness and truth) and find out what pleases the Lord.
>
> Have nothing to do with the fruitless deeds of darkness, but rather expose them. It is shameful even to mention what the disobedient do in secret. But everything exposed by the light becomes visible—and everything that is illuminated becomes a light. (Ephesians 5:8–13; emphasis added)

PERMISSION TO SHARE

It took me six and a half years of researching Migdal Eder before I felt God releasing me to tell others about it. The same diligence is true of my study of the Mount of Olives and my numerous excursions and interviews with important people regarding the Garden Tomb. I tried to shrink away from exposing the great potentiality of this location being the real tomb of Yeshua, but I felt the Lord God telling me, "No, no—you're *going to do it.*"

I am now convinced this is why God gave us the revelation of that unspeakably beautiful beam of light. That's when Yeshua said to my soul, "*Now* are you sure about it?" Other than the Lord Himself causing such a thing to happen, it would otherwise be physically impossible to replicate. To this day, when I go to that spot on the Mount of Olives, I literally shake.

Now, every time I take a tour group to Israel, I lead them to that site and show them what I believe to be the real tomb of Yeshua. Some are thoroughly fascinated, while others get angry about my nontraditional disclosure. Some even want to leave.

I suppose it will be that way until Yeshua comes again and places His feet upon the Mount of Olives. Then all the world will know. But the vision that Lian and I had at the site of that long-buried tomb was far from the only evidence we uncovered.

64

PROSKULIO

I was able to eventually speak face to face with the man who
had been managing the site of that tomb for well over twenty years.

Most scholars know that it's extremely unusual to have a rolling
stone at an ancient burial site. This practice was reserved only for
wealthy and prominent people.

FEW ROLLING-STONE TOMBS

As a matter of fact, most authoritative sources agree that only four rolling-
stone entrances have been discovered among the Jewish tombs in the area.
Consider the following examples:

Biblical Archaeology Review:

Israeli archaeologist Amos Kloner, an expert on ancient tombs in
Israel… Points out that "98 percent of the Jewish tombs from this
period…were **closed with square blocking stones.**… That **only
four of the huge disk-type "rolling stones" have been discovered**

from the time of Jesus, versus hundreds of the **square blocking** types.[302] (Emphasis added)

Zondervan Handbook of Biblical Theology:

In the vicinity of Jerusalem there are 1,000 or more rock-cut tombs. Israeli archaeologist Amos Kloner, who has examined **more than 900** such tombs, **found only four tombs dating from the late Second Temple period** (the time of Jesus) that were **closed by a rolling stone:**

1. the tomb of the Queen Helena of Adiabene
2. the family tomb of King Herod of Jerusalem
3. one nearby Herod's Family Tomb
4. another located in the upper Kidron Valley[303] (Emphasis added)

In spite of what some website or amateur archeologists might say otherwise, there's a sound reason we can be certain that our Lord and Savior was buried with a *rolling stone* in front of the cave: Scripture itself says so, over and over again.

Proskulio[304] is the Greek word used to describe the stone in front of the tomb of Yeshua, as recorded at least five different times in the Gospels of Matthew, Mark, and Luke.[305] The word means "to roll" or "roll (up to)." There is no other shade of meaning, so we know it was a stone *that rolled* and it wasn't just a typical, and much more prevalent, square block.

Barnes' Notes on the Bible:

Being cut out of a rock, there was no way by which the disciples could have access to it **but by the entrance,** at which the guard was placed, and **consequently it was impossible for them to steal him away.** The sepulcher, thus secure, was rendered more so **by rolling a great stone** at its entrance.[306] (Emphasis added)

Expositor's Greek Testament:

[This method] of shutting the door of the tomb; the **Jews called the stone *golal*, the roller.**[307] (Emphasis added)

Gill's Exposition of the Scripture:

The stone rolled to the door, was **what the Jews call, from its being rolled to,** and from the door of the sepulcher; and which, they say, was a large and broad stone, **with which the mouth of the sepulcher was stopped** above: and it was at the shutting up of the sepulcher with this stone, that mourning began.[308] (Emphasis added)

Apparently, there *used to be a rolling stone* in front of the *cave grave* at the Church of the Pater Noster on the Mount of Olives. In 2005, I was able to eventually speak face to face with the man who had managed the site of that tomb for well over twenty years. He told me there actually *was* a rolling stone there, years ago. I was floored. He also explained that because people were so frequently handling the stone and leaning on it, those in charge of the site were afraid it might fall on someone—so it was removed in 1989. He had no idea where it had been taken. But he was certain it was indeed a *rolling* grave stone. For me, that revelation was just another confirmation that this was the place.

COINCIDENCES OR CONCLUSIONS?

Think of it. The Mount of Olives is the most contextually valid site of the crucifixion, meeting all the requirements of the red heifer sin offering as well as the detailed description of the site of Jesus' ultimate sacrifice found in Hebrews 13. It is also where David deposited the most famous skull in Israel's entire history, therefore making it the "place of the skull"—

Golgotha. And, it is the place David retrieved Goliath's sword—the very one the young man had used to separate the giant's body from his head. And all of that happened at Israel's oldest altar of the worship of Yahweh, at the top of the Mount of Olives—the place to which Jesus will return in all His glory.

On top of all this, in these last days, and only within the last century, an ancient cave just happened to collapse. And in that collapse, a first-century tomb was resurrected before the eyes of the world—a tomb that had originally been sealed with a rolling stone. And, that tomb is near the top of the Mount of Olives. How many more "coincidences" like this would it take to finally draw a reasonable conclusion?

And of course, the entire deal was sealed for me when my wife and I were treated to a sign from God—a shaft of *light*—right in that spot.

PART XII

FROM THE BEGINNING TO THE END

Trust in the Lord with all your heart, and do not lean on your own understanding. In all your ways acknowledge him, and he will make straight your paths. Be not wise in your own eyes; fear the Lord, and turn away from evil.

~Proverbs 3:5–7, ESV

65

THE HOLY SPIRIT OF POWER

*If you're walking in His Word, the enemy will not like it,
and he will oppose you.*

When we teach others according to biblical principles and truth that is proven right from the Scriptures, it takes a huge burden off of us. We don't have to worry about what will happen as a result of our presentation, because the consequences for what we do in obedience to the Holy Spirit and the clear Word of God are on Him.

God doesn't want us waffling, worrying about *what if* this happens, or *what if* that happens, as a result of our decisions. If we speak something in full accordance with His Word and the best supporting evidence He has revealed, then He wants us to be confident that He will use it for Kingdom work, as well as for our personal benefit.

> For God gave us a spirit not of fear but of power and love and self-control. (2 Timothy 1:7, ESV)

When we walk in the power of the Holy Spirit, He gives us sound wisdom. He is with us and will never forsake us.

I have counsel and sound wisdom; I have insight; I have strength. (Proverbs 8:14, ESV)

If any of you lacks wisdom, you should ask God, who gives generously to all without finding fault, and it will be given to you. (James 1:5, ESV)

Biblical principles are for our protection. They're there to guide us and take us through to the end. If you're walking according to God's principles, He will get you to where you want to go, and ultimately it will be to the new heavens and the new earth, the *New Jerusalem*. God will enable you to achieve the things in life that He wants you to achieve, but it has to be done His way. That's the way God operates.

THE BIG FIVE

There are certain requirements if you're going to live by biblical principles. In my opinion, the "Big Five" are the following:

1. **Live for the cause that's greater than yourself.** It's all about Yeshua. It's not about us. We are small people, and He's a big God. Live for Yeshua and the Kingdom of God. He will use you, equip you, anoint you, and bless you.

In so doing, strive to be a light in this dark world and a witness to who Yeshua is in your life. You can't be a light if you're walking in the latest *political correctness* of this world system, a system controlled by the Chaldean spirit. It can only happen if you're walking in *biblical principles*. The only way to walk in biblical principles is to be grounded in the truth of the Word of God and possess a real, born-again connection to the Holy Spirit.

They triumphed over [Satan] by the blood of the Lamb and by the word of their testimony; they did not love their lives so much as to shrink from death. (Revelation 12:11, ESV)

2. **Be very clear about what you believe.** If you're a child of the living God, certain matters are simply nonnegotiable. For example, if you're considering living with someone outside of marriage, aborting a child, or having an affair, there are clear biblical principles that cover those issues. There's no need to even pray about those matters! You already know the answer to how God sees them!

If you get an offer for something that you know is ungodly, but you start considering it, you're on the path to making a terribly wrong decision. You're on a path to destruction. You're being swayed by the Chaldean spirits. They are trying to possess what is not theirs—*your life.* God's rock-solid principles don't move. Stand firm.

3. **Expect spiritual warfare.** If you're walking in His Word, the enemy will not like it and will oppose you. He'll try to take you out of God's direction, provision, and blessing. You'll have conflict in this world because there are lost or biblically immature people who don't like the firm biblical principles. Some won't want to be part of your life anymore because they don't like the way you're living. Believe me, I know.

You have to make a decision to follow Yeshua and leave all the consequences to God—even if following Him doesn't appear to be the logical, worldly path. Suit up in God's armor—not the armor of this world, but the supernatural armor God has clearly revealed to us. That's our power. The world doesn't understand it, but once you consistently walk in that power, you'll be overwhelmed by its effectiveness. The Holy Spirit doesn't always give you *logical,* but He always gives you *supernatural...* He gives you *biblical.* Live in it...daily.

4. **Don't be anxiety-ridden about life.** It is true—our world is going crazy, just like the Bible said it would. We are nearing the end of all things and the beginning of Yeshua's righteous rule and reign. Without setting any dates—something I never do—I *can* say that it won't be much longer before Jesus sets His feet, once again, on the Mount of Olives. On that day, the new Kingdom reign and the restoration of all things will begin. This is the most prophetic time the world has ever seen, and we are living

right in the midst of it. We have been raised up for "such a time as this." Embrace *your time to shine*…for Yeshua.

5. **Keep your eyes on Jesus.** Keep moving forward, in Him. Make your decisions based upon the Word of God, no matter how loudly the Chaldean spirits of this fallen world system scream at you to do otherwise. They are only doing the bidding of Satan, the great "masquerader." You are doing the bidding of the King of Kings.

> **Let us fix our eyes on Jesus**, the author and perfecter of our faith, who for the joy set before him **endured the cross, scorning its shame**, and sat down at the right hand of the throne of God. **Consider him who endured such opposition from sinful men**, so that you will **not grow weary and lose heart**. (Hebrews 12:2–3; emphasis added)

Many times we don't see—until we are far in the future, looking back—that the biblically correct decisions we made "way back when" were not only wise, but were supernatural life-changers as well. Life simply has to be carried out through a daily walk of faith, by the power of the Holy Spirit.

> For I have given you an example, that you also should do just as I have done to you. (John 13:15, ESV)

Yeshua set an example for us to know how to live. If you're going to live by biblical principles, you have to believe in the absolute sovereignty of God; He is in control of everything. You must believe that He's big enough, powerful enough, and loving enough, and is present with you in every step of life, so you don't have to worry about what's ahead.

He's on it. God's got this. His promises to you were sealed at the cross and punctuated by the empty tomb.

66

WALKING IN GOD'S FAVOR

Before I was a believer in Yeshua,
I prayed religiously every day as an Orthodox Jew—
but it was just mumbled words.

The Bible says if we trust in God in all situations, the favor of God is upon us. And who doesn't want *the favor* of the Almighty God and Creator of the Universe upon them?

> Let not steadfast love and faithfulness forsake you; **bind them** around your neck; **write them** on the tablet of your heart. **So you will find favor and good success in the sight of God and man.** (Proverbs 3:3–4; emphasis added)

Knowing we're walking in the favor of God in these profoundly prophetic times is critical. These days are so fraught with dangers, uncertainties, deception, and destruction that we need, *as never before,* to know we're safe in His special care and protection.

ESTHER

God knew we would need examples of people who walked before us in His will to show us the way. One such example is that of Queen Esther.

> Then Queen Esther answered, "If **I have found favor in your sight,** O king, and if it please the king, let my life be granted me for my wish, and my people for my request. (Esther 7:3; emphasis added)

Esther went to the king, who was a nonbeliever, and because the favor of God was upon her, she received the earthly king's favor. Using this as an example, we can see that if we trust God, we can expect Him to go before us and to overshadow us with His protection. The question is always, "Am I walking in God's favor?" The answer must be "yes" if we are trusting Him to go before us.

NOAH

Noah is another example of someone who found favor in the eyes of God.

> So the Lord said, "I will blot out man whom I have created from the face of the land, man and animals and creeping things and birds of the heavens, for I am sorry that I have made them." **But Noah found favor in the eyes of the Lord.** (Genesis 6:7–8, ESV; emphasis added)

If you're walking in obedience, God will give you favor in every area of your life.

> My sheep hear my voice, and I know them, and they follow me. (John 10:27, ESV)

If you're listening to God, His favor is upon you. Scripture says Noah not only listened to God, but He trusted God. It's an important key. If we want to walk in the favor of God, then we have to put our full trust in Him and obey Him.

> Jesus said to them, "Not everyone who says to me, 'Lord, Lord,' will enter the kingdom of heaven, but only the one who does the will of my Father who is in heaven." (Matthew 7:21, ESV)

> If you love me, keep my commands. (John 14:15, ESV)

> Whoever claims to live in him must live as Jesus did. (1 John 2:6, ESV)

These verses are not about keeping or losing salvation. They're about living within *God's favor*—precisely because we *are* saved, and He wants to bless us as we serve Him.

Are you listening to God? Are you trusting Him? Are you doing His will? Are you abiding in His Word? Are you studying it out to its end... in context?

It is crucial to know (Hebrew: *yada*) God's Word intimately. Study it, research it, read it, walk in it, dig into it over and over again, and don't be ashamed to speak its truth. Then, as you pray, you can claim those truths found in God's Word and take Him at His Word, walking in it by faith. In this way, you will have the *favor of God* upon you at all times.

What is the favor of God? It is His acceptance and approval, His support, His divine energy, His provision, and His joy.

> Trust in the Lord with all your heart, and do not lean on your own understanding. In all your ways acknowledge him, and he will make straight your paths. Be not wise in your own eyes; fear the Lord, and turn away from evil. (Proverbs 3:5–7, ESV)

This is the way Noah lived. It's the way Lot lived. Both lived in the midst of some of the most horrific settings of life the world has ever known. God brought his destroying wrath on those worlds, even though His own dear servants were living in the midst of those days. Yet, because they were faithful, because they were living under God's favor, He protected them. He delivered them out of the wrath He poured out on the unbelieving world.

With those facts in mind, consider the following:

Jesus said to them, **"Just as it was in the days of Noah, so also will it be in the days of the Son of Man.** People were eating, drinking, marrying and being given in marriage up to the day Noah entered the ark. Then the flood came and destroyed them all. **It was the same in the days of Lot.** People were eating and drinking, buying and selling, planting and building. But the day Lot left Sodom, fire and sulfur rained down from heaven and destroyed them all. **It will be just like this on the day the Son of Man is revealed."** (Luke 17:26–30; see also Matthew 24:37–39; emphasis added)

By faith Noah, when warned about things not yet seen, in holy fear built an ark to save his family. By his faith he condemned the world and became heir of the righteousness that is in keeping with faith. (Hebrews 11:7)

If God did not spare the ancient world when he brought the flood on its ungodly people, **but protected Noah, a preacher of righteousness,** and seven others; if he condemned the cities of Sodom and Gomorrah by burning them to ashes, and made them an example of what is going to happen to the ungodly;

And if **he rescued Lot, a righteous man,** who was distressed by the depraved conduct of the lawless (for that righteous man, living among them day after day, was tormented in his righteous soul by the lawless deeds he saw and heard)—if this is so, then

the Lord knows how to rescue the godly from trials and to hold the unrighteous for punishment on the day of judgment. (2 Peter 2:5–9; emphasis added)

These are just a few of many similar passages demonstrating why we should strive to sincerely live under the favor of God.

The Bible is not a restaurant; we can't choose a word here and a word there like at an all-you-can-eat buffet. We have to be grounded in the Word according to its context. If we are, we will walk in God's favor and then, sometimes, even the favor of nonbelievers will fall on us. Our responsibility as ambassadors for the Kingdom of Yeshua is to listen to God and trust Him.

The Bible says that if what we pray for is in the will of God, He will answer our prayers. Before I was a believer in Yeshua, I prayed religiously every day as an Orthodox Jew—but it was just mumbled words, rote and memorized. None of it was in the will of Yahweh. God is not looking for us to practice mere religion; He's looking for a sincerely desired and genuine relationship. That is *what* and *who* He favors.

How were you saved? By trusting that God would do what He said He would do. All you did was confess your sins and repent, believing that He died in your place, rose again, and gave you the Holy Spirit to help you until He returns. It was all about *faith*, taking God at His Word. That's how we must endeavor to pray—with faith and expectation that God will do what He says He will do, in spite of our circumstances.

Noah found favor by listening to God and trusting Him enough to move forward, even when things didn't appear to make sense. Whatever God told him to do, he did in faith. He actually built a ship in his own backyard because God told him to do so. Since he acted in faith—*he took God at His Word*—Noah found favor in the eyes of God.

What is your testimony? Do the people around you see you as a person who walks with God? Do they describe you that way to others? Is the light of Yeshua Jesus shining through you in every aspect of your interactions and responses to life? Are you listening to and obeying God even when you don't completely understand what the outcome will be—like Noah, Lot, and Esther?

When people see you walking in God's favor, they'll ask what's different, and doors will open for you to share His love.

> But in your hearts revere Christ as Lord. Always be prepared to give an answer to everyone who asks you to give the reason for the hope that you have. But do this with gentleness and respect. (1 Peter 3:15)

God wants to give you favor so you can be a powerful and unswerving ambassador for His Kingdom.

67

WHAT DOES IT MATTER?

*This blessing was given so God's people might know
and hear the voice and heart of God Himself.*

Our journey has been about sharpening our spiritual archeological skills. Hopefully, I've been able to encourage you to dig, and then dig even deeper. I pray you will do this for the rest of your own personal *journey to Zion*, always asking the hard questions, searching out the answers in their proper context, and never giving up your pursuit of biblical truth.

From the beginning words of the first verse of Genesis all the way to Revelation's very end, the soon-coming reign of Jesus Christ is unfolded before us, especially if we know what we are looking for. It is the declaration of God that, in the culmination of all things, Satan loses and God's blood-bought children win. This is what Satan is desperately trying to hide from us and the world.

In the midst of life's daily routine—fooling even Satan himself—*God with us* eased quietly upon the scene of His own creation, then fulfilled every jot and tittle of the ancient biblical prophecies of His coming and of the redemption of His children. As you've now seen, from His arrival in a very special birthing stall to the winding down of His earthly ministry on Golgotha's cross—every bit of it, and everything in between—was always centered on Migdal Eder and the Mount of Olives.

The significance of these two bombshells seems to have largely been hidden from the eyes of God's children for several thousand years. But now we know why. And now we know the truth. More importantly, we know why these truths *matter.* And you are now equipped to share these life-altering truths with others, especially the Jewish people the Lord might put in your path.

Let me encourage you to fervently pray for the Jewish people of Israel and everywhere else around the world. You are promised all manner of special blessings in God's Word when your heart is directed toward taking the Word of God to Israel and reaching out to the Jews of the world with the gospel of Yeshua. And, if you think of it, from time to time, please pray for me, as we are still operating and ministering in the very heart and heat of that great spiritual battle, right in the middle of the planet's spiritual ground zero. We are just small people who serve an unfathomably big God. Pray that He keeps us in His will and in the center of His favor and blessing, guiding our footsteps day by day.

In the meantime, *the spirit of the Chaldeans* runs rampant throughout Israel, the world at large, and right in the midst of much of today's institutional church. It will continue to do so right up to the end. At least you now know exactly what that spirit is, how it operates, and what it "looks" like in Israel, as well as in the church. You are way ahead of the game. You are being equipped to help the rest of the church get caught up to Satan's last-days ploys; you're putting on the *armor of God.*

Pray that the Lord of Heaven will continue to empower our ministry so that *together* we can pull those demonic blinders off unbelievers everywhere, Jew or Gentile, as we strive to help build up the true Temple of God, the *one new man.*

The god of this age has blinded the minds of unbelievers, so that they cannot see the light of the gospel that displays the glory of Christ, who is the image of God. (2 Corinthians 4:4)

My people are destroyed for lack of knowledge. Because you have rejected knowledge, I also will reject you from being priest for Me; because you have forgotten the law of your God, I also will forget your children. (Hosea 4:6, NKJV)

The Spirit clearly says that in later times some will abandon the faith and follow deceiving spirits and things taught by demons. (1 Timothy 4:1)

Before we part company, please allow me to pray an especially holy blessing over you in these last few moments. The words I wish to speak over you come from God's Word, in the sixth chapter of the book of Numbers. These are not just "any" words. The words of this prayer, "known as the Aaronic blessing" are infused with Holy Spirit power.[309]

This prayer was given by Yahweh to the first high priest, Aaron. In Leviticus 9:22, it is recorded that Aaron blessed the people, first from the brazen altar of sacrifice, and afterwards when the priests came out of the Tabernacle. This blessing was given so that the Lord's people might know the voice and heart of God Himself. Through it, they would understand the depths of the supreme love and mercy that He was directing their way. It was as if God Himself had laid His hands upon their heads and spoke over them.

Please receive this blessing upon yourself now—in that same holy way in which it was first intended:

The LORD bless you and keep you, The LORD make his face to shine upon you and be gracious to you; The LORD lift up his countenance upon you and give you peace. *Amen.*

My dear fellow pilgrim and spiritual archeologist, thank you for taking this journey with me. If I don't get to personally meet you in this life, I'll look forward to seeing you one day soon—in the light of His glory... in Yeshua's Zion.

ABOUT THE AUTHOR

Messianic Rabbi Zev Porat was born and raised in Israel in a deeply devout Jewish Orthodox family and tradition. His journey from orthodoxy to faith in *Yeshua Ha Mashiach* is a lengthy saga of profound supernatural interventions and amazing revelations from Heaven's throne, as greatly expanded upon within the pages of this book.

Zev, and his wife Lian, currently reside in Tel Aviv, Israel.

To discover more about Zev's life and global ministry,
visit his website at:
www.messiahofisraelministries.com.

NOTES

1. The story of the Muslim imam is a prominent feature in the book that I and Carl Gallups coauthored: *The Rabbi, The Secret Message, and the Identity of Messiah* (Crane, MO: Defender Publishing, 2007). The rabbis he's led to Yeshua are written about and photographically documented at the website, www.messiahofisraelministries.com.

2. *Yeshua.* Hebrew word for Jesus.

3. Knesset and Likud Party. The Knesset is the unicameral legislature of Israel. The Likud Party, officially known as Likud—National Liberal Movement—is the major center-right to right-wing political party in Israel founded by Ariel Sharon.

4. Although I use the entirety of almost all these passages, several portions of each are reproduced here:

Isaiah 53:5: "But he was pierced for our transgressions, he was crushed for our iniquities; the punishment that brought us peace was on him, and by his wounds we are healed."

Isaiah 9:6: "For to us a child is born, to us a son is given, and the government will be on his shoulders. And he will be called Wonderful Counselor, Mighty God, Everlasting Father, Prince of Peace."

Micah 5:2: "But you, Bethlehem Ephrathah, Though you are little among the thousands of Judah, Yet out of you shall come forth to Me The One to be Ruler in Israel, Whose goings forth are from of old, From everlasting." (NKJ)

Psalm 2:10–12: "Therefore, you kings, be wise; be warned, you rulers of the earth. Serve the Lord with fear and celebrate his rule with trembling. Kiss his son, or he will be angry and your way will lead to your destruction, for his wrath can flare up in a moment. Blessed are all who take refuge in him."

Psalm 110:1: "The Lord says to my lord: 'Sit at my right hand until I make your enemies a footstool for your feet.'"

Psalm 22:16–18: "Dogs surround me, a pack of villains encircles me; they pierce my hands and my feet. All my bones are on display; people stare and gloat over me. They divide my clothes among them and cast lots for my garment."

Isaiah 7:14: "Therefore the Lord himself will give you a sign: The virgin will conceive and give birth to a son, and will call him Immanuel."

5. *Yeshu.* In Hebrew, this is a derogatory name for Yeshua. It is a play on words that represents a Hebrew acronym that declares, "Let his name forever be cursed."

6. *Yad L'Ac*him (Hebrew: "hand for brothers") is an Orthodox Jewish organization operating in Israel that focuses on outreach, counter-missionary work (anti-Christian at its core), and opposition to interfaith marriage.

7. Zev Porat. "Zev Porat Testimony / Messiah of Israel Ministries." Accessed 9/5/20. https://www.messiahofisraelministries. org/zev-porat-testimony.

8. *Aliyah.* Hebrew word for a Jewish person moving to Israel to become a legal Israeli citizen.

9. *HELPS Word-studies:* 4461 rhabbí—a rabbi; a teacher-scholar recognized by the Jewish public for accumulating a great number of Bible facts, i.e. respected for his accumulation of knowledge. "Rabbi." **Explained by Jesus himself as** *(1320 /didáskalos),* **"teacher"** *(Mt 23:8),* Used by the Jews in addressing their teachers. (Emphasis added) NT #4461. "Rhabbi," https://biblehub.com/greek/4461.htm.

10. *Meyer's New Testament Commentary:* The prohibitions, Matthew 23:8 ff., have reference to the **hierarchical** meaning and usage which were **at that time associated** with the titles in question. The teacher's titles in themselves **are as legitimate and necessary** as his functions; but **the hierarchy, in the form which it assumed…was contrary to the spirit and mind of Jesus.** (Emphasis added). https://biblehub.com/commentaries/matthew/23-8.htm.

Benson Commentary: The Jewish [expositors] were called rabbis, fathers, and masters, by their…disciples, whom **they required both to believe implicitly what they affirmed, without asking** any further reason, and **to obey unreservedly** what they enjoined, **without seeking for any further authority.** The things forbidden here are, 1st, **a vain-glorious affectation of such titles** as these, **the ambitious seeking of them,** and **glorying in them.** (Emphasis added). https://biblehub.com/commentaries/matthew/23-8.htm.

Expositor's Greek Testament: **Do not seek** [for the purpose of prominence over others] **to be called** [rabbi], **if others call you this** it will **not be your fault.** (Emphasis added). https://biblehub.com/commentaries/matthew/23-8.htm. *Pulpit Commentary:* After stating the customs of the Pharisees, Christ proceeds to give his own disciples **a lesson in humility.**... They are **not to be eager** for such distinctions, indicative of spiritual superiority. The prohibition must be understood in the spirit, and not in the letter (comp. 1 Corinthians 11:1; 1 Timothy 1:2). Our **Lord does not forbid respect** for teachers or different grades in his Church (see 1 Corinthians 12:28; Ephesians 4:11-13); **that which he censures is the inordinate grasping at such personal distinctions, the greedy ambition** which loves the empty title, and **takes any means** to obtain it. (Emphasis added). https://biblehub.com/commentaries/matthew/23-8.htm.

11. Gallups and Porat, *Rabbi, the Secret Message and the Identity of Messiah.*

12. For the only two books in the world (as of this writing) published by major Christian publishers on the life, death, and Messiah note of Rabbi Kaduri, see: Gallups and Porat, *The Rabbi, the Secret Message, and the Identity of Messiah*; and Gallups, *The Rabbi Who Found Messiah* (Washington, DC: WND Books, 2014).

13. Joffe, Lawrence. "Rabbi Yitzhak Kaduri: Mercurial Jewish Mystic Who Threw His Weight behind Rightwing Israeli Politicians," UK Guardian, 1/30/06. https://www.theguardian.com/news/2006/jan/31/guardianobituaries. israel.

"Shas politicians exploited his reputation, while others literally cashed in on his name. Kaduri was once delivered by helicopter to bless a sausage factory in a development town. Aparatchiks then collected monetary pledges from towns-folk who believed they could purchase heaven's favour via this holy conduit."

14. See note 10, Gallups and Porat.

15. Lawrence Joffe. "Rabbi Yitzhak Kaduri," *The Guardian*, 1/30/06. Accessed 9/ 30/20. https://www.theguardian.com/ news/2006/jan/31/guardianobituar-ies.israel.

16. This entire section was taken from a book Gallups and Porat, *The Rabbi, the Secret Message and the Identity of Messiah.*

17. Ibid.

18. Ibid.

19. Jewish Kabbalists originally developed their own transmission of sacred

texts within the realm of Jewish tradition, and often use classical Jewish Scriptures to explain and demonstrate its mystical teachings. These teachings are held by followers in Judaism to define the inner meaning of both the Hebrew Bible and traditional rabbinic literature and their formerly concealed transmitted dimension, as well as to explain the significance of Jewish religious observances. One of the fundamental Kabbalistic texts, the Zohar, was first published in the thirteenth century, and the almost universal form adhered to in modern Judaism is Lurianic Kabbalah.
See: Wikipedia contributors. "Kabbalah," Wikipedia, Free Encyclopedia. Accessed 11/5/20. https://en.wikipedia.org/w/index.php?title=Kabbalah&oldid=986868235.

20. The details of that story are recounted in Gallups and Porat, *The Rabbi, The Secret Message, and the Identity of Messiah.*

21. See note 10, Gallups and Porat.

22. Zionism. "A worldwide Jewish movement that resulted in the establishment and development of the state of Israel and that now supports the state of Israel as a Jewish homeland." From Dictionary.com. https://www.dictionary.com/browse/zionist.

23. Your Dictionary. "ZION—word meaning," yourdictionary.com. Accessed 2/25/21. https://www.yourdictionary.com/zion.

24. Watts, Isaac. "We're Marching to Zion," Library.timelesstruths. Accessed 1/21/21. https://library.timelesstruths.org/music/Were_Marching_to_Zion.

25. The editors of *Encyclopaedia Britannica.* "Zion," *Encyclopaedia Britannica.* Accessed 2/16/21. https://www.britannica.com/place/Zion-hill-Jerusalem.

26. *Yeshua Ha Mashiach.* Hebrew for "Jesus the Messiah."

27. Romans 11:24. *Pulpit Commentary*, Biblehub.com. https://biblehub.com/commentaries/romans/11-24.htm.

28. Also known as "replacement theology," or "supersessionism." See https://en.wikipedia.org/wiki/Supersessionism.

29. Romans 11:26. *Barnes' Notes on the Bible*, Biblehub.com. https://biblehub.com/commentaries/romans/11-26.htm.

30. Romans 11:26. *Meyer's New Testament Commentary*, Biblehub.com. https://biblehub.com/commentaries/romans/11-26.htm.

31. See Romans 3:1–2.

32. Let me emphasize: I am not attempting to belittle individual Catholic

people or clergy who sincerely love the Lord Jesus Christ and are born again by believing upon His name alone for their salvation. And, as stated in the text to which this footnote applies, both Catholics and Protestants have erected tourist traps in Israel that are not true to scriptural locations or teachings. I will clearly prove this before this book comes to an end. You'll see the evidence of my contentions with your own eyes. But, I am adamant about the fact that the institutionalized Roman Catholic system is largely responsible for the massive confusion among the Jewish people concerning the genuine gospel of Jesus Christ. And for this reason, the Catholic Church has been a huge hindrance to the last-days work of bringing Jews to Christ, especially in Israel. Again, I have lived in Israel all of my life. I know firsthand of the truth of this matter.

33. Jewish Virtual Library, "Christian-Jewish Relations: The Inquisition." Accessed 1/3/21. https://www.jewishvirtuallibrary.org/the-inquisition.

34. The *Chaldean spirit* is a demonic principality that expresses itself through sorcery, witchcraft, astrology, and the like. Its name flows from a certain historical people group, synonymous with Babylon. That spirit is spoken of throughout the New Testament and is especially emphasized in Revelation as the driving force of evil throughout the planet. It is the spirit of Babylon (Chaldean spirit) against which the final wrath and judgment of God is coming upon the planet. We will undertake an even deeper look at this principality, and those stated truths, in subsequent chapters.

35. Jewish Encyclopedia. "Demonology" (Demons in the Bible). Accessed 12/2/20. http://www.jewishencyclopedia.com/articles/5085-demonology.

36. *The Theosophal Glossary:* **Chaldeans, or Kasdim.** At first a tribe, then a caste of learned Kabbalists. They were the savants, the magians of Babylonia, astrologers and diviners. H. P. Blavatsky, The Theosophal Glossary. https://library.indstate.edu/about/units/rbsc/cordell/PDFs/blavatsky_h_1892x_theosophical.pdf. (p. 75).

Also see: R Campbell Thompson. *The Devils and Evil Spirits of Babylonia: Being Babylonian [Chaldean] and Assyrian Incantations Against the Demons, Ghouls, Vampires, Hobgoblins, Ghosts, and Kindred Evil Spirits, Which Attack Mankind*, Vol. 1 "Evil Spirits." (London: Luzac, 1903). https://publicdomainreview.org/collection/spells-against-the-evil-spirits-of-babylonia-1903.

37. For an excellent scholarly resource and in-depth biblical study on the Garden's location as being within the area of Jerusalem, see: Gallups, Carl. *Gods of*

Ground Zero: The Truth of Eden's Iniquity, (Crane, MO: Defender Publishing, 2018). (I served as a research assistant to the author of this book).

38. A few examples describing these power structures are found in Daniel 10, Romans 8:38, Ephesians 3:10, Colossians 1:16, and Colossians 2:15.

39. I recommend two scholarly studies (supported by renowned scientific truths and discoveries) of the Bible's clear teaching about dimensional realms of reality, the physical entities that occupy those realms, portals between those dimensions, and even the science and biblical examples of "time travel." See: Gallups, Carl. *Gods of the Final Kingdom* (Crane, MO: Defender Publishing, 2018.), and Heiser, Michael S. *The Unseen Realm: Recovering the Supernatural Worldview of the Bible* (Lexham Press, 2015).

40. While there are certainly varying theological opinions concerning this matter, and I'm aware that this belief is controversial in some circles of theology, I am of the opinion that the Scriptures most closely present the scenario I have described here. This, after all, appears to be exactly what Paul was speaking of in Ephesians 6 when he spoke of the various dark authorities that operate within certain "principalities" and in the halls of the unseen realms. Paul warns the believer that we must constantly be "suited up" for those occasions when we might come into contact with, or come under the potential influence of, those demonic forces. This same principle applies to what Daniel encountered in Daniel 10. This is when the angel revealed to the prophet the realities of the spiritual forces with which that angelic being had engaged in very real battle. These demonic battles occurred within the national domains and principalities of the Persian and Greek empires of Daniel's day.

41. Matthew 12:43. *Barnes' Notes on the Bible*, Biblehub.com. https://biblehub.com/commentaries/matthew/12-43.htm.

42. Matthew 12:43. *Pulpit Commentary*, Biblehub.com. https://biblehub.com/commentaries/matthew/12-43.htm.

43. The *institutional church* is different than the true body of born-again, blood-bought, Spirit-filled believers found throughout the world—even among the various denominations of Christianity. The merely institutional church is sometimes referred to by scholars as the "visible" church, whereas the "invisible" church is made up of those who have been sealed by the Holy Spirit unto the day of salvation (Ephesians 1:13–14).

44. Babylonia is sometimes called "Shinar" or the "land of Babylon," but usually it is called the "land of the Chaldeans." Its inhabitants are a few times referred to as "Babylonians," but typically as Chaldeans.
The name "Shinar" occurs eight times in the Hebrew Bible, in which it refers to Babylonia. "Shinar" was the Hebrew name of a land that included both Babylon and Erech—i.e., both northern and southern Babylonia. See: Emil G. Hirsch, George A. Barton., "Shinar," *Jewish Encyclopedia*, accessed 12/27/20, http://www.jewishencyclopedia.com/articles/13582-shinar.
45. Genesis 2:10–14 lists four rivers in association with **the Garden of Eden:** Pishon, Gihon, Hiddekel (the Tigris), and Phirat (the Euphrates). These lands lie north of Elam, immediately to the east of **ancient Babylon, which does lie within the region being described.** (Emphasis added)
See: Speiser, E.A. (1994). "The Rivers of Paradise." In Tsumura, D. T.; Hess, R. S. (eds.). *I Studied Inscriptions from Before the Flood.* Eisenbrauns. https://www.google.com/books/edition/I_Studied_Inscriptions_from_Before_the_F/g5MGVP6gAPkC?hl=en&gbpv=1&bsq=Speiser,+%22The+Rivers+of+Paradise%22+Cush&pg=PA38&printsec=frontcover.
46. See: Gallups, *Gods of Ground Zero.*.
47. *Jamieson-Fausset-Brown Bible Commentary:* **Land of Shinar**—The fertile valley **watered by the Euphrates and Tigris** was chosen as the center of their union and the seat of their power. (Emphasis added).
Pulpit Commentary: **Babylonia** (cf. Genesis 10:10). The derivation of the term is unknown, though it probably meant **the land of the two rivers.** Its absence from ancient monuments (Rawlinson) suggests that it was **the Jewish name for Chaldaea.** (Emphasis added). See: Genesis 11:2, "Commentaries," Biblehub.com, https://biblehub.com/commentaries/genesis/11-2.htm.
48. Driscoll, Mark. "What Is the Spirit of Babylon?" Realfaith.com. Accessed 12/ 22/20. https://realfaith.com/daily-devotions/what-is-the-spirit-of-babylon.
49. Also see: R Campbell Thompson. *The Devils and Evil Spirits of Babylonia: Being Babylonian and Assyrian Incantations Against the Demons, Ghouls, Vampires, Hobgoblins, Ghosts, and Kindred Evil Spirits, Which Attack Mankind,* Vol. 1 "Evil Spirits." (London: Luzac, 1903). https://publicdomainreview.org/collection/spells-against-the-evil-spirits-of-babylonia-1903.
Isaiah 23:13. *Pulpit Commentary*, Biblehub.com. https://biblehub.com/commentaries/isaiah/23-13.htm.

50. Isaiah 23:13. *Barnes' Notes on the Bible*, Biblehub.com. https://biblehub.com/commentaries/isaiah/23-13.htm.

51. Chaldean. כַּשְׂדָּי adj. 1 Chaldean. 2 astrologer. [From כַּשְׂדִּים (= Chaldeans), which is related to Akka. mat Chaldu, dissimilated from mat Kashdu (= land of the Chaldeans).... According to others Akka. Kashdu and Heb. כַּשְׂדִּים lit. mean "conquerors," and are connected with Akka. kashādu (= to conquer).] כִּשּׁוּף m.n. PBH magic, sorcery, witchcraft. [Verbal n. of כִּשֵּׁף. See כשׁף.]. See: Klein Dictionary, כִּשָּׁלוֹן. "Chaldean," Sefaria, accessed 12/22/20, https://www.sefaria.org/Klein_Dictionary%2C_%D7%9B%D6%B7%D6%BC%D7%A9%D6%B0%D7%82%D7%93%D6%B4%D6%BC%D7%99?lang=bi.

52. Revelation 11:8. *Meyer's New Testament Commentary*, Biblehub.com. https://biblehub.com/commentaries/revelation/11-8.htm.

53. Revelation 11:8. *Barnes' Notes on the Bible*, Biblehub.com. https://biblehub.com/commentaries/revelation/11-8.htm.

54. Revelation 11:8. *Jamieson-Fausset-Brown Bible Commentary*, Biblehub.com. https://biblehub.com/commentaries/revelation/11-8.htm.

55. N.T. #169. (GK. *Akathartos*) Impure spirit: *Strong's Exhaustive Concordance* | foul, unclean. From *a* (as a negative particle) and a presumed derivative of kathairo (meaning cleansed); impure (ceremonially, morally [lewd] or specially, [demonic])—foul, unclean. See: https://biblehub.com/greek/169.htm.

56. Mark Driscoll is the pastor of Trinity Church in Scottsdale, Arizona. He holds a master's degree in exegetical theology from Western Seminary in Portland, Oregon. Driscoll has debated Deepak Chopra on one of his multiple appearances on ABC's *Nightline*; discussed marriage with Barbara Walters on *The View*; bantered with the hosts at *Fox and Friends*; cohosted *Loveline* with Dr. Drew; and argued for the truth of God's Word on separate occasions with Piers Morgan and D. L. Hughley on CNN. See: https://realfaith.com/about.

57. Ibid. Driscoll, "What Is the Spirit of Babylon?"

58. Robert Morris is the founding senior pastor of Gateway Church, a multicampus megachurch with an estimated weekly attendance of thirty-six thousand as of 2016, and one of the largest churches in the United States. It is located in the Dallas-Fort Worth Metroplex. Morris is featured on the weekly television program *The Blessed Life* and is the bestselling author of twelve books, including *The Blessed Life*, *From Dream to Destiny*, *The God I Never Knew*, and *The Blessed Church*.

59. Morris, Robert. *Truly Free: Breaking the Snares That So Easily Entangle (Beware the Chaldeans)*, (Nashville: W Publishing Group, Imprint of Thomas Nelson, 2015) p. 50. https://www.google.com/books/edition/Truly_Free/8Re MBQAAQBAJ?hl=en&gbpv=1&dq=Chaldeans:+as+it+were+demons.+The+r oot+word+means+to+lay+waste+or+to+destroy.+And+the+actual+word+means +wanderers.&pg=PA50&printsec=frontcover.

60. "[The Lord says] **I will** turn you around, **put hooks in your jaws** and **bring you out with your whole army**—your horses, your horsemen fully armed, **and a great horde** with large and small shields, all of them brandishing their swords." (Ezekiel 38:4; emphasis added)

61. Sanctification is the continual process of growing in the Lord and in the pure knowledge of His Word. This work is done in and through the Holy Spirit of God's leadership and guidance, and through the development of our own spirit of humility and teachability concerning the ways of the Lord.

62. In the midst of my personal quest, I wanted to know more about the Roman Catholic claim on these sites in Jerusalem and all around Israel. I was angry because these sites have turned so many Jews totally away from the gospel. I had to have a deeper understanding. So…I went to the Vatican to see for myself. I had more *spiritual archeology* to do.

Once inside St. Peter's Basilica, I looked up at all the statues and the startling intensity of patterns and artwork, and immediately I was overcome with an extremely deep feeling of *spiritual warning*. The spirit of the place was discernible. And, to me, it was not holy at all. As a result, I will never step foot in the Vatican again.

63. Loyola Press. "Stations of the Cross." Accessed 12/12/20. https://www.loyolapress.com/catholic-resources/liturgical-year/lent/stations-of-the-cross/stations-of-the-cross.

64. Even *Haaretz*, a mainstream Orthodox Israeli publication, states the following about the "Christianized" Via Dolorosa: Via Dolorosa—No way. The "Way of the Suffering" comprises 14 stations supposedly tracking the route taken by Jesus on Good Friday. But there's a problem: the path in fact evolved first in European cathedrals and church courtyards and was only subsequently transposed to Jerusalem, well after the Crusader period. See: Haaretz. "Jesus Sites in Jerusalem: Are They Real?" Haaretz. Accessed 1/11/21. https://www.haaretz.com/archaeology/.premium.

MAGAZINE-jesus-sites-in-jerusalem-are-they-real-1.5477044.

65. Codina, Victor, S. J. "Why Do Some Catholics Oppose Pope Francis?" *America Magazine*, 9/12/19. https://www.americamagazine.org/faith/2019/09/12/why-do-some-catholics-oppose-pope-francis.

66. Wamsley, Laurel. "Vatican OKs Receiving COVID-19 Vaccines, Even If Research Involved Fetal Tissue," NPR, 12/21/20. https://www.npr.org/sections/coronavirus-live-updates/2020/12/21/948806643/vatican-oks-receiving-covid-19-vaccines-even-if-research-involved-fetal-tissue.

67. Pope Francis and the Vatican. "In New Film, Pope Francis Affirms Gay People 'Are Children of God,' Expresses Support for Legalizing Civil Unions," 10/21/20, https://thecatholicsun.com/in-new-film-pope-francis-affirms-gay-people-are-children-of-god-expresses-support-for-legalizing-civil-unions.

68. See: Matthew 10:15, 11:23–24; Luke 10:12, 17:29; Romans 9:29; 2 Peter 2:6; Jude 7; and Revelation 11:8.

69. *Jamieson-Fausset-Brown Bible Commentary:* **The great city**, wherein all the martyrdoms of saints have taken place. **Babylon** marks its idolatry, **Egypt its tyranny, Sodom** its desperate corruption, **Jerusalem** its pretensions to sanctity on the ground of spiritual privileges, while all the while it is the murderer of Christ in the person of His members. **All which is true of Rome.** (Emphasis added) https://biblehub.com/commentaries/revelation/11-8.htm.

Matthew Poole's Commentary: Most judicious interpreters, by **the great city here, understand Rome,** which is seven or eight times (under the name of Babylon) so called in this book, Revelation 14:8 Revelation 16:19 18:10, 16,18,19,21. (Emphasis added) https://biblehub.com/commentaries/revelation/11-8.htm.

Pulpit Commentary: "**The great city**" **is referred to in Revelation** 16:19; Revelation 17:18; Revelation 18:10–19 (**Babylon-Rome**). Its signification is always the same, viz. the type of what is ungodly and of the world, and it is always consigned to punishment. (Emphasis added, parenthesis in original). https://biblehub.com/commentaries/revelation/11-8.htm.

70. By Philip Pullella, Ahmed Eljechtimi. "Conversion Is Not Your Mission, Pope Tells Catholics in Morocco," Reuters, 3/31/2019. https://www.reuters.com/article/us-pope-morocco/conversion-is-not-your-mission-pope-tells-catholics-in-morocco-idUSKCN1RC0EI.

71. Universalism. The belief that all humankind will eventually be saved. See:

"Universalism," Merriam-Webster Dictionary. https://www.merriam-webster. com/dictionary/universalism.

72. Day, Michael. "Pope Francis Assures Atheists: You Don't Have to Believe in God to Go to Heaven," Independent UK, 10/5/15. https://www.independent. co.uk/news/world/europe/pope-francis-assures-atheists-you-don-t-have-believe-god-go-heaven-8810062.html.

73. Israel, especially Jerusalem, is that ground zero of which I speak. For a thorough and in-depth study of this truth see: Gallups, *Gods of Ground Zero*.

74. When I reference the Catholic Church in this historically accurate manner, I'm not making any general judgment upon individual Catholic people (many of whom are more than likely genuine believers in the same way that a number of Protestants are genuine believers). What I'm referencing is the monolithic and pervasive Roman Catholic *institution* and certain ecclesiastical systems within it, as well as other specific pronouncements and activities emanating from the Vatican down through the ages, which certainly appear to be very effective tools in the hands of Satan.

75. Ephesians 3:15.

76. For a study of the Divine Council of God, see: Gallups, *Gods and Thrones*, and Heiser, *The Unseen Realm*.

77. *Expositor's Bible Commentary on Ezekiel 28:* **The cherub is the warden** of the "holy mountain of God," and no doubt also **the symbol and bearer of the divine glory.** (Emphasis added) See: "Ezekiel 28," *Expositor's Bible Commentary*, Biblehub.com. http://biblehub.com/commentaries/expositors/ezekiel/28. htm.

The Pulpit Commentary on Ezekiel 28: The splendor of the King of Tyre of Ezekiel 28 had suggested the idea of Eden the garden of God. This, in its turn, led on to that of the cherub that was the warder of that garden (Genesis 3:24; emphasis added). See: "Ezekiel 28," *Pulpit Commentary*, Biblehub.com. http:// biblehub.com/commentaries/pulpit/ezekiel/28.htm.

78. Dr. Lehman Strauss, "Bible Prophecy (A Principle of Prophetic Interpretation; Isaiah's Prophecies; Micah's Prophecies)," Bible.org. Accessed 11/4/17. https://bible.org/article/bible-prophecy.

Author's Note: A compound prophecy, or a compound reference, is one that either contains several layers of meaning and context or one that begins as a reference to one thing or person, but then shifts to a symbolic reference to something or someone else. See several examples of this well-known biblical phenomenon in the above-listed reference material by Dr. Strauss.

79. "Ezekiel 28," *Coffman's Commentaries on the Bible*, Studylight.org. https://www.studylight.org/commentaries/bcc/ezekiel-28.html.

80. Robert Jamieson, A. R. Fausset, and David Brown, *Commentary Critical and Explanatory on the Whole Bible* (Ezekiel 28), 1871. http://www.biblestudy-tools.com/commentaries/jamieson-fausset-brown/ezekiel/ezekiel-28.html.

81. "Ezekiel 28:11–19," *The Bible Exposition Commentary: Old Testament*, Biblesoft PC Study Bible, copyright from 1988–2008 *Bible Exposition Commentary: Old Testament* © 2001–2004 by Warren W. Wiersbe. All rights reserved. Accessed 12/14/17.

82. "Ezekiel 28:18," *Coffman's Commentaries on the Bible* (See reference to FF Bruce, *New Layman's Bible Commentary*, p.886). https://www.studylight.org/commentaries/bcc/ezekiel-28.html.

83. I am using a lot of material in the next three chapters from the book *Masquerade: Preparing for the Greatest Con Job in History*. That book was written by Pastor Carl Gallups and was published by Defender Publishing in March 2020, with aforeword by Pat Boone. Used by written permission.
For even deeper study, see *Masquerade*, especially "Part IV—Unmasking the Enemy."

84. Andrew Lloyd Weber. "The Phantom of the Opera Musical." See: https://en.wikipedia.org/wiki/The_Phantom_of_the_Opera_ (1986_musical).

85. "Ezekiel 28," *Guzik Bible Commentary—Enduring Word*, (Against Satan—King of Tyre), Enduring Word. https://enduringword.com/bible-commentary/ezekiel-28.

86. *Guzik Bible Commentary—Enduring Word*. This chapter [Ezekiel 28] and Isaiah 14 throw light on the fall of Satan, and indicate that he was a created being who fell through pride…. Here we have the most graphic and illuminating portrayal of Satan to be found in the whole Bible. His original power and greatness, wisdom and beauty, and exalted position are all set forth. See: "Ezekiel 28," Guzik Bible Commentary—Enduring Word (Against Satan—King of Tyre), Enduring Word. https://enduringword.com/bible-commentary/ezekiel-28.

87. "Ezekiel 28," *Guzik*. https://enduringword.com/bible-commentary/ezekiel-28.

88. Matt Slick, "Was Lucifer Originally an Angel of Worship?" CARM. Accessed 8/11/19. https://carm.org/questions/about-demons/ was-lucifer-originally-angel-worship.

89. "Ezekiel 28:13," *Jamieson, Fausset, and Brown Commentary* (from *Jamieson, Fausset, and Brown Commentary*, Electronic Database. Copyright © 1997, 2003, 2005, 2006 by Biblesoft, Inc. All rights reserved).

90. Britannica. "Musical instrument—Classification of instruments." Accessed 4/2/21. https://www.britannica.com/art/musical-instrument/ Classification-of-instruments.

Instruments have been classified in various ways, some of which overlap. The Chinese divide them according to the material of which they are made—as, for example, stone, wood, silk, and metal. Writers in the Greco-Roman world distinguished **three main types of instruments: wind, stringed, and percussion.**

91. *Talk of the Nation*, NPR. "'The Power of Music' to Affect the Brain," NPR, 6/1/11. https://www.npr.org/2011/06/01/136859090/ the-power-of-music-to-affect-the-brain.

92. See Gallups, *Masquerade*.

93. I will address this designation of Satan's wicked character in an upcoming chapter.

94. "Isaiah 14," *Lange's Commentary on the Holy Scriptures: Critical, Doctrinal, and Homiletical*, Studylight.org. https://www.studylight.org/commentaries/lcc/ isaiah-14.html#_ftnref21.

95. "Isaiah 14," *Arno Gaebelein's Annotated Bible*, Studylight.org. https://www. studylight.org/commentaries/gab/isaiah-14.html.

96. "Isaiah 14:13," *E. W. Bullinger's Companion Bible Notes*, Studylight.org. https://www.studylight.org/commentaries/bul/isaiah-14.html.

97. "Isaiah 14," *Ironside's Notes on Selected Books*, Studylight.org. https://www. studylight.org/commentaries/isn/isaiah-14.html.

98. "Isaiah 14," *The Bible Exposition Commentary: Old Testament*, Biblesoft PC Study Bible,1988–2008, *Bible Exposition Commentary: Old Testament*, 2001–2004 by Warren W. Wiersbe. All rights reserved. Accessed 12/14/17.

99. *Barnes' Notes on the Bible:* His object was…**to exalt himself above the stars; to be elevated above all inferior beings; and to be above the gods** [angelic beings]. (Emphasis added) See: https://biblehub.com/commentaries/isa-iah/14-13.htm.

Jamieson-Fausset-Brown Bible Commentary: "The stars" are often also **used to express heavenly principalities** (Job 38:7). (Emphasis added) See: https://biblehub.com/commentaries/isaiah/14-13.htm.

Gill's Exposition of the Entire Bible: **I will exalt my throne above the stars** of God; which he has made and set in the heavens, and preserves; **meaning the angels**, Job 38:7. (Emphasis added) See: https://biblehub.com/commentaries/isaiah/14-13.htm.

100. In the Scriptures, we find that Gabriel was responsible for carrying the messages of God's decrees (Daniel 8:16; 9:21; Luke 1:19 and 26). Michael was charged with overseeing issues of prayer and spiritual warfare (Daniel 10:13, 21; 12:1; Jude 9; Revelation 12:7). And Satan, the shining one, was the worship leader of Heaven, and the guardian cherub of the Garden of Eden, at the very beginning (Isaiah 14:11; Ezekiel 28:13).

101. See Gallups, *Masquerade.*

102. Isaiah 14:12. "Parallel Translations," Biblehub.com. https://biblehub.com/isaiah/14-12.htm.

103. Hebrew: *Helel ben shachar.* Interlinear text for Isaiah 14:12. https://biblehub.com/interlinear/isaiah/14-12.htm.

104. "OT 1966. *Helel,*" Biblehub.com, https://biblehub.com/hebrew/1966.htm.

105. *Strong's Exhaustive Concordance:* Lucifer—**From halal** (in the sense of brightness); the morning-star—lucifer. see HEBREW halal." https://biblehub.com/hebrew/1966.htm.

106. "Isaiah 14:12," *Keil & Delitzsch Commentary on the Old Testament,* Studylight.org, https://www.studylight.org/commentaries/kdo/isaiah-14.html.

107. Hebrew 1242, Boqer. https://biblehub.com/hebrew/1242.htm.

108. Hebrew 3117, Yom. https://biblehub.com/hebrew/3117.htm.

109. Numbers 24:17. *Cambridge Bible for Schools and Colleges:* A metaphor for a glorious King; cf. Revelation 22:16. According to an early Jewish interpretation, found in the Targum, this verse was a prediction of the Messiah. https://biblehub.com/commentaries/numbers/24-17.htm.

Jamieson-Fausset-Brown Bible Commentary: There shall come a Star out of Jacob, and a Scepter shall rise out of Israel—This imagery, in the hieroglyphic language of the East, denotes…pre-eminently, the Messiah. https://biblehub.com/commentaries/numbers/24-17.htm.

110. Guardian Cherub. See Ezekiel 28:13.

111. *Ellicott's Commentary for English Readers*: "And the day star arise.—An amplification of "until the day dawn." "Day star" occurs nowhere else in the New Testament. Christ calls Himself "the bright morning star" (Revelation 22:16)." https://biblehub.com/commentaries/2_peter/1-19.htm.

112. *Jamieson-Fausset-Brown Bible Commentary*: And **very early in the morning**, on the first day of the week, they came unto the sepulcher at **the rising of the sun**—not quite literally, but "**at earliest dawn**"; according to a way of speaking, not uncommon, and occurring sometimes in the Old Testament. https://biblehub.com/commentaries/mark/16-2.htm.

113. *Gill's Exposition*: Early, when it was yet dark; as it was when she set out, **the day just began to dawn**; though by that time she got to the sepulcher, the sun was rising. https://biblehub.com/commentaries/john/20-1.htm.

114. "Isaiah 14:12," *Barnes' Notes on the Bible*, Biblehub.com. https://biblehub.com/commentaries/isaiah/14-12.htm.

115. "Isaiah 14:12," *Clarke's Commentary on the Bible*, Biblehub.com. https://biblehub.com/niv/isaiah/14-12.htm.

116. https://biblehub.com/parallel/isaiah/14-12.htm.

117. https://biblehub.com/parallel/isaiah/14-12.htm.

118. "OT 1984, Halal," See the *Brown-Driver-Briggs* definitions of word usage. II. [הָלַל] verb be boastful, Qal Imperfect 2masculine plural Psalm 75:5; Participle Psalm 5:6 2t.; —be boastful Psalm 75:5 Participle boastful ones, boasters Psalm 5:6); Psalm 73:3; Psalm 75:5. https://biblehub.com/hebrew/1984.htm.

119. "OT 3314. *Yiphah*," Biblehub.com. https://biblehub.com/hebrew/3314.htm.

120. "OT 3313, *Yapha*," Biblehub.com. https://biblehub.com/hebrew/3313.htm.

121. Isaiah 14:11. *Matthew Henry's Commentary on the Bible*, Biblehub.com. https://biblehub.com/commentaries/isaiah/14-11.htm.

122. Numbers 4:23. *Hebrew Lexicon*, biblehub.com. https://biblehub.com/lexicon/numbers/4-23.htm.

123. *Strong's Concordance* (Hebrew): 6633. Verb—tsaba *(from primary root: lisbo)*: to wage war, serve; 6635. Noun—tsaba: army, war, warfare. See: https://biblehub.com/hebrew/6635.htm; https://biblehub.com/hebrew/6633.htm.

124. Song of Solomon 3:8. *Benson's Commentary*, Biblehub.com. https://bible-hub.com/commentaries/songs/3-7.htm.

125. Song of Solomon 3:8. *Pulpit Commentary*, Biblehub.com. https://bible-hub.com/commentaries/songs/3-7.htm.

126. Song of Solomon 3:8. *Jamieson-Fausset-Brown Bible Commentary*, Bible-hub.com. https://biblehub.com/commentaries/songs/3-7.htm.

127. I urge you to read Isaiah 11:1–5 as well. Similar imagery of the coming Redeemer and certain other elements of the Ephesians 6 armor are also employed there: "Righteousness will be his belt, and faithfulness the sash around his waist" (Isaiah 11:5).

128. *Cambridge Bible for Schools and Colleges:* The fully developed image of His arming Himself with His own attributes has no exact parallel in the O.T. It is reproduced and further elaborated in the N. T. it suggests the figure of the Christian armor (Ephesians 6:14 ff.; 1 Thessalonians 5:8). See: https://bible-hub.com/commentaries/isaiah/59-17.htm.

*Barnes' Notes on the Bible:*Paul (in Ephesians 6:14–17; compare 2 Corinthians 6:7) has carried out [Isaiah 59] to greater length, and introduced more particulars in the description of the spiritual armor of the Christian. See: https://biblehub.com/commentaries/isaiah/59-17.htm.

Gill's Exposition of the Entire Scripture: The apostle has borrowed these phrases from hence, and applied them to the Christian armor, Ephesians 6:14. See: https://biblehub.com/commentaries/isaiah/59-17.htm.

Biblical Illustrator: Just as in Ephesians 6:1–24. The manifold self-manifestations of the inner life of the soul are symbolized under each of the different pieces of armour. See: https://www.studylight.org/commentaries/eng/tbi/isaiah-59.html.

John Trapp Complete Commentary: Christ did; and so must every Christian, [Ephesians 6:14] where the apostle Paul soundeth the alarm, and describeth his weapons as here, defensive and offensive, alluding likely to this text. (Emphasis added) See: https://www.studylight.org/commentaries/eng/jtc/isaiah-59.html.

129. Isaiah 59:17. *Lange's Commentary on the Holy Scriptures: Critical, Doctrinal, and Homiletical,* Studylight.org. https://www.studylight.org/commentaries/lcc/isaiah-59.html.

130. Isaiah 59:17. *Ellicott's Commentary for English Readers*, Biblehub.com, https://biblehub.com/commentaries/isaiah/59-17.htm. See also: Hebrew Lexi-

con for this verse at: https://biblehub.com/lexicon/numbers/4-23.htm.

131. Exodus 30:17–21; 40:30–32.

Also see the following Jewish Encyclopedia entry:

The priests in the sanctuaries wore no shoes (see "Silius Italicus," iii. 28; Theodoret on Ex. iii., quæstio 7; Yer. Sheḳ. v. 48d). Moses and Joshua were told to take off their shoes on holy ground (Ex. iii. 5; Josh. v. 15). "No one was allowed to walk on the Temple ground with shoes on or with dust on his feet" (Ber. ix. 5; compare Iamblichus, "Pythagoras," § 105).

Morris Jastrow, Jr., W. Max Muller, Marcus Jastrow, Kaufmann Kohler, "Barefoot," Jewish Encyclopedia, (accessed 8/21), https://jewishencyclopedia.com/articles/2519-barefoot.

132. Exodus 3:5.

133. Joshua 5:15.

134. Isaiah 59:17. *Cambridge Bible for Schools and Colleges*, Biblehub.com. https://biblehub.com/commentaries/ephesians/6-15.htm.

135. Hewitt, Howard. "Story of Bethlehem Sheep More Than Legend," Wabash, 4/14/14. https://blog.wabash.edu/immersionlearning201314/2014/03/14/story-of-bethlehem-sheep-more-than-legend/#:~:text=The%20shepherds%20of%20Bethlehem%20were,days%20(one%2Dyear).&text=When%20his%20time%20had%20come,to%20Jerusalem%20to%20be%20sacrificed.

From the article: **The shepherds of Bethlehem were in charge of raising sheep for the temple sacrifices.** According to the laws of the time the sheep that were used for the offerings had to be a one-year-old male sheep that had been outside for 365 days (one-year). Since these sheep needed to remain outside the shepherds were also outside, not using the cave during the awful winter (rainy season). You can see this in Luke 2: 8, "That night some shepherds were in the fields outside the village, guarding their flocks of sheep." **Once the sheep were of age the shepherds would bring them to the city of Jerusalem to be sacrificed for the Sabbath (Friday). It was important that the sheep that was to be sacrificed did not possess any blemishes** (broken legs, or injuries). **Once the sheep's blood was completely spilled for all of the sins the priest would return to the people and proclaim, "It is finished."**

136. Matthew 2:7. *Young's Literal Translation*, Biblehub.com. https://biblehub.com/luke/2-7.htm.

137. Matthew 2:7. *Literal Standard Translation*, Biblehub.com. https://bible-hub.com/luke/2-7.htm.

138. Oslo II Accord: The Interim Agreement on the West Bank and the Gaza Strip commonly known as Oslo II or Oslo 2 was a key and complex agreement in the Israeli–Palestinian peace process. The Oslo Accords envisioned the estab-lishment of a Palestinian interim self-government in the Palestinian territories but did not promise an independent Palestinian state. See: Wikipedia. "Oslo II Accord." Accessed 1/21/21. https://en.wikipedia.org/wiki/Oslo_II_Accord

139. Wikipedia. "Area C—West Bank." Accessed 12/28/20. https://en.wikipedia.org/wiki/Area_C_(West_Bank).

140. *Barnes' Notes on the Bible:* And thou, O **tower of the flock**—"'**Tower of Eder**,' which is interpreted 'tower of the flock,' about a mile from Bethlehem," says Jerome who lived there, "and fore-signifying (in its very name) by **a sort of prophecy the shepherds at the Birth of the Lord." There Jacob fed his sheep Genesis 35:21**, and there (since it was hard by Bethlehem) the shepherds, keeping watch over their flocks by night, saw and heard the Angels singing, "Glory to God in the highest, and on earth peace, good will toward men." **The Jews inferred from this place that the Messiah should be revealed there.** https://biblehub.com/commentaries/micah/4-8.htm.

Jamieson-Fausset-Brown Bible Commentary: Jerome takes the Hebrew for "flock," Eder or Edar, as **a proper name,** namely, a village near Bethlehem, for which it is put, Bethlehem being taken to represent the royal stock of David (Mic 5:2; compare Ge 35:21). https://biblehub.com/commentaries/micah/4-8.htm.

Gill's Exposition of the Entire Bible: And thou, O tower of the flock…The words "Migdal Eder" are left by some untranslated, and think that place to be intended so called, which was near to Bethlehem, Genesis 35:19; and perhaps is the same which Jerome calls the tower of Ader, about a mile from Bethle-hem: this is supposed to be the place where the shepherds were watching over their flocks at the time of Christ's birth, the tidings of which were first brought to them here; and the Jewish doctors speak of it as near Jerusalem. https://biblehub.com/commentaries/micah/4-8.htm.

141. Biblical lineage is traced through the father. Arnold Fruchtenbaum. "The Genealogy of Messiah," 4/20/18. https://jewsforjesus.org/publications/issues/issues-v05-n06/the-genealogy-of-the-messiah: When one examines all

the genealogies in the Hebrew Scriptures, several facts become quite obvious. Other than extremely infrequent exceptions, only the male line is traced in those genealogies. Usually, only men's names appear, again, with a few exceptions. However, the lineages of the women is not given. This is not an intentional slight against women in general, as some might suggest. Rather it is simply a biblical fact that it was the lineage of the father who determined both national and tribal identity.

142. "Ephrathah" is a former name of the location, and there were two different places with the name "Bethlehem," so Micah adds the details for clarity of location. See: http://www.hisplacechurch.com/resources/uploads/1983.

143. Wikipedia. "Alfred Edersheim." Accessed 1/11/21 https://en.wikipedia.org/wiki/Alfred_Edersheim.

144. Edersheim, Alfred. *The Life and Times of Jesus the Messiah* (Chapter VI: "The Nativity of Jesus the Messiah"). Accessed 1/12/21 (1883) 180. https://www.ccel.org/ccel/edersheim/lifetimes.vii.vi.html.

145. Ibid.

146. Tourist Israel: The Guide, "Getting from Jerusalem to Bethlehem." Accessed 12/23/20. https://www.touristisrael.com/get-jerusalem-bethlehem/19515/.

147. The term "remnant" in the biblical sense, and especially the Christian sense, means those who are born-again believers in Yeshua, and not necessarily all of those whose names might be on a church roll. Nor are they necessarily all those who claim to be a Christian as a mere title of their adherence to a faith system. Jesus said it like this: "Not everyone who says to me, 'Lord, Lord,' will enter the kingdom of heaven, but only the one who does the will of my Father who is in heaven" (Matthew 7:21).

148. Griffin, Sherry Driskell. "Shepherds Did Not Follow a Star—They Knew Where to Go." Accessed 1/12/21. https://heavenslibrary.online/savior/.

149. "A passage in the Mishnah (Shek. vii. 4.) leads to the conclusion, that the flocks, which pastured there, were destined for Temple-sacrifices, and, accordingly, that the shepherds, who watched over them, were not ordinary shepherds. The latter were under the ban of Rabbinism, on account of their necessary isolation from religious ordinances, and their manner of life, which rendered strict legal observance unlikely, if not absolutely impossible. The same Mishnic passage also leads us to infer, that these flocks lay out all the

year round, since they are spoken of as in the fields thirty days before the Passover—that is, in the month of February, when in Palestine the average rainfall is nearly greatest."

See: Edersheim, *The Life and Times of Jesus the Messiah.* https://www.ccel.org/ccel/edersheim/lifetimes.vii.vi.html.

150. Mishnah Bekhorot 5:4. "English Explanation of Mishnah Bekhorot 5:4," Sefaria.org, accessed 6/12/21, https://www.sefaria.org/English_Explanation_of_Mishnah_Bekhorot.5.4.2?lang=bi.

151. Mishnah: The first major written collection of the Jewish oral traditions known as the Oral Torah. It is also the first major work of rabbinic literature. Maimonides. "Commentary on Tractate Avot with an Introduction (Shemona perakim)." World Digital Library. Accessed 2/3/21. https://www.wdl.org/en/item/3964.

152. "Migdal Eder and the Birth of Christ," Bible Things in Bible Ways. Accessed 1/1/21, https://biblethingsinbibleways.wordpress.com/2020/05/21/migdal-eder-and-the-birth-of-christ.

153. Dr. Jürgen Buehler. "The Tower of the Flock," International Christian Embassy Jerusalem, 10/22/12, https://int.icej.org/news/commentary/tower-flock.

154. Micah 4:8. *Pulpit Commentary*, Biblehub.com. https://biblehub.com/commentaries/micah/4-8.htm.

155. Micah 4:8. *Gill's Exposition of the Entire Bible*, Biblehub.com. https://biblehub.com/commentaries/micah/4-8.htm.

156. Micah 4:8. *E. W. Bullinger's Companion Bible Notes*, Studylight.org. https://www.studylight.org/commentary/micah/4-8.html.

157. International Standard Bible Encyclopedia Online. "Eder (1)." Accessed 1/12/21. https://www.internationalstandardbible.com/E/eder-(1).html.

158. See: OT # 4029, Migdal-Eder. "Hebrew," Biblehub.com. https://biblehub.com/hebrew/4029.htm.

159. **In the interest of academic integrity,** I must point out that, for ages, scholars disagreed about the exact location of Migdal Eder. Some put it in and around Jerusalem, and not anywhere near Bethlehem. However, numerous other scholars, *as I,* see the clear biblical connections (both Old and New Testaments) to Migdal Eder at Bethlehem. The scenario of the angels, the shepherds, the manger, the swaddling bands, the significance of the shepherd's

fields and their priestly work, modern archeology and exploration, etc., add up to Migdal Eder being the one located at the Bethlehem fields. However, as an example of the different interpretations among various scholars expressed in a single commentary, I have provided this one from *Benson's Commentary of* the Old and New Testaments: Micah 4:8. And thou, O tower of the flock—Or, of Eder, as Archbishop Newcome and many others translate the word, considering it as a proper name; a tower in or near Bethlehem; see Genesis 35:21. Or, as some think, a tower near the sheep-gate in Jerusalem, (Nehemiah 3:1; Nehemiah 3:32) put here for the whole city. See: https://www.studylight.org/ commentary/micah/4-8.html.

160. Micah 4:8. *Pulpit Commentary*, Biblehub.com. https://biblehub.com/ commentaries/micah/4-8.htm.

161. Micah 4:8. *Barnes' Notes on the Bible*, Biblehub.com. https://biblehub. com/commentaries/micah/4-8.htm.

162. Gary H. Everett's 2011 edition of *Study Notes on the Holy Scriptures* is a culmination of thirty years of personal Bible study. Everett received his master of divinity from Southwestern Baptist Theological Seminary in 1992. He is currently pursuing his doctor of ministry at this same seminary. He has taught in Bible colleges for ten years and served as a pastor for five. For thirteen years, he has been a missionary in Kampala, Uganda, under Dr. Robert B. Nichols of Calvary Cathedral International in Fort Worth, Texas. https://www.logos.com/ search?filters=author-5464_Author&sortBy=Relevance&limit=30&page=1&o wnership=all&geographicAvailability=all.

163. Micah 4:8. *Gary Everett's Study Notes on the Scriptures*, Studylight.org. https://www.studylight.org/commentary/micah/4-8.html.

164. Edersheim, *The Life and Times of Jesus the Messiah*. Accessed 1/12/21. https://www.ccel.org/ccel/edersheim/lifetimes.vii.vi.html.

165. Torah Life Ministry. "The Unique Tamid Sacrifice—Why Does It Matter?" Torahlifeministry.com, 9/15/16. https://torahlifeministry.com/blog/ item/185-the-unique-tamid-sacrifice-why-does-it-matter.html. "According to ancient Jewish sources outside the Bible, the morning sacrifice/offering of the Tamid took place at 9 a.m. The evening sacrifice/offering took place at 3 p.m. (See Mishnah, Tamid 3:7; Josephus, Antiquities 14.4.3; Philo, Special Laws, 1:169)."

166. Luke 2. "Literal Standard Version," Biblehub.com. https://biblehub.com/lsv/luke/2.htm.

167. For a detailed scholarly study on this topic see: David I. Macht. "A Scientific Appreciation of Leviticus 12:1–5." Accessed 2/2/21. https://www.jstor.org/stable/3259207?seq=1.

168. I will expand upon this amazing truth in a few chapters from this one. Beracah is a specific valley mentioned in the Hebrew Bible (Old Testament). It was named the "Valley of Blessings" ("blessing" is "Berakhah" in Hebrew) by Jehoshaphat, king of Judah after Jehovah God's victory over Moab and Ammon, as recorded in 2 Chronicles 20:1–30. The valley is on the main road from Hebron to Jerusalem. See: https://en.wikipedia.org/wiki/Beracah#cite_note-1.

169. *Thayer's Greek Lexicon:* STRONGS NT 4683: σπαργανόω σπαργανόω, σπαργάνω: 1 aorist ἐσπαργάνωσα; perfect passive participle ἐσπαργανωμένος: (σπράγανον a swathing band); to wrap in swaddling-clothes: an infant just born, Luke 2:7, 12. (Ezekiel 16:4; (Euripides, Aristotle), Hippocrates, Plutarch, others.) See: Sparganoό," Greek # 4683. "Thayer's Greek Lexicon," Biblehub.com. https://biblehub.com/hebrew/2854.htm.

170. From GK. *Sparganon* (**a strip**; from a derivative of the base of *sparasso* meaning **to strap or wrap with strips**); to swathe (an infant after the Oriental custom)—wrap in swaddling clothes.

171. *Benson's Commentary:* The design of the prophet is to mark out that state of impurity wherein the Hebrews were found in Egypt, plunged in idolatry and ignorance, and oppressed with cruel servitude. See: https://biblehub.com/commentaries/ezekiel/16-4.htm.

Matthew Poole's Commentary: Nor swaddled: this usage for the continued preservation of the infant, for strengthening it, setting its limbs, and keeping them in their right and orderly posture, is most necessary to be observed, and yet there was none that would do this for this infant: so forlorn was the state of the Jews in their birth, without beauty, weltering in blood, without strength, new-born, without friend that might act the mother's or midwife's office. See: https://biblehub.com/commentaries/ezekiel/16-4.htm.

Pulpit Commentary: When this was done, the child was wrapped in swaddling clothes (Luke 2:7), but these too were wanting in the picture which Ezekiel draws. See: https://biblehub.com/commentaries/ezekiel/16-4.htm.

172. "In relation to the…idea of Israelite leaders as terrible shepherds, Jesus fulfills what the Israelites could not. He embodies the perfect Israelite, the one who fulfilled all the Law, the true leader of Israel. Being both truly God and truly man, **Jesus is able to represent both Israel and God at the same time in this single metaphor.**" See: Murawski, Bryan. "John 10-Shepherd Metaphors in the New Testament," Bethany Bible Church. Accessed 1/12/21. https://www.bethanybiblechurch.com/ john-10-shepherd-metaphors-in-the-old-testament.

173. *Jamieson-Fausset-Brown Bible Commentary* on Job: Image from childbirth (Job 38:8, 9; Eze 32:2; Mic 4:10). Ocean at its birth was wrapped in clouds as its swaddling bands. See: https://biblehub.com/commentaries/job/38-9.htm. *Matthew Poole's Commentary on Job:* Having compared the sea to a new-born infant, he continues in the same metaphor, and makes the clouds as swaddling-bands. (Emphasis added)

174. The Greek word for *manger* is Strong's #5336. Phatné. It is also interpreted as a "stall," or sometimes, as a feeding trough, depending on the context. See: https://biblehub.com/greek/5336.htm. The angels said: You will find a baby, wrapped in swaddling cloths, lying *in a manger* (Luke 2:12; emphasis added).

In the case of Jesus, the context would most likely mean the lower level birthing room at the Tower of the Flock rather than some indiscriminate feeding trough for a farm animal. An example of the use of this word as *a stall* (manger), is found in Luke 13:15: "The Lord answered him, 'You hypocrites. Doesn't each of you on the Sabbath untie your ox or donkey from **the stall** (*phatné*—manger) and lead it out to give it water?'" (Emphasis added)

175. Ibid. The Greek word for manger is Strong's #5336, *phatné*.

176. OT 3045. *Yada.* https://biblehub.com/hebrew/3045.htm.

177. NT 1097. *Ginóskó. Helps Word Studies:* ginōskō—properly, to know, especially through personal experience (first-hand acquaintance). 1097 /ginōskō ("experientially know") is used for example in Lk 1:34, "And **Mary [a virgin] said to the angel, 'How will this be since I do not know** (1097 /ginōskō = sexual intimacy) a man?'" See: https://biblehub.com/greek/1097.htm.

178. Edersheim, *The Life and Times of Jesus the Messiah.* https://www.ccel.org/ ccel/edersheim/lifetimes.vii.vi.html.

179. Study to shew thyself approved unto God, a workman that needeth not to be ashamed, rightly dividing the word of truth. (2 Timothy 2:15, KJV).

180. For an excellent study on what the Bible says about portals and different physical dimensions of reality, see Gallups, *Gods of the Final Kingdom*.

181. The name, expressing the concept of wrestling, **clinging firmly** to God, **and overcoming**, and God's confirming of his covenant with Jacob, indicates that Israel is to be understood as Jacob's covenant name. The name spoke of his being bound with a bond of life and love to God…. It was to be through Abraham's seed (Gen 15:5; 17:1–8) that God would bring in the Messiah and the sure redemptive victory over Satan, sin, and its effects. (Emphasis added) Bible Dictionaries—*Baker's Evangelical Dictionary of Biblical Theology*—Israel. https://www.biblestudytools.com/dictionary/israel.

182. Spiritual Israel as the Church. See: Got Questions. "What Is Spiritual Israel," GotQuestions.org, accessed 6/21/21, https://www.gotquestions.org/spiritual-Israel.html.

183. According to the Bible, the region was named after the Hebrew patriarch Jacob, also known as *Israel* (from Yisrae'el, **meaning to "persevere with God"**) and, by extension, his nation. See: https://www.ancient.eu/israel/#:~:text=According%20to%20the%20Bible%2C%20the,%2C%20by%20extension%2C%20his%20nation.

184. As an example, consider that Mahmoud Ahmadinejad was president of Iran from 8/3/05–8/3/13, and during that time he repeatedly hurled hate-filled speeches against Israel. Ahmadinejad **refused to call Israel by name**, instead **calling it the "Zionist regime."** He continually called for the "elimination of the Zionist regime." See: Hughes, Dana; Bingham, Amy (9/26/12). "Iran's Ahmadinejad Says America Entrusted Itself to the Devil." ABC News. https://abcnews.go.com/Politics/OTUS/irans-ahmadinejad-america-entrusted-devil/story?id=17328593.

185. Ein Gedi, literally "spring of the kid (young goat)," is an oasis and a nature reserve in Israel, located west of the Dead Sea, near Masada and the Qumran Caves. Ein Gedi was listed in 2016 as one of the most popular nature sites in the country. Today, it site attracts about one million visitors a year. See: Zafrir RinatAlmog Ben Zikri. "Israeli Nature Spots Draw 2 Million Visitors, Tons of Trash During Passover Holi-

day," Haaretz.com, 5/1/16. https://www.haaretz.com/israel-news/.
premium-nature-spots-draw-2-million-visitors-tons-of-trash-1.5377688.

186. 2 Samuel 15:30. *Benson Commentary*, Biblehub.com. https://biblehub.
com/commentaries/2_samuel/15-30.htm.

187. 2 Samuel 15:30. *Gill's Exposition of the Entire Bible*, Biblehub.com.
https://biblehub.com/commentaries/2_samuel/15-30.htm.

188. See: Smith, Colin. "Striking Parallels and Contrasts," Unlocking the
Bible, 11/30/18. https://unlockingthebible.org/lifekey/striking-parallels-and-
contrasts. See also: Chris Katulka, "Similarities between Jesus and King David
(Part I)," Friends of Israel Blog, 4/19/13. https://www.foi.org/2013/04/19/
similarities-between-jesus-and-king-david-part-1. (Part 2—https://www.foi.
org/2013/04/26/similarities-between-jesus-and-king-david-part-2).

189. Acts 1:11. *Ellicott's Commentary for English Readers*, Biblehub.com.
https://biblehub.com/commentaries/acts/1-11.htm.

190. Acts 1:11. *Bengel's Gnomen*, Biblehub.com. https://biblehub.com/com-
mentaries/acts/1-11.htm.

191. Acts 1:11. *Gill's Exposition of the Entire Bible*, Biblehub.com. https://bible-
hub.com/commentaries/acts/1-11.htm.

192. I Kings 11:7. *Cambridge Bible for Schools and Colleges*, Biblehub.com.
https://biblehub.com/commentaries/1_kings/11-7.htm.

193. Ezekiel 11:23. *Ellicott's Commentary for English Readers*, Biblehub.com.
https://biblehub.com/ezekiel/11-23.htm.

194. Ussishkin, David. "The Necropolis from the Time of the Kingdom of
Judah at Silwan, Jerusalem." (May 1970). *Biblical Archaeologist*. 33 (2): 33–46.

195. Westhead, Rick. "Jerusalem's Mount of Olives Cemetery Running
Out of Rom," *Toronto Star*, 12/16/12. https://www.thestar.com/news/
world/2012/12/16/jerusalems_mount_of_olives_cemetery_running_out_of_
room.html.

196. Ibid.

197. For this and more info on the Mount of Olive connections to Jesus' life
and ministry, see: https://loveisrael.com/places/mount-of-olives.

198. Windle, Bryan. "Three Tombs of Jesus: Which is the Real One?" *Bible
Archeology Report*, 4/20/19. https:// biblearchaeologyreport.com/2019/04/20/
three-tombs-of-jesus-which-is-the-real-one.

199. Ossuary: a container or room in which the bones of dead people are placed.

200. Dr. Heiser, Michael, S. "Thinking Clearly About the 'Jesus Family Tomb'," Associates for Biblical Research. 3/26/10. http://www.biblearchaeology.org/post/2010/03/26/Thinking-Clearly-About-the-Jesus-Family- Tomb. aspx

201. Cascone, Sarah. "A New Study Suggests That Jesus's Tomb Is 700 Years Older Than Previously Thought," Artnet.com, 11/29/17. https://news.artnet.com/art-world/jesus-burial-site-older-than-we-thought-1163408#:~:text=New%20scientific%20testing%20adds%20 credence,National%20Technical%20University%20of%20Athens.

202. Ibid.

203. Staff, Biblical Archeological Society. "Where Is Golgotha, Where Jesus Was Crucified?" Accessed 1/22/21. https://www.biblicalarchaeology.org/daily/ biblical-sites-places/jerusalem/where-is-golgotha-where-jesus-was-crucified.

204. For more on this topic see: Wikipedia. "The Garden Tomb." Accessed 1/9/21. https://en.wikipedia.org/wiki/The_Garden_Tomb.

205. For more information, see: Wikipedia. "Charles George Gordon." Accessed 1/9/21. https://en.wikipedia.org/wiki/Charles_George_Gordon.

206. In 1842, heavily relying on Robinson's research, Otto Thenius, a German theologian and Bible scholar from Dresden, was the first to publish a proposal that the rocky knoll north of Damascus Gate—which, as Thenius noticed, resembled a skull—was the biblical Golgotha. The site he suggested contains a few natural cavities as well as a manmade cave, which Christians call Jeremiah's Grotto and Muslims initially called Al-Adhamiyah, a name later corrupted to El-Heidhemiyeh. Thenius went so far as to suggest that Jeremiah's Grotto was, in fact, the tomb of Christ. See: Wikipedia. "The Garden Tomb," (Discovery: Otto Thenius). Accessed 1/21/21. https://en.wikipedia.org/wiki/The_Garden_Tomb. See: Charles W. Wilson, *Golgotha and The Holy Sepulchre* (1906, The Committee of the Palestine Exploration Fund), pp. 103–120. See: Otto Thenius, *Golgatha et Sanctum Sepulchrum in Zeitschrift fir die historische Theologie (1842).*

207. W. Harold Mare. "The Place of Christ's Crucifixion and Burial," Journal: *Bible and Spade* (First Run), Volume: BSP 03:2 (Spring 1974). Accessed 1/21/21. https://www.galaxie.com/article/bsp03-2-01. Maudlin, Leon. "Gor-

don's Calvary," Leon Maudlin Blog. Accessed 1/21/21. https://leonmauldin. blog/2011/03/15/gordons-calvary.

208. Chadwick, Jeffery R. "Revisiting Golgotha and the Garden Tomb," BYU Religious Studies Center, Religious Educator Vol. 4 No. 1 2003. Accessed 1/4/21 https://rsc.byu.edu/vol-4-no-1-2003/revisiting-golgotha-garden-tomb.

209. Zondervan Academic. "The History of Jerusalem in the Bible," Accessed 2/2/21. https://zondervanacademic.com/blog/ the-history-of-jerusalem-in-the-bible.

210. Aven, Beth. "A Scholarly Conundrum," Biblearcheology.org, Spring 2002 Edition.https://biblearchaeology.org/research/new-testament-era/2308-golgotha-a-reconsideration-of-the-evidence-for-the-sites-of-jesus-crucifixion-and-burial.

211. Gabriel Barkay, "The Garden Tomb," published in *Biblical Archaeology Review* March/April 1986. https://www.baslibrary.org/ biblical-archaeology-review/12/2/2.

212. Matthew 27:60. *Ellicott's Commentary for English Readers*, Biblehub.com. https://biblehub.com/commentaries/matthew/27-60.htm.

213. John 19:41. *Expositor's Greek Testament*, Biblehub.com. https://biblehub. com/commentaries/john/19-41.htm.

214. John 19:41. *Bengel's Gnomen*, Biblehub.com. https://biblehub.com/com-mentaries/john/19-41.htm.

215. See also: Gallups, *Gods of Ground Zero* (Chapter 39, "Garden of Sorrows").

216. John 19:41. *Pulpit Commentary*, Biblehub.com. https://biblehub.com/ commentaries/john/19-41.htm.

217. Dr. Ernest L. Martin (PhD). *Secrets of Golgotha: The Lost History of Jesus' Crucifixion* (Second Edition), Academy for Scriptural; 2nd edition (June 1, 1996). Read the entire book online here: https://www.askelm.com/golgotha/ Golgotha%20Chap%2000.pdf.

218. A. Michas, Peter. "The Rod of an Almond Tree in God's Master Plan," Wine Press Publishing; 2nd edition (May 1, 1997). (Intro statement for book on Amazon site), https://www.amazon.com/Almond-Tree-Gods-Master-Plan/ dp/1579210074/ref=sr_1_1?dchild=1&keywords=The+Rod+of+an+Almond+ Tree+in+God%E2%80%99s+Master+Plan%2C&qid=1612304479&s=book s&sr=1-1.

219. Matthew 27. *Vincent's Word Studies*, (Verse 33), Studylight.org. https://www.studylight.org/commentaries/eng/vnt/matthew-27.html.

220. Dr. Livingston. "Golgotha." Accessed 1/12/21, https://biblearchaeology.org/research/new-testament-era/2308-golgotha-a-reconsideration-of-the-evidence-for-the-sites-of-jesus-crucifixion-and-burial.

221. Ibid.

222. Dr. James D. Tabor. "Locating Golgotha: Archeology," 2/26/16. https://jamestabor.com/locating-golgotha.

223. Topo is a combining form used like a prefix meaning "place" or "local." It is often used in scientific and other technical terms. Topo- comes from the Greek *tópos*, meaning "place" or "commonplace." See: Topo. Dictionary.com, https://www.dictionary.com/browse/topo-.

224. From Dr. James Tabor's article on Golgotha: There is a late Jewish tradition, known also by Christian fathers like Origen, **that Adam's skull was buried** in Jerusalem, which accounts for the tradition so common in medieval art of placing a skull at the foot of the cross. Some have speculated that the name **might be related to "Goliath,"** based on the text of Samuel that mentions David bringing his severed head to Jerusalem (1 Samuel 17:54). Others have seen the name as describing a despicable **place of execution, where skulls and bones** would be strewn about. Still others, have seen it more as a physical description—**perhaps of a craggy rock-like hillock that gave the appearance of a skull.**

What none of these texts explicitly say is anything about a hill called Golgotha or Calvary, which is so familiar in Christian tradition, **but as we will see, that notion does have support in other texts.** So the question is—where is Golgotha? Can it be located? And why would it be called the "place of the Skull." (Emphasis added)

Dr. James D. Tabor. "Locating Golgotha: Archeology," 2/26/16, https://jamestabor.com/locating-golgotha.

225. For David and Goliath as a metaphor for Yeshua and Satan, See: Dr. Redpath, Alan. "Vanquishing the Enemy," Moody Media. Accessed 1/23/21. https://www.moodymedia.org/articles/vanquishing-enemy. Also s Dr. Bob Deffinbaugh. "14. David and Goliath (1 Samuel 17:1–58)," Bible.org. Accessed 1/12/21. https://bible.org/seriespage/14-david-and-goliath-1-samuel-171-58.

226. 1 Samuel 21:1. *Cambridge Bible for Schools and Colleges*, Biblehub.com. https://biblehub.com/commentaries/1_samuel/21-1.htm.

227. 1 Samuel 21:1. *Jamieson-Fausset-Brown Bible Commentary*, Biblehub.com. https://biblehub.com/commentaries/1_samuel/21-1.htm.

228. Encyclopedia.com. "Mount of Olives." Accessed 1/21/21. https://www. encyclopedia.com/philosophy-and-religion/bible/biblical-proper-names/ mount-olives.

229. 1 Samuel 21:9. *Cambridge Bible for Schools and Colleges*, Biblehub.com. https://biblehub.com/commentaries/1_samuel/21-9.htm.

230. 1 Samuel 21:9. *Keil and Delitzsch Biblical Commentary on the Old Testament*, Biblehub.com. https://biblehub.com/commentaries/1_samuel/21-9.htm.

231. Dr. Taylor Marshall. "Golgatha: The Word Symbolizes a Beautiful Reality." Accessed 2/2/21. https://taylormarshall.com/2013/03/golgatha-word-symbolizes-beautiful.html.

232. Richard A. Shenk, PhD (Biographical Profile). https://bcsmn.edu/profile/ rick-shenk.

233. For Dr. Shenk's statements on this, see: 1. Holloway, Henry. "Bible Bombshell as 'David vs Goliath Skull Found Where Jesus Was Crucified'," UK Star, 10/19/19. https://www.dailystar.co.uk/news/weird-news/bible-bombshell-david-vs-goliath-20649333. 2. Waters, Conny. "Skull of Biblical Giant Goliath Is Buried on the Hill Golgotha in Jerusalem—New Claim," Ancient Pages, 11/7/19. https://www.ancientpages.com/2019/11/07/skull-of-biblical-giant-goliath-is-buried-on-the-hill-golgotha-in-jerusalem-new-claim.

234. Marshall. "Golgatha."" https://taylormarshall.com/2013/03/golgatha-word-symbolizes-beautiful.html.

235. Hebrew—*Nob*. (Definition), Abarim Publications. Accessed 1/11/21. https://www.abarim-publications.com/Dictionary/n/n-b-he.html.

236. Britannica Editors. "Mount of Olives." Accessed 1/11/21. https://www. britannica.com/place/Mount-of-Olives.

237. Isaiah 10:32. *Cambridge Bible for Schools and Colleges*, Biblehub.com. https://biblehub.com/commentaries/isaiah/10-32.htm.

238. Isaiah 10:32. *Gill's Exposition of the Entire Bible*, Biblehub.com. https:// biblehub.com/commentaries/isaiah/10-32.htm.

239. Isaiah 10:32. *Jamieson-Fausset-Brown Bible Commentary*, Biblehub.com. https://biblehub.com/commentaries/isaiah/10-32.htm.

240. Isaiah 10:32. *Barnes' Notes on the Bible*, Biblehub.com. https://biblehub.com/commentaries/isaiah/10-32.htm.

241. "The exact location of the mountain known in the ancient sources as Mount Scopus is not known. It is described as being in the north-eastern part of the ridge that prominently *includes the Mount of Olives,* which dominates Jerusalem from the east."
See: Wikipedia. "Mount of Scopus" (Modern Era). Accessed 1/21/21, https://en.wikipedia.org/wiki/Mount_Scopus#:~:text=The%20exact%20location%20of%20the,dominates%20Jerusalem%20from%20the%20east.

242. Dr. Richard T. Ritenbaugh. "Isaiah 10:27–34," Bibletools.org. Accessed 1/23/21. https://www.bibletools.org/index.cfm/fuseaction/Topical.show/RTD/cgg/ID/14380/Sennacherib-as-Gods-Tool.htm.

243. "Olives, Mount of," (*Smith's Bible Dictionary*), Classic.net.bible.org. Accessed 1/22/21. http://classic.net.bible.org/dictionary.php?word=Olives,%20Mount%20Of.

244. Compound Prophecy. See: Dr. Lehman Strauss, "Bible Prophecy (A Principle of Prophetic Interpretation; Isaiah's Prophecies; Micah's Prophecies)," Bible.org. Accessed 11/4/17. https://bible.org/article/bible-prophecy.
Author's note: A compound prophecy, or a compound reference, either contains several layers of meaning and context or begins as a reference to one thing or person, but then shifts to a symbolic reference to something or someone else. See several examples of this well-known biblical phenomenon in the above listed reference material by Dr. Strauss.

245. Ibid. For scholarly examples of Sennacherib as a type of Satan, see: Guzik, David, et al.

246. Isaiah 10:32. *Matthew Henry's Concise Commentary*, Biblehub.com. https://biblehub.com/commentaries/isaiah/10-32.htm.

247. Isaiah 11:1. *Maclaren's Exposition of the Bible*, Biblehub.com. https://biblehub.com/commentaries/isaiah/11-1.htm.

248. Isaiah 11:1. *Cambridge Bible for Schools and Colleges*, Biblehub.com. https://biblehub.com/commentaries/isaiah/11-1.htm.

249. Isaiah 11:1. *Pulpit Commentary*, Biblehub.com. https://biblehub.com/commentaries/isaiah/11-1.htm.

250. Isaiah 11:1. *Barnes' Notes on the Bible*, Biblehub.com. https://biblehub.com/commentaries/isaiah/11-1.htm.

251. Romans 15:12. *Expositor's Greek New Testament*, Biblehub.com. https://biblehub.com/commentaries/romans/15-12.htm.

252. Romans 15:12. *Bengel's Gnomen*, Biblehub.com. https://biblehub.com/commentaries/romans/15-12.htm.

253. Romans 15:12. *Gill's Exposition of the Entire Bible*, Biblehub.com. https://biblehub.com/commentaries/romans/15-12.htm.

254. For scholarly examples of Sennacherib as a type of Satan, see: 1. Guzik, David. "No Deal With the Devil," *Enduring Word*, 2/16/20, https://enduringword.com/no-deal-with-the-devil. 2. John W. Ritenbaugh. "Satan (Part 3): Demons," Bibletools.org. https://www.bibletools.org/index.cfm/fuseaction/Audio.Details/ID/169/Satan-Part-3.htm. 3. Verheyden, Joseph. "The Devil in Person, the Devil in Disguise: Looking for King Sennacherib in Early Christian Literature," Brill: Over Three Centuries of Scholarly Publishing. Accessed April 2, 2021, https://brill.com/view/book/edcoll/9789004265622/B9789004265622_013.xml.

255. See Gallups, *Gods of Ground Zero*, for a detailed and scholarly study of why Jerusalem is the center of Satan's lusts and the reasons for his eternal desire to possess it as his very own.

256. Martin. *Secrets of Golgotha: The Lost History of Jesus' Crucifixion*. https://www.askelm.com/golgotha/Golgotha%20Chap%2000.pdf.

257. Ernest L. Martin bio: From 1960 to 1972, Dr. Martin taught history, theology and elementary meteorology at the Ambassador College campus in Bricket Wood, England, where he became dean of faculty. He earned his PhD at Ambassador College.

Between 1969 and 1973, Ambassador College entered an alliance with Hebrew University in Israel that had been negotiated by Dr. Martin. This commenced a five-year archaeological program with students from Ambassador College working on Dr. Benjamin Mazar's excavation near the Western Wall of the Temple Mount. During this period, Martin supervised 450 participating college students during summer months. The partnership was mentioned in a *Time* magazine article. ("Education: Digging for Credit," 9/3/73, via content.time.com).

Following the eventual closure of the Ambassador College campus in England, Martin became chairman of the Department of Theology at Ambassador College in Pasadena, California, in 1973.

Dr. Martin was a dear friend of the famed theologian, commentary writer, and biblical scholar F. F. Bruce. (See *Secrets of Golgotha: The Lost History of Jesus' Crucifixion* p. 412).

F.F. Bruce: Frederick Fyvie Bruce FBA (1910–1990), usually cited as F. F. Bruce, was a British biblical scholar who supported the historical reliability of the New Testament. His first book, *New Testament Documents: Are They Reliable?* (1943), was voted by the American evangelical periodical *Christianity Today* in 2006 as one of the top fifty books "which had shaped evangelicals." (Grass, Tim (2012). *F. F. Bruce: A Life. Milton Keynes: Paternoster.* p. 40. ISBN 978-0-8028-6723-0.)

258. Dr. James D. Tabor bio: James D. Tabor served as chair (2004–2014) of the Department of Religious Studies at the University of North Carolina, where he has taught since 1989. He is currently professor of ancient Judaism and early Christianity. Previously he held positions at the University of Notre Dame and the College of William and Mary. He received his PhD from the University of Chicago in 1981 in ancient Mediterranean religions. https://jamestabor.com/about-dr-tabor/.

259. Dr. Douglas Jacoby bio: Douglas Jacoby is a Bible teacher who has served as a minister on church staff for twenty years, in London, Birmingham, Sydney, Stockholm, Philadelphia, Indianapolis, and Washington DC. He also serves as adjunct professor of theology at Lincoln Christian University and professor of theology in the Rocky Mountain School of Theology and Ministry. With degrees from Drew, Harvard, and Duke, Douglas has written thirty-five books, recorded nearly nine hundred podcasts, and spoken in over one hundred universities, and in over five hundred cities, in 126 nations around the world. Douglas has led twenty-five tours to the biblical world. https://www.douglasjacoby.com/about.

260. Dr. Nikos Kokkinos bio. University of Oxford, Faculty of Classics, Ancient History, Academic Visitor | Graeco-Roman Near East. Archaeologist and ancient historian. Kokkinos was born in Alexandria, Egypt, in 1955 of Greek parentage. His early education in Egypt and Greece included both Semitic and European languages. Nikos' doctoral dissertation, "The Herodian Dynasty," written in the Ashmolean Library under the supervision of the distinguished Professor Fergus Millar, was long preceded by a popular book, *The Enigma of Jesus the Galilaean* (1980), which became temporarily a Greek

bestseller, and by his study of Antonia Augusta (1992), a development of his undergraduate work. His contribution to Chronos, Kairos, Christos (1989) has converted many scholars to his dating of the crucifixion, while he was a member of a team of ancient historians and archaeologists who took academia by storm with their worldwide publicized theory of centuries of darkness (1991). See: https://oxford.academia.edu/oxfordacademiaedu. See also: https://nikos-kokkinos.webs.com/biographicalsketch.htm.

261. Dr. N. F. Hutchinson. See: Section 5.3, "Surveys in Palestine by Captains Mieulet and Derrien, of the French Etat Major," *Palestine Exploration Fund Quarterly Statement* 5.3 (July 1873): 113–115. https://biblicalstudies.org.uk/articles_peq_01.php.

262. Wikipedia. "Helmut Koester." Accessed 4/5/21. https://en.wikipedia.org/wiki/Helmut_Koester.

263. In 2 Samuel 24:9 and 1 Chronicles 21:5, the census ordered by King David, Miphkad, has etymological reference to *counting*—specifically for the "counting of heads—or *skulls*." It this perhaps yet another reference to Golgotha as the "skull place"? In Nehemiah 3:31, the Miphkad gate is rendered the "Inspection Gate."

264. Mélbourne O'Banion. "The Law of the Red Heifer: A Type and Shadow of Jesus Christ," *Studia Antinqua*, Volume 4 | Number 1 | April 2005. https://scholarsarchive.byu.edu/cgi/viewcontent.cgi?article=1041&context=studiaantiqua.

265. The Golden Gate, as it is sometimes referred to in Christian writing, is the only eastern gate of the Temple Mount. It is one of only two gates that used to offer access into the city from that side in Jesus' day. It has been walled up since medieval times.

266. Martin, *Secrets of Golgotha*, pp. 4–5.

267. Tabor, "Locating Golgotha: Archeology."

268. The **Talmud** is the source from which the code of Jewish **Halakhah** (law) is derived. It is made up of the **Mishnah and the Gemara**. The **Mishnah** is the original written version of the oral law and the **Gemara** is the record of the rabbinic discussions following this writing down. It includes their differences of view. See: "The Talmud." BBC. Accessed 1/30/21. https://www.bbc.co.uk/religion/religions/judaism/texts/talmud.shtml.

269. *Parah* is the name of a treatise in the Mishnah and the Tosefta, included in the order Tohorot. The Pentateuchal law (Numbers 19) decrees that a red heifer, "wherein is no blemish, and upon which never came yoke," shall be burned and her ashes mixed with spring water, that the compound so obtained may be used to sprinkle and cleanse everyone who becomes unclean. The burning of the heifer and the preparation of the ashes, as well as the fetching of the water and its mixture for sprinkling, were attended by strict ceremonies. The treatise Parah contains a detailed description of these ceremonies, as well as various regulations concerning the purity of the water for sprinkling and its different effects.

   One or more of the preceding sentences incorporates text from a publication now in the public domain: Singer, Isidore; et al., eds. (1901–1906). "Parah." *The Jewish Encyclopedia* (New York: Funk & Wagnalls). Retrieved 5/20/15. Reproduced word-for-word at: https://en.wikipedia.org/wiki/Parah.

270. Dr. Douglas Jacoby. *The Red Heifer Sacrifice and the Crucifixion.* (1997, Revised 2001). https://www.douglasjacoby.com/the-red-heifer-sacrifice-and-the-crucifixion.

271. Martin, *Secrets of Golgotha*, pp. 4–5.

272. Tabor, "Locating Golgotha: Archeology." 2/26/16. https://jamestabor.com/locating-golgotha.

273. Jacoby. *The Red Heifer Sacrifice and the Crucifixion*

274. To see more teaching and helpful photographs and drawings, see: "Red Heifer Bridge." Accessed 1/21/21. http://templemountlocation.com/redHeiferBridge.html.

275. *Shekalim* is the fourth tractate in the order of Moed in the Mishnah. Its main subject is the half-shekel tax that ancient Jews paid every year to make possible the maintenance and proper functioning of the Temple in Jerusalem. See: Wikipedia. "Shekalim." Accessed 1/12/21. https://en.wikipedia.org/wiki/Shekalim_(Tractate)#cite_ref-1.

276. Martin, *Secrets of Golgotha: The Lost History of Jesus' Crucifixion."* chapter 2.

277. Kokkinos. University of Oxford, Faculty of Classics, Ancient History, Academic Visitor | Graeco-Roman Near East.

278. Tabor. "Locating Golgotha: Archeology."

279. See: Wikipedia. "Gospel of Nicodemus." Accessed 2/1/21. https://en.wikipedia.org/wiki/Gospel_of_Nicodemus.

280. Reid, George (1913). "Acta Pilati." In Herbermann, Charles (ed.). *Catholic Encyclopedia*. (New York: Robert Appleton Company).

281. See: Gospel of Nicodemus. "The Gospel of Nicodemus, or Acts of pilate," Accessed 1/12/21, from "The Apocryphal New Testament" (M.R. James—Translation and Notes— IX, 5) (Oxford: Clarendon Press, 1924). http://www.earlychristianwritings.com/text/gospelnicodemus.html.

282. See: Acts 5:30, 10:39; Galatians 10:13.

283. John W. Ritenbaugh. "Eden, The Garden, and The Two Trees (Part Three)," Biblestudy.org, Accessed 2/1/21. https://www.bibletools.org/index.cfm/fuseaction/Library.sr/CT/TRANSCRIPT/k/2037.

284. Tabor. "Locating Golgotha: Archeology."

285. Dr. N. F. Hutchinson. "Palestine Exploration Quarterly: Notes on Our Lord's Tomb" (1870: pp. 379–381). See also: Tabor. "Locating Golgotha: Archeology," 2/26/16, https://jamestabor.com/locating-golgotha.

286. Dr. N. F. Hutchinson. "Further Notes on our Lord's Tomb" (1873: pp. 113–115). See also: Tabor. "Locating Golgotha: Archeology," 2/26/16, https://jamestabor.com/locating-golgotha.

287. Melito of Sardis (Died c. 180) was the bishop of Sardis near Smyrna in western Anatolia and a great authority in early Christianity. Melito held a foremost place in terms of bishops in Asia due to his personal influence and his literary works, most of which have been lost. What has been recovered, however, has provided great insight into Christianity during the second century. See: https://en.wikipedia.org/wiki/Melito_of_Sardis.

288   From that hour the holy mother of God remained especially in the care of John, as long as she had her habitation in this life. And when the apostles had divided the world by lot for preaching, **she settled in the house of his parents near Mount Olivet.** ...Then Mary, undressing herself, put on better garments. And, taking the palm which she had received from the hands of the angel, **she went out to the mount of Olivet,** and began to pray. See: http://www.rosarychurch.net/answers/ap082000.html.
Tabor. "Locating Golgotha: Archeology."

289. The **Talmud** is the source from which the code of Jewish **Halakhah** (law) is derived. It is made up of the **Mishnah and the Gemara.** The **Mishnah** is the original written version of the oral law.

290. Jacoby. "The Red Heifer Sacrifice and the Crucifixion."

291. Following are examples of this view:

Ellicott's Commentary for English Readers: We then (who are all "priests unto God") "have an altar of which," on the very principles of their Law, "they that serve the Tabernacle (see Hebrews 8:5) have no right to eat." **The stress is laid on the sacrifice**, of which we eat, **not upon the altar itself.** If separately interpreted, **the altar will be the** place of sacrifice, **the Cross.** https://biblehub.com/commentaries/hebrews/13-10.htm.

292. *Cambridge Bible for Schools and Colleges:* But of our Sacrifice, which is Christ, and from (ἐξ) **our Altar, which is the Cross**—on which, as on an Altar, our Lord was offered—we may eat. https://biblehub.com/commentaries/hebrews/13-10.htm.

Bengel's Gnomen: It is **chiefly eaten in the Sacred Supper**, where His body is set forth as given up for us, and His blood shed for us, **in that single sacrifice of the cross.** https://biblehub.com/commentaries/hebrews/13-10.htm.

Dr. Koester, Helmut. "Outside the Camp," *Harvard Theological Review*, 1962 (55), pp.299–315. https://www.jstor.org/stable/1508726?refreqid=excelsior%3A644e02edb9af6203518cb010c7c05750&seq=1. See also: Martin, *Secrets of Golgotha: The Lost History of Jesus' Crucifixion*, pp. 14–15.

293. Martin, *Secrets of Golgotha,* pp. 14–15

294. Hebrews 13:10. Vincent's Word Studies, Biblehub.com. https://biblehub.com/commentaries/hebrews/13-10.htm.

295. Hebrews 13: 10. Gill's Commentary on the Entire Bible, Biblehub.com. https://biblehub.com/commentaries/hebrews/13-10.htm.

296. Jacoby, "The Red Heifer Sacrifice and the Crucifixion."

297. Tabor, "Locating Golgotha: Archeology."

298. Martin, Secrets of Golgotha, chapter 1.

299. "Garden Tomb," See theholyland.net. Accessed 1/21/21. https://www.seetheholyland.net/tag/gordons-calvary.

300. Mauldin, Leon. "Gordon's Calvary." Accessed 2/1/21. https://leon-mauldin.blog/2011/03/15/gordons-calvary.

301. Sacred Destinations. "Church of the Pater Noster, Jerusalem." Accessed 2/23/21. http://www.sacred-destinations.com/israel/jerusalem-church-of-pater-noster.

302. Jeffrey R. Chadwick. "Revisiting Golgotha and the Garden Tomb," *Religious Educator* Vol. 4 No. 1, 2003. https://rsc.byu.edu/vol-4-no-1-2003/revisiting-golgotha-garden-tomb.

303. "Sealing the Tomb of Jesus," (An excerpt from *Zondervan Handbook of Biblical Theology*), Olivetree.com. Accessed 2/2/21. https://www.olivetree.com/blog/sealing-tomb-jesus.

304. Strong's #4351, Proskulio. Strong's Concordance Proskulio: to roll to—Definition: to roll to—Usage: I roll to, roll up against. https://biblehub.com/greek/4351.htm.

305. See: Matthew 27:60, 28:2; Mark 15:46, 16:4; and Luke 24:2.

306. Matthew 27:60. *Barnes' Notes on the Bible*, Biblehub.com. https://biblehub.com/commentaries/matthew/27-60.htm.

307. Matthew 27:60. *Expositor's Greek Testament*, Biblehub.com. https://biblehub.com/commentaries/matthew/27-60.htm.

308. Matthew 27:60. *Gill's Exposition of the Scripture*, Biblehub.com. https://biblehub.com/commentaries/matthew/27-60.htm.

309. The Aaronic Blessing

Pulpit Commentary: In Leviticus 9:22 it is recorded that Aaron blessed the people, first by himself from the brazen altar of sacrifice, and afterwards in conjunction with Moses, when they came out of the tabernacle; and that he might so bless the people is mentioned as one object of his consecration (Deuteronomy 21:5; and cf. 1 Chronicles 23:13). ... And this act of blessing was far from being a mere expression of good will, or from being a simple prayer... For that name in which the blessing was given was not inoperative, but was mighty with untold spiritual efficacy where rightly used as the name of blessing.... Both, therefore, in its form and its contents this benediction is one of the most profound and most fruitful of the Divine oracles; and this indeed we might have expected, because (if we may venture to say so) God is never so entirely and absolutely himself as in blessing. See: Numbers 6:23. Pulpit Commentary, Biblehub.com. https://biblehub.com/commentaries/numbers/6-23.htm.